PLOTS AND DEEDS

Stanford Studies in Middle Eastern and
Islamic Societies and Cultures

PLOTS AND DEEDS

Agrarian Annihilation and
the Fight for Land Justice in Palestine

Paul Kohlbry

STANFORD UNIVERSITY PRESS

Stanford, California

Stanford University Press
Stanford, California

Library of Congress Cataloging-in-Publication Data
Names: Kohlbry, Paul author
Title: Plots and deeds : agrarian annihilation and the fight for land justice in Palestine / Paul Kohlbry.
Other titles: Stanford studies in Middle Eastern and Islamic societies and cultures
Description: Stanford, California : Stanford University Press, 2026. | Series: Stanford studies in Middle Eastern and Islamic societies and cultures | Includes bibliographical references and index.
Identifiers: LCCN 2025022082 (print) | LCCN 2025022083 (ebook) | ISBN 9781503645103 cloth | ISBN 9781503645110 paperback | ISBN 9781503645127 ebook
Subjects: LCSH: Land tenure—Palestine | Palestinian Arabs—Land tenure | Agriculture—Economic aspects—Palestine | Peasants—Palestine—Economic conditions | Land settlement—Government policy—Israel | Land use, Rural—Palestine
Classification: LCC HD850 .K64 2026 (print) | LCC HD850 (ebook) | DDC 333.3/15694—dc23/eng/20250721
LC record available at https://lccn.loc.gov/2025022082
LC ebook record available at https://lccn.loc.gov/2025022083

Cover design: Ann Weinstock
Cover art: Nabil Anani, *Olive Pickers at Dawn*, 2011

The authorized representative in the EU for product safety and compliance is: Mare Nostrum Group B.V. | Mauritskade 21D | 1091 GC Amsterdam | The Netherlands | Email address: gpsr@mare-nostrum.co.uk | KVK chamber of commerce number: 96249943

Contents

Acknowledgments

All books are collective projects in some way or another, and this one is no different.

My biggest debt is to the people I spent time with in Palestine. Long before I imagined that I would ever write a book, I learned so much from working with the Palestinian Grassroots Anti-Apartheid Wall Campaign, especially from Jamal Juma', Dawood Hamoudeh, Hadeel Hunaiti, and Maren Mantovani. I am thankful to the many, many people who put up with my questions, took time out of their day to talk to me, and shared their stories and insights, especially in Bruqin, Farkha, and Qarawat Bani Zeid. Special thanks are due to the staff of the Palestinian Land Authority, and later the Land and Water Settlement Commission, in Salfit and Dura. Bassam Kharajeh, Mohammed Nazzal, and Shlomy Zaharia met with me numerous times, and provided me with documents that I would not otherwise have been able to get. Ghada al-Madbouh and Penny Mitchell of the Palestinian American Research Center, as well as Raja Khalidi, Omar Tesdell, and Haim Yacobi all helped me stay in the country, or made important introductions and suggestions during the early days of research. Steve Keller and Hadeel always helped me land on my feet when I came back to Ramallah.

I began this project at Johns Hopkins University. I was fortunate enough to have some excellent mentors in Jane Guyer, Michael Levien, Christopher Nealon, Tom Özden-Schilling, and Deborah Poole. In Baltimore, Önder Celik,

Victor Kumar, Emma McGlennen, Mac Skelton, Thomas Thornton, and Chris Westcott read almost everything that I wrote, and their suggestions improved it all immensely.

I finished this project as I moved to Providence, then to Chicago, and then to Ithaca. Beshara Doumani, Barbara Oberkoetter, and Alex Winder made the Palestinian Studies program at Brown University a great place to work. Kathleen Cavanaugh and Ben Laurence did the same during my year in the Pozen Center for Human Rights at the University of Chicago, and were kind enough to set up a book workshop for me, even after I had left. When I arrived at the Department of Anthropology at Cornell, Sarah Besky welcomed me into the Agrarian Studio and the intellectual community it has made, for which I am very grateful.

Over the years, many people have helped me figure out what this book is about. Amiel Bize, Beshara Doumani, Cameron Hu, Marc Kohlbry, Callie Maidhof, Kareem Rabie, Jeff Reger, Sobhi Samour, Sherene Seikaly, Jeremy Siegman, and Alex Winder have all provided critical feedback, perspective, and encouragement. The comrades of the Agrarian Question Group, Kellan Anfison, Gabi Kirk, Graham Pitts, and China Sajadian, all read many drafts of many things, and our conversations shaped the core ideas in this book. Past, present, and visiting members of the Agrarian Studio at Cornell—Hadia Akhtar Khan, Natacha Bruna, Pinaki Chandra, Ashawari Chaudhuri, Liam Greenwell, Suraj Kushwaha, Tamar Law, Jessie Mayall, Steven McCutcheon, Alex Nading, Yui Sasajima, Devika Shekhawat, Finn West, and Roderick Wijunamai—were also subjected to many chapters (often more than once), and always provided generous feedback. Members of Hadia's writing group, Amiel, Nataya Friedan, and Katy Lindquist, offered comments that helped me rethink some bits of the argument near the end.

A few people read the manuscript in its entirety. I am immensely grateful to Sarah, Darryl Li, and Kareem for providing extensive feedback on an earlier version of this manuscript. Cameron and China also read this whole thing all the way through, and then parts of it again after I had torn it up and started over.

I've presented some of this material at different venues over the years. Thanks are due to the Department of Near Eastern Studies at Cornell, New Directions in Palestinian Studies at Brown, the Palestine Economic Policy

Research Institute in Ramallah, the Capital in the Web of Sovereignty workshop at the Centre for Anthropological Research on Museums and Heritage in Berlin, the Palestinian Agricultural Development seminar series hosted by the Margaret Ansetee Centre for Global Studies at Cambridge, and the Military Surplus seminar at the Centre for Research in the Arts, Social Sciences and Humanities at Cambridge, for giving me opportunity to think through some of my ideas out loud.

Fieldwork would not have been possible without funding. I am grateful for financial support from the Foreign Language and Area Studies Program, Wenner-Gren Foundation, Palestinian American Research Center, the National Science Foundation, and the Programs in Jewish Studies and Women, Gender, and Sexuality at Johns Hopkins.

It has been a pleasure to work with Kate Wahl, Thane Hale, Emily Smith, and the rest of the team at Stanford University Press. I am very grateful to Kate for her willingness to take on this project at a rather weird time, and to her editorial guidance as I was finishing it up. Thanks are also due to Nabil Anani for allowing me to use his painting for the cover of this book. I am also very thankful to the two sets of anonymous reviewers whose incisive comments made this manuscript far better, and to Lys Weiss of Post Hoc Academic Publishing Services for doing the final copyediting.

Finally, I am so lucky to have met Wenfei Xu along the way. I appreciate her suggestions that I try to explain what I'm talking about to readers who might not have spent the past decade reading about peasants, her help with the maps, her encouragement during setbacks, and her patience with this project at the times when it felt like there was no end in sight. Hairui Marc Kohlbry joined us when the manuscript was out for the final round of peer review, and he has been workshopping some very interesting shrieks and squeals as I've been putting the finishing touches on it. I hope when he is old enough to read this book, justice will not feel so far out of reach.

PLOTS AND DEEDS

Introduction

RECENTERING PEASANTS, RETHINKING LAND

WHAT COMES TO MIND WHEN YOU THINK OF RURAL PALESTINE? IF you have encountered artistic, literary, or religious depictions of the region, you may envision a pastoral scene, likely of a village inhabited by peasant families and surrounded by terraces planted with olive groves. If you are familiar with the political situation from one of the many books, documentaries, or human rights reports about the Israeli occupation, then a far less peaceful scene probably comes to mind. Perhaps it is one in which armored bulldozers are razing homes, or villagers are clinging to uprooted olive trees. These are powerful images, and generations of artists, travelers, scholars, and journalists have woven them into enduring narratives in which this rural landscape is emblematic of *the land* of Palestine. But too often, these narratives idealize or ignore the people who live there. They might celebrate peasant farmers for being rooted in the land or mourn their inevitable disappearance, but they rarely consider what such farmers do, what they have to say, or how they have changed over time.

What might we learn from rural Palestine if we understand the people living there not as an inert feature of the landscape, but as a force that is actively shaping it? *Plots and Deeds* centers peasant farming in the study of

Palestine in order to understand what land means for Palestinians. To do so, I tell the stories of three villages in the central highlands of Palestine where property ownership and peasant labor are a living part of emerging collective identities, dynamic agrarian projects, and contested land defense politics. When we foreground those who own and work the land, we can rethink the question of Palestine as an agrarian question and see how daily struggles in the highlands are part of a global fight for land justice.

I did not come to Palestine intending to write a book about land or peasants. Instead, I came as a young activist. I knew little about farming, and my knowledge of rural Palestine largely came from reports detailing the many human rights violations those living there had experienced. I lived in the city of Ramallah in the mid-2000s and worked for the Palestinian Grassroots Anti-Apartheid Wall Campaign, better known as Stop the Wall. It was the protests in highland villages like Nil'in, Bil'in, and Nabi Saleh against Israel's theft of their land and water that introduced me to one aspect of life in rural Palestine. Over time, I came to learn that these protests were part of a century-long tradition of popular resistance that had made the peasant an important figure for anticolonial politics and international solidarity.[1]

What was happening in these villages seemed at odds with what was happening in Ramallah. Financed by Western donors and international financial institutions, the Palestinian Authority (PA), the nonsovereign government that has administered parts of the West Bank since the 1990s, embarked on a new sort of nationalist program in which private sector development and liberal markets were supposed to lead to the creation of an independent Palestinian state. After the withdrawal of Israeli troops from the city, Ramallah became the epicenter of what has come to be known as "neoliberal Palestine."[2] Banks began to provide mortgages and personal loans. Luxury housing and commercial buildings seemed to be sprouting everywhere. New bars and restaurants opened to serve the growing numbers of entrepreneurs, consultants, diplomats, and activists like me. Visitors to Ramallah were often shocked by the sight of Palestinians driving high-end cars or sipping cappuccinos. A gulf seemed to be appearing between the "bubble" of Ramallah and the refugee camps and villages that supplied the city with cheap labor, and where military occupation was still very present.[3]

But rural places were changing, too. Working with Stop the Wall gave me the opportunity to spend time in highland villages across the West Bank, and in the late 2000s I visited Nabi Saleh to interview young protesters who had been shot by Israeli soldiers. Driving through the village at that time, I encountered the aftermath of these protests. Black circles had been burned into the road by flaming tires, spent tear gas grenades were strung together and displayed like strings of Christmas lights on the walls lining the street, and windows were boarded up to protect against bullets and shells. On certain days, I could smell the lingering stench of sewage left behind by the chemical "skunk" water that Israeli troops sprayed indiscriminately on demonstrators and homes. A few years later, just a stone's throw away from a military observation tower at the village entrance, I noticed that something else had appeared: three billboards for a new Palestinian real estate development in the area. For low monthly payments, they offered Palestinian buyers land with a title deed. While these advertisements included the traditional agrarian imagery of olive trees and terraced hillsides, they were offering something very new: single-family homes, secure property rights, and great returns on investment.

I began research for what eventually became *Plots and Deeds* in order to understand this jarring confluence of rural land defense, settler colonial dispossession, and capitalist real estate development. This research project soon took me a bit farther north of Nabi Saleh, to the villages of Bruqin, Qarawat Beni Zayd (Qarawa for short), and Farkha. In the hills shared by these three villages, I met farmers who had set up a cooperative to sell organic olive oil and established an experimental farm. On the hill across from that farm, I found that developers were converting agricultural land into real estate. Nearby, I spent time with the young communist activists organizing voluntary work crews to reclaim and replant land so as to prevent the Israeli authorities from confiscating it. And I accompanied the PA surveyors who were slowly mapping and titling the area. I found that many of the forces that are transforming Palestine, and indeed rural places across the planet, were converging in the central highlands.

Fieldwork allowed me to talk to the people living in these villages and pay closer attention to the landscape. One summer night in 2013, I was walking outside of Bruqin with a companion from the village. We could see the lights of the nearby settlement and military tower keeping watch over the

FIGURE 1. Field site in the central highlands.

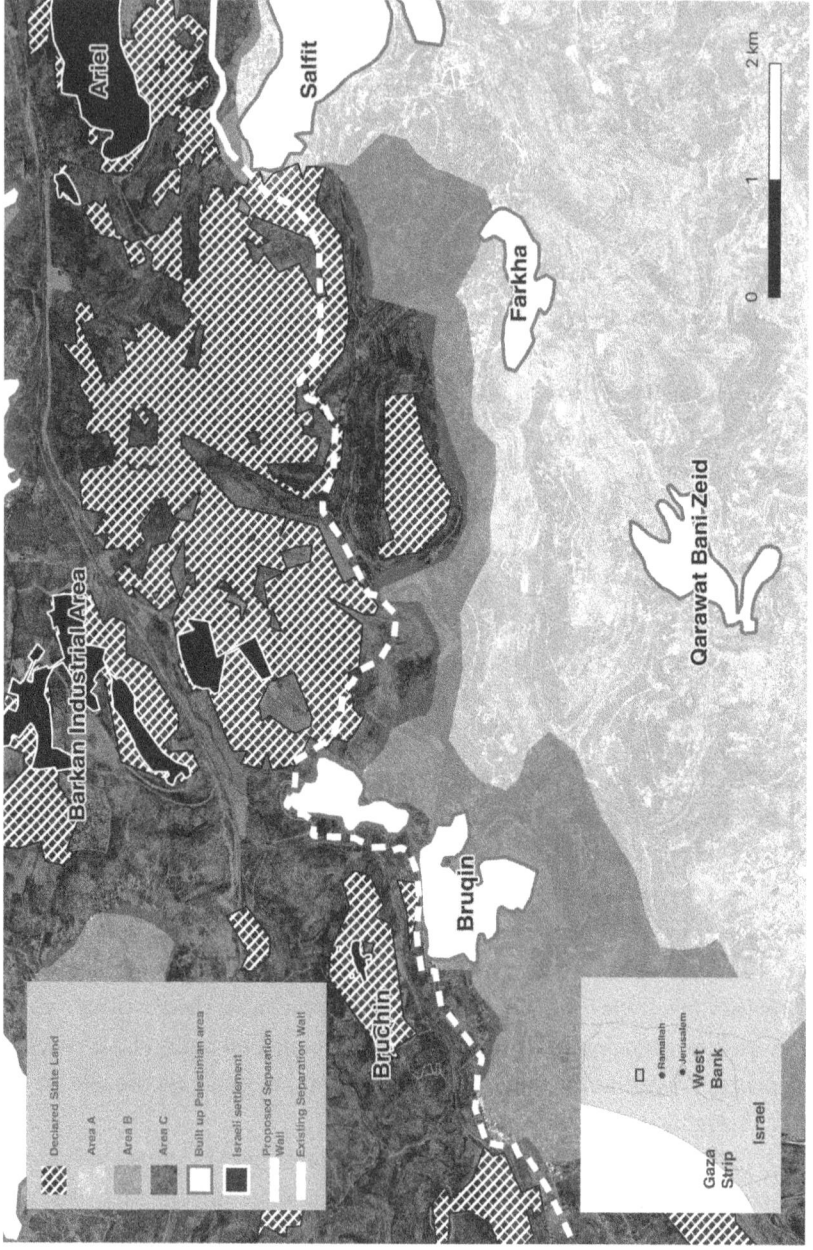

Legend:
- Declared State Land
- Area A
- Area B
- Area C
- Built up Palestinian area
- Israeli settlement
- Proposed Separation Wall
- Existing Separation Wall

Ariel

Barkan Industrial Area

Salfit

Farkha

Bruchin

Bruqin

Qarawat Bani-Zeid

Ramallah
Jerusalem
West Bank
Gaza Strip
Israel

0   1   2 km

Map by Wenfei Xu based on data from B'Tselem.

area. Shortly before my arrival, the Israeli government had confiscated more land from the village to expand the settlement. Earlier in the day, I had met farmers who had been attacked by soldiers and evicted for "trespassing" on their own land, and had had crops polluted by sewage that flowed from the Israeli homes and factories on the hilltops. Pointing to the ground in front of us, my companion told me that the men and women of the village had once planted these hilltops with seasonal crops, taking advantage of every bit of arable land. Gazing at rocks and overgrown bushes, it was hard for me to imagine that anything had ever grown there.

Several years later, on a cloudy spring day, I was visiting the land of a farmer in Qarawa. His plot was planted with olive saplings as well as beans, peas, and other vegetables. On one terrace stood a small, cinderblock structure that provided a shaded spot where one could sit and enjoy a meal. The day he invited me to visit, we sampled some fruits and vegetables while his older children worked, one taking a weed-whacker to the spring grass, the other encouraging a donkey, hitched to a plow, to stay its course. He did not have plans to invest heavily in agriculture, he told me, and farming had become more of a "hobby." Instead, he thought of his land "as an investment, as real estate" that he would one day pass on to his children.

Land confiscation, environmental damage, and military violence in places like Bruqin have been very well documented for a long time.[4] The activists and organizations that have been doing this documenting are part of a human rights movement that, since the 1980s, has worked tirelessly to gather evidence of Israeli crimes and advocate for the rights of Palestinians.[5] As a result of their work, what Israel does to Palestinians in the occupied territories is no longer hidden from public scrutiny. Another result is that everyone from legal experts to radical activists to interested observers now talks about justice in Palestine through the frameworks of human rights and international law.[6]

Land commodification in places like Qarawa has received far less attention. Part of the reason for this has to do with the pervasiveness of human rights thinking, which means that researchers pay scant attention to economic issues unless those issues are directly related to the Israeli occupation. But even among the recent revival of "political economy" in Palestinian studies, there is little discussion of the transformation of land ownership in

Palestine's villages.[7] This absence is made even more troubling given that land has a great deal of personal and political importance for Palestinians, in addition to being the most valuable financial asset that many own. As a result, critical scholarship on political economy has yet to explore what changes to the land mean for those who live in villages like Bruqin and Qarawa, or how the confiscation of land on one hilltop might be connected to its commodification on the other.

When we begin to map connections between land grabs, settlement expansion, rising prices, and real estate speculation, the outlines of what I call *agrarian annihilation* come into view. Like others across historic Palestine, the people who live in the central highlands have experienced the decimation of their land base. Israeli colonization and incorporation of villagers as wage labor has driven both the dispossession and devaluation of agricultural land. These processes have inadvertently created opportunities for Palestinian developers, with increasing land sales putting new pressures on peasant farming. Together, coercive state actions and the invisible (but no less important) power of capital dispossess rural landowners while making agrarian livelihoods increasingly unviable—even unthinkable—for those who have managed to hold onto their land. Calling this process "agrarian change" is an understatement, as sometimes the changes are so drastic that it is impossible to know that agrarian activity existed in certain areas in the first place, much less if it could be possible in the future.

How are those facing annihilation demanding justice? In the highlands, peasant land tenure and farming practices are intertwined with land defense, and together they provide an ethical and political repertoire for what we should think of as *land justice*. The struggles I explore in the chapters that follow include claiming private property, losing village control over land, asserting the rights of cultivation, and reestablishing collective agrarian presence. And while I will argue that it is illuminating to understand them as *peasant* struggles, those involved in them bear little resemblance to the heroic revolutionaries or tragic victims that populate so many agrarian imaginaries. Instead, they engage with colonial law, treat land as a commodity, rework traditional farming practices, and transform rural landscapes. They teach us that land justice is fundamentally a demand for *return*—both the return of the land that was taken, and a return to the land—that emerges from ordinary practices and small experiments that are transforming agrarian life.

Students, scholars, and activists have much to gain by thinking about rural Palestine from the ground up. Doing so reveals the changing roles that peasants have played, and continue to play, in the question of Palestine. It enriches accounts of both land grabbing and settler colonialism. And it allows us to understand the global significance of what is happening in the central highlands, a place that connects Palestine to the vast array of peoples and movements demanding land justice.

"PEASANTS" IN PALESTINE?

It might seem anachronistic to be talking about "peasants" today. But they still exist, not as a residual presence, but as a significant portion of the world's farming population. Peasants are farmers with a specific labor process, one in which the household dwells on and cultivates the land and consumes some of what is produced there.[8] While they often sell agricultural surplus on the market or find other work off the farm, their control of land means that they do not totally rely on selling commodities, or on their labor, to survive.[9] A growing body of research on agroecology has found that peasant farming (also called "smallholder" and "family farming") is far more productive than once believed, and far more ecologically and socially sustainable than industrial models.[10] Peasants are also an important political force, nationally and internationally. One of the world's largest social movements is La Via Campesina, which is made up of 180 organizations representing some 200 million "peasants, landless workers, indigenous people," and other agrarian constituencies.[11] Such organizations are working to transform the global food system, defending land and territory, and confronting climate change, putting them at the center of the most pressing struggles for justice we are facing today.

Scholars of Palestine do not talk about peasants much anymore. This absence is a result of the unfortunate separation between Palestinian studies and agrarian studies, which is itself symptomatic of a wider problem in the study of the Middle East and North Africa.[12] It was not always this way. In the 1960s, scholars studied the dispossession and proletarianization of the remaining Palestinian peasants in Israel.[13] In the 1980s, research based on extensive fieldwork explored similar dynamics in the occupied territories, with far more attention paid to peasant social relations and farming practices.[14] But while scholarship on Palestine increased dramatically in the 1990s—leading some to complain of "the Palestine industry"—researchers were heading to cities and refugee camps, not villages.[15] For almost three decades, villages and peasants have only appeared in a few anthropological monographs, tellingly about oral history and memory.[16] For North American scholars, at least, the peasantry had disappeared.

Over the past decade, there has been a slow resurgence of interest in agrarian issues in Palestine. Some researchers have tracked the effects of fair trade certification on Palestinian olive oil and weaponization of environmental protection laws against the Palestinian foraging.[17] Others have studied rain-fed cultivation and its attendant forms of knowledge and practice, and have rethought the meaning of agricultural development under settler colonialism.[18] For critics of the existing political order, small-scale farming is a pillar of "economic resistance" to Palestinian neoliberalism and Israel settler colonialism.[19] Still marginal in most of these discussions, however, is much consideration of agrarian political economy, meaning that the questions of "who owns what?" "who does what?" "who gets what?" and "what do they do with it?" are often relegated to the background, or never considered at all.[20]

There is no better place to begin to ask these questions than in the highlands of Palestine. This region has been inhabited for millennia, and until relatively recently hosted a primarily agrarian society. Winter rainfall sustained a typical Mediterranean polyculture of olives, wheat, and grapes, while the drier eastern slopes were devoted to grazing. Villages were home to longstanding clans, and integrated into regional (and later global) markets through networks of rural notables and urban merchants. In 1948, with the destruction of historic Palestine and the expulsion of 750,000 Palestinians, the highlands in the Galilee region became part of the state of Israel. In 1967, Israel occupied the West Bank, including the highlands that make up the mountainous spine of the territory. Israel has been the effective sovereign ever since, although the PA has administered noncontiguous islands of territory since 1995. Despite these radical political and economic changes, many rain-fed agricultural practices and local forms of identification have survived until this day.[21]

Most of the people who cultivate the land in Farkha, Qarawa, and Bruqin can be understood as peasant farmers. There are around 14,730 dunums (a dunum is about a quarter of an acre) of agricultural land in these three villages, and those that live there typically own small plots of land that they inherited or purchased.[22] Average farm sizes are small in the central highlands, ranging between 7.5 and 8.5 dunums, or about 2 acres.[23] Most farms are controlled and owned by individuals, most of whom are older men.[24] They reside near their farms in villages and towns, and they rely on their own labor, and that of their families.[25] They engage in rain-fed farming—primarily olives, but not so long ago wheat and, in some places, grapes, figs, and other fruits—for both subsistence agriculture and commodity production, consuming much of what they grow, and selling the surplus on the market. The men and women who cultivate the land in these three villages are part of a larger population of cultivators living in the West Bank highlands, and have much in common with millions of others who make up the world's peasantries.[26]

These farmers face dire conditions. Since 1967, Israeli settler colonialism—in particular land confiscations, trade restrictions, and policies encouraging Palestinian labor migration—has been the main driver of de-agrarianization in the West Bank. The Oslo Peace Accords led to the creation of the PA in 1993, but limited Palestinian self-rule did little to improve rural livelihoods. Israel replaced much of its Palestinian labor force with other migrant workers. It also expanded settlements, which it surrounded with walls, fences, and military checkpoints, cutting off access to more and more agricultural land. The PA has done little to support village agriculture, but its land titling projects have helped the companies and individual investors buy up rural land. Today, those who still insist on farming do so in a hostile political economy, one that values their property but can do without their labor—or indeed their very presence—on the land.

As a result, many of those who live in the central highlands are no longer engaged in agriculture. Most of those who are also hold other jobs; for three-quarters of all Palestinian farmers, agriculture is a "secondary activity" alongside their primary employment.[27] Many farmers spend far less time on the land, some only visiting for the olive harvest, and agriculture now accounts for less of a household livelihood than it once did. Viewed narrowly as a primary occupation or a source of income, peasant farming might seem to be of little importance.

Given this state of affairs, does it make sense to talk about peasants in Palestine, or indeed anywhere in the world? Calling today's rural producers "peasants," some scholars argue, no longer captures the agricultural practices or class relations that characterize rural life.[28] Others claim precisely the opposite, pointing to the growth of self-identified "peasant" social movements and arguing that peasant farming represents a radical alternative to the capitalist food system, one that, rather than disappearing, is growing worldwide.[29]

Beyond their diminishing numbers and economic marginalization, however, I believe that it is critical to center peasant farming in our discussions of Palestine for three key reasons. First, peasant agriculture remains a fluctuating part of household livelihood and a vital safety net for village residents during periods of crisis. While farming is no longer the primary concern for rural households or occupation of its members, what people grow in their groves and gardens still supplements household diets and incomes. And when Israeli closures of checkpoints and border crossings prevent people from reaching their jobs and stop goods from circulating, those who still control land return to agriculture. As I will discuss in chapter 1, the very forces that drive agrarian annihilation are, paradoxically, those that continue to throw people back into peasant agriculture *and* politicize it in new ways.

Second, peasant labor is still important for rural identity and land defense. Today, cultivators in the central highlands self-identify as both "peasants" (*fallahin*) and "farmers" (*muzara'in*). More important than the specific word, however, are the social relations and responsibilities that peasant labor creates. "It matters to simple commodity producers," the anthropologist Michel-Rolph Trouillot points out, "that they work on the land rather than on the sea, that they produce fruits rather than hats, that they can both sleep and work in the same room or not."[30] Peasant farming requires family labor and various forms of cooperation and as a result engenders powerful forms of solidarity and connections to place. These relations can be the basis of a shared responsibility to defend village land and a desire for what some have called autonomy, but I think is better understood as agrarian self-determination.[31] In other words, peasant farming shapes how people fight for land, and the kinds of values they fight to defend.

Finally, peasant farming is a political resource for Palestinians. The colonization of the highlands since the late 1970s has put the people living there on the front lines of a national struggle for land. Peasant farming, in particular the hope that agricultural self-sufficiency would lessen Palestinian dependence on Israel, influenced theories of "popular protection," "resistance economy," and "self-reliant agricultural development," which in turn have influenced the activities of various groups and movements.[32] Peasant farmers are also a source of "traditional" or "Indigenous" knowledge, so important to organic agriculture, agroecology, and food sovereignty efforts underway in Palestine today.[33] Outside of Palestine, food and farming make Palestinians legible to new international audiences and political movements, creating forms of solidarity that have only grown since Israel's war in Gaza in 2023. "The scale of massacres in Gaza and the openly genocidal intentions of the far-right Israeli government," opens a 2024 account from a delegation of nine peasant organizations, "have led La Via Campesina to intensify its solidarity work with Palestinian farmers."[34] Peasant farming is a vital resource for anticolonial struggle, and part of a powerful agrarian political imaginary that inspires global solidarity.

Peasants still exist in Palestine, and they still matter. Their labor helps families survive and informs wider struggles for land defense and agrarian self-determination. But what (and who) a peasant is, is not fixed. Instead, as farmers and their allies create new political movements or rework agricultural systems, their social and political identities shift as well. And it is because of what peasant farming provides to people now, and what it may offer them in the future, that we should be concerned about agrarian annihilation.

AGRARIAN ANNIHILATION

There are different ways to understand the destruction of rural Palestine. Some scholars have shown how the colonial history of property and enclosure structure Israeli colonization.[35] Some have looked at the relationship between labor migration and Israeli settlement.[36] And some have explored how the PA has seized village land for the benefit of private developers.[37] Each reveals something different about dispossession in the West Bank: the specific mechanisms that Israel uses to seize land, the exploitation and management of a captive population, and the continuities between settler colonialism and neoliberal capitalism. I build on these accounts across *Plots and Deeds*, just as I try to reorient some of their insights to illuminate the experiences and struggles of those who cultivate the land.

I also draw on scholars working in the field of critical agrarian studies to make sense of the relationships between capital and dispossession.[38] In the wake of the large-scale land deals that followed the 2008 financial crisis, scholarly and activist research has drawn our attention to the centrality of land dispossession for contemporary capitalism and illuminated the complex ways that rural populations resisted or accommodated the loss of their lands.[39] However, the scholarship on land grabbing and "new enclosures" has had little to say about settler colonialism, and nothing to say about Palestine.[40] Reviewing more than a decade of research on the subject, a group of senior scholars asked: "Are the new terminologies and analyses of land grabbing useful amidst the world's current crises that are rooted in questions of land and territorial control—Russia's war in Ukraine or Israel's occupation of and attacks on Palestine?"[41] The answer is yes, these terminologies and analyses can be useful, but only if we develop concepts to help make sense of the contradictory ways that conquest, law, and accumulation transform land politics in settler colonies.

The concept of agrarian annihilation is one such concept, and helps clarify the relationship between the destruction of land, of people, and of imagination. I sketch an outline of annihilation in chapter 1, before tracing its effects in the subsequent chapters. In a word, annihilation results when state dispossession and neglect converge with the indirect domination of capital. Land expropriation exists alongside what geographer Shiri Pasternak, in her study of settler colonial jurisdiction in Canada, calls "colonialism without dispossession," or the processes—often banal and bureaucratic—that result in the "diminishing capacity of communities to reproduce their social, economic, and legal orders."[42] In the highlands, moments of assault and enclosure punctuate slower, incremental changes that make farmers abandon their land by limiting the time they can spend on it, the sorts of crops they grow, and their ability to make a living doing so. Peasant agriculture is not simply disappearing. It is being actively destroyed.

Conquest is at the root of annihilation. For Zionism the territorial goal has always been a settler colonial one: the acquisition of as much land as possible with as few Arabs as possible. Achieving this objective required establishing overlapping arrangements of Jewish ownership, sovereignty, and presence on the land, on the one hand, and the elimination of the Palestinians as a people with the ability to exercise a sovereign claim over a territory, on the other.[43] In the West Bank, conquest is an ongoing process carried out by the Israeli military and police as well as quasi-state and private actors that include settler organizations, vigilante groups, and paramilitaries. Like other settler colonial projects, these different forces share a commitment to settler dominance, but do not always operate together. Instead, different logics—security, counterinsurgency, profit, territorial expansion, revenge—create multiple frontiers within the West Bank itself. While large-scale bombings and massacres make headlines, it is the regular acts of mundane violence that make conquest a grinding, ever present reality for Palestinians.

Law legitimizes conquest and paves the way for further dispossession. Prior to 1948, the Zionist movement acquired land primarily through market acquisitions. After 1948, the new state created a legal regime to facilitate and manage the seizure of Palestinian land. In 1967, both private and state power began to orchestrate the acquisition of Palestinian land in the occupied territories. And after 1995, the Oslo Accords divided the West Bank into Areas A, B, and C, giving Israel additional tools to dispossess Palestinians. Through a regime of physical, bureaucratic, and legal barriers, Israel has made Area C—which accounts for around 60 percent of the West Bank and more than two-thirds of its agricultural land—effectively off limits to Palestinian farmers.[44] This arrangement, which on paper was supposed to be an interim measure, is now more than three decades old and constitutes a permanent layer of colonial jurisdiction over Palestinian territory, one that now functions as a large land reserve for future colonization.

For cultivators, colonization results not only in land dispossession, but also in land destruction. In the highlands, Israeli settlement is a housing project, with some industrial zones as well. To build additional residential buildings or factories, the Israeli authorities raze pastures and cultivated areas, and remove trees and structures along the path of walls and near checkpoints to create sterile buffer zones. Sewage and industrial waste flow out of these restricted areas, damaging agricultural land that is still technically under Palestinian control. Destruction is at once immediate and drawn out, with the uprooting of trees and demolition of homes accompanying slower processes of environmental degradation and invisible ecological change.[45]

In the context of land dispossession and destruction, the transformation of peasants into wage laborers emerges as a slow process of displacement. Shortly after 1967, the military government facilitated the incorporation of peasants and refugees into the Israeli economy as cheap wage laborers, turning many villages into commuter dorms and drawing thousands of people out of agriculture. While these numbers have diminished since the 1990s, many Palestinians still have no other choice but to work either inside Israel illegally, or in the West Bank settlements. From the perspective of the settler state, peasants are part of a disposable reserve army of labor. As the agricultural economist Hisham Awartani put it in his important dissertation on rain-fed agriculture in the early 1980s, Israeli occupation "accelerated the desertion of land and its eventual transfer to Israeli control, undermined the productive potential of a major economic sector, and transformed a large segment of deeply rooted Palestinians into roaming 'mercenaries.'"[46] From the perspective of individual workers, work in Israel paid better than working the land. But from a national perspective, de-agrarianization posed a grave political danger.

An invisible web of agricultural subsidies and trade regulations ensured that peasant farmers received little protection from market forces. After an early attempt to modernize Palestinian agriculture in the 1970s, Israel withdrew any significant government support for Palestinian farmers. Instead, various trade barriers and restrictions allowed Israeli producers to dump cheap goods in the occupied territories, while preventing Palestinians from selling their products in Israeli markets.[47] While the Oslo Accords were supposed to guarantee the free movement of goods after the 1990s, Israel's control over most of the arable land and water resources, alongside its singular ability to impede and halt the movement of people and commodities, maintained Israeli domination and undermined Palestinian food production.[48] While the PA has limited powers to affect this situation, it has never prioritized agriculture in the allocation of government resources. The abandonment of cultivators by all public authorities has meant that, for decades, they have effectively faced the full force of the colonial state and market alone.

Dispossession and displacement invite the sorts of Palestinian capital accumulation that further chip away at peasant agriculture. Since the mid-2000s, Palestinian developers and speculators have bought up cheap agricultural and formerly agricultural land in the highlands. Through a series of land titling projects, the PA has facilitated the emergence of new land markets across the West Bank. Like other places where "yesterday's agriculture is today's 'not-yet-urban,'" land is becoming valuable as potential real estate, incentivizing farmers to sell their land and discouraging agricultural investment.[49] In the highlands, war and development are not opposites; instead, they exist on a continuum, with war zones giving way to wealth for those who happen to own land in the right place.[50]

Agrarian annihilation unfolds at different scales and temporal rhythms, each eroding the capacity of peasant farming to sustain life. Since 1967, agriculture has declined in the highlands of the West Bank. From 29.9 percent in the 1980s, agriculture dropped to account for only 5.6 percent of GDP in the occupied territories by the time I began my fieldwork in the early 2010s.[51] As farmers spent less time on their land and cultivate fewer crops, the landscape lost the diverse agricultural environments that characterized highland farming. Coping strategies like monocropping, chemical inputs, and time-saving measures resulted in new forms of market dependency, unexpected ecological damage, and the diminution of farming knowledge. Different losses—economic, legal, cultural, and ecological—reinforce one another, and compound over time. Farmers may lose legal ownership of land decades before they are actually prevented from accessing it, just as it takes a generation or two before the loss of farming knowledge is truly felt. While Palestinian farmers may still legally own and perhaps even access some of their land, their ability to make a living farming it is greatly diminished, if not taken away entirely.

These compounding effects create very different kinds of problems. Farmers lose land regardless of whether it is confiscated by the state, fraudulently taken by settlers, or sold to developers. But these losses are not experienced or understood in the same way. People might band together to fight the state, go to court to prove they did not collude with settlers, or blame themselves for giving up their land. When the Israeli state uproots olive trees, activists join protests and human rights organizations document violations of international law. But when land is slowly ruined and abandoned, farmers find that they have little political support or legal recourse. It is from the social and ethical problems annihilation creates for Palestinians, and the political and economic projects they enact to hold onto the land, that different elements of land justice emerge.

LAND JUSTICE

In my usage across this book, "land justice" is a political proposition and a research question.[52] It proposes that realizing justice for those who have been dispossessed, displaced, and excluded from land should be at the heart of any emancipatory political project. It asks that we study the conditions that give rise to injustice, and seek to understand the different ideas and idioms that animate struggles for land. When we study land justice, our thesis is that those who live on and from the land produce valuable theories of justice and ways to enact it. Our task is thus not only to document these ideas and practices, but to critically engage with their limits and possibilities.

We might usefully distinguish between five different demands for land justice. First, the demand for political self-determination and freedom from colonial occupation or imperial control. Second, for the redistribution of land, usually from large landlords to peasants, tenants, or landless people. Third, for democratization, for example, through strengthening local authority over land, or by decommodifying it entirely and placing it under public control or common ownership. Fourth, for reparation, through compensation or the return of stolen land. Fifth, for regeneration, for example, of land damaged by war or depleted through industrial farming. Struggles for land justice often include many, and sometimes all, of these different demands. They hail from diverse political traditions, cross urban and rural spaces, and are increasingly part of globalized networks. And as a growing number of these movements begin to identify and think with the Palestinian cause, it is becoming increasingly important to map out the meanings of land justice in Palestine.

In the chapters that follow, I argue that property, labor, and land defense each provide different vantage points for examining the formation of land justice in Palestine. In the highlands, land justice is not a program or platform; instead, it is a collection of claims and practices that emerge from the mundane choices, and the extraordinary sacrifices, people make to hold

onto the land. Each of these chapters focuses on an element of this formation: private property, village control over land, the rights of cultivation,
and reestablishing collective agrarian presence. And each demonstrates
how communist activists, human rights lawyers, development economists,
and land surveyors—each working with various movements and NGOs—
have all had a hand in transforming how people own, work, and defend their
land. Property, labor, and land defense are deeply rooted in the highlands,
just as they are part of extensive transnational legal regimes and political
movements.

Property provides a generative entry point for thinking about land justice. Property ownership organizes one's relationship to land in terms of abstract legal rights. These rights are part of a property regime that, following
the anthropologist Katherine Verdery, produces relatively stable patterns of
"values, cultural meanings, and social and power relations" that shape how
people relate to one another and, importantly, the idioms they use to make
claims.[53] When people make property claims, they are not only making
claims to a specific plot of land, but also asserting or demanding inclusion as
a rights-bearing member of a political community.[54] As a result, such claims
often operate simultaneously at multiple scales, bringing together intimate
local conflicts and national battles for political recognition and sovereignty.

Today in the West Bank, private property is the most widespread property regime. The private ownership of agricultural land has existed in parts
of the highlands since the late Ottoman period, and later, under the British Mandate (1920–48) and then as part of the kingdom of Jordan (1950–
67), became increasingly widespread. In chapter 2, I demonstrate how even
though the Israeli authorities suspended land titling after 1967, colonization
made private ownership increasingly important for Palestinian land rights.
After the mid-2000s, Palestinian land titling and real estate development
have entrenched and expanded the reach of private ownership. As I show
in chapter 3, land titling has facilitated the commodification of family land,
making it accessible to new, nonresident owners. These struggles over property have given rise to a discourse about justice in which ownership grounds
claims to precolonial presence, demands for local control over village land,
and conduct based on fair prices and transparent market interactions. Because property rights make Palestinian claims legible to various local and

international authorities, the failure of the law to protect Palestinian rights in one domain has done little to slow the gradual spread of private property in the West Bank.

Labor is the second angle from which to consider land justice. Following Marx, we might think of labor as akin to a metabolic interchange between humans and nature.[55] And in the peasant labor process, returning to Trouillot, "land is both the object and instrument of labor, in addition to being the place of work."[56] This labor process is the foundation of some of the most important social relationships and cultural values for peasants, and working the land is often generative of various sorts of access and ownership rights.[57] Finally, from leaving their villages as migrant workers or staying as contract farmers, peasants have long been unevenly integrated into dominant political and economic orders. Thus, these relationships, values, and rights that are part of the peasant labor process, like property, are at once local and transnational.

Peasant farming remains the main form of agricultural work in the highlands, even though far fewer people rely on agriculture for their main livelihood. It is at the foundation of what Palestinian thinkers have variously referred to as "attachment," the "relationship between people and land," or "feelings of belonging (intima')."[58] The work of cultivation is the subject of chapter 4. Using the idiom of "building" ('amr) the land as an entry point, I show how the long-term work of cultivation inscribes peasant values into the landscape in surprisingly durable ways. As agricultural land is transformed into real estate, some men have turned to their lives of working the land both to criticize those whom they see as engaging in speculative or wasteful behavior and to assert their rightful claim on the new wealth promised by property ownership. Chapter 5 traces the origins of numerous projects underway in the highlands—voluntary work, an olive oil cooperative, home gardens, and an experimental farm—to the 1970s, when Palestinian organizers and thinkers began to incorporate aspects of peasant labor into insurgent approaches to agricultural development and grassroots organizing. I argue that all of these projects share a commitment to getting people to come back to the land, and allow us to see how a rural politics of return takes shape through collective forms of agrarian labor. While labor is enmeshed with class inequality and patriarchal power, it also provides a dynamic way for making claims to land, even in the absence of ownership, and an approach to land justice that is both processual and open-ended.

Land defense provides a third perspective for thinking about land justice. Land defense encompasses the various ways that Indigenous peoples resist colonial dispossession and displacement *through* asserting their political authority, legal control, and historical presence in specific territories. Peasants were part of some of the first land defense struggles against Zionist settlement and were at the forefront of anticolonial resistance during the British Mandate.[59] However, it was the Palestinians who were able to remain in what became Israel after 1948, and the land defense committees they organized to resist the expropriation of their land in the 1960s, that had a direct impact on the development of land defense in the West Bank. Since the 1970s, legal contestation, tree planting, land reclamation, sit-ins, protest marches, and other tactics have all left their mark on physical and political landscape of the highlands.

Property ownership and peasant labor both shape rural land defense. Like colonized peoples across the globe, Palestinians find themselves forced to contest dispossession by working through the colonial legal system.[60] But unlike many Indigenous struggles, as chapter 2 shows, in the West Bank Palestinians have little option but to defend land through private property claims. While legal efforts may slow, but not prevent, dispossession, property has provided a way for landowners, lawyers and human rights organizations, and now the PA and private companies, to demonstrate to international audiences how the Israeli occupation violates liberal norms. In chapters 2 and 3, I investigate how anticolonial struggles also provide part of the moral and political language for criticizing the spread of private ownership, and the commodification of land, in the highlands. One of the main ways the Israeli authorities establish legal control over territory is by declaring untitled and uncultivated land to be state property, leading Palestinians to use tree planting to prevent dispossession. By situating this practice as an adaptation of peasant labor, chapter 4 shows how tree planting both includes and exceeds legal claims, often with unexpected political and ecological effects. The back-to-the-land efforts I describe in chapter 5 are also inseparable from land defense. They grapple with displacement and search for ways to enable those who had left to work in Israel, or who had never farmed at all, to build new attachments to village land. Land defense, then, provides a framing that is at once more specific and more capacious than "resistance," insofar as it allows us to see not only the forms of colonial power that Palestinians fight against, but also the kinds of land justice they are fighting to achieve.

Land justice provides the grounds for reconceptualizing the question of Palestine as an agrarian question. In *The Question of Palestine*, the literary scholar and public intellectual Edward Said famously treated the Palestinian question as a contest between "an affirmation" of a people that "identified itself with the land it tilled and lived on" and "a denial" that Palestinians are "a population with an indissoluble bond with the land."[61] As a result, he pointed out, "Palestine itself is a much debated, even contested, notion. The very mention of the name on the one hand constitutes for the Palestinian and his partisans an act of important and positive political assertion, and on the other, for the Palestinian's enemies it is an act of equally assertive but much more negative and threatening denial."[62] Too often, as historian Beshara Doumani reminds us, efforts to assert Palestinian presence fall into narratives of "erasure/affirmation" or "colonization/resistance" that cannot explain "how the Palestinians became a people and what their relationship is to place" and turn "a blind eye to internal contradictions."[63] Asking questions about agrarian property ownership and labor provides an alternative to these sorts of narratives. In doing so, we learn how the injustices suffered at the hands of landlords and brokers take on newfound significance, how agrarian toil becomes the basis for novel moral and political claims as property values change, and how fights over land are not only conducted proudly against the Israeli state, but also often involve painful confrontations over inheritance with the relatives or plot boundaries with neighbors. It is only by exploring how, and for whom, land becomes home, property, territory, and homeland that we can grasp *how* Palestinians affirm their connection to place, and defend it.

Tracing the demands and projects that emerge from this matrix of property, labor, and land defense illuminates the different, and often contradictory, meanings that land justice takes in Palestine. Such contradictions often disappear from accounts that emphasize movements that fight against private property and for the creation of a commons.[64] In Palestine, references to enclosure and commons tend to align with this bigger political project and theoretical framing; as one recent essay put it, "the *musha'a* [commons] of Palestine may guide our transition from one disastrous world and outlook to another: to the commune and the commons."[65] But these accounts rarely dwell on the complicated valences of property ownership, or the changing forms of agricultural labor, and they cause us to pass over the ways that Palestinians rework peasant practices and values as they grapple with the changing agrarian political economy.[66] This grappling includes resistance, of course, as well as moral complaints, ambiguous negotiations, and enthusiastic support for secure land rights and profitable investment. Today, the sheer number of demands for land justice across the world testifies both to the continuing importance of land for so many people, and to the long histories of violence that have given control of so much of it to so few. As one front of this global land war, the central highlands have much to teach us about the present meaning and possible futures of land justice, in and beyond Palestine.

ETHNOGRAPHY AND SOLIDARITY

Plots and Deeds is based on interviews, participant observation, and archival research. I began this project in 2013, taking trips back to the highlands until 2022. My fieldwork involved formal interviews with everyone who had an interest in rural land, as well as informal conversations during visits to villages, walks with farmers, and time spent hanging around government offices and with survey teams.[67] From the beginning of May 2016 until I left in January 2017, I spent a few days each week accompanying survey teams working for the Palestinian Land Authority (PLA) and later for the Land and Water Settlement Commission (LWSC). The time that I was not in the villages was spent looking for archival materials in state archives, libraries, village councils, and personal collections.[68] It became quite clear over these years that historical narratives, personal stories, and even rumors are always potentially constitutive of legal and political claims to land.[69]

My relationships with the people I spent time with—as an "international," a man, a stranger, and a friend—shaped what people told me, what they kept to themselves, and what they hoped I would write. The term "international" is used widely in the West Bank to refer to the many foreigners who come as aid workers, consultants, journalists, activists, and diplomats.

Being an international and holder of a US passport meant that I enjoyed a privilege that Israel denies to West Bank Palestinians: mobility. I was able to access archives in Jerusalem and carry out interviews in Tel Aviv and Haifa as easily as I was able to reach the various cities and villages in the highlands. It also granted me easier access to people working for the World Bank, the Office of the Quartet, and various NGOs. Finally, it meant that people would often try to convey to me, regardless of what I was asking, the ways that they suffered under Israeli occupation, with the directive that I should relay their stories to the outside world. It is the latter issue that I wrestled the most with in writing this book: how to convey the injustice that Palestinians face while also critiquing the ways this injustice is usually conveyed.

My gender also informed what I learned about land, and *Plots and Deeds* is based mostly on male voices. My opportunities to speak with women about land and property were, for the most part, limited to chance encounters during my time with surveyors, in public meetings, or in the company of legal aid workers. Many of the spaces I had access to were male spaces, and as a result my interviews and casual conversations were with men. My arguments in the book are thus not "the whole story" about land; instead, they often represent a critical engagement with the assumptions and concerns of men.

Often, I was a stranger in the places where I was doing research. When I accompanied survey teams or visited a new village, my presence as an outsider meant that people were curious about my presence and, while usually happy to talk to me, were not quite sure what the point was if I was not working for a human rights organization or development NGO. Sometimes people assumed I was an Israeli, speaking to me in Hebrew; once, I was even offered unsolicited directions to the nearest settlement. There were a few instances where my presence aroused suspicion; in one, which I recall in chapter 3, several young men were convinced I was a land broker. In sum, being a stranger meant that my perspective was limited, and provided me a way to reflect on the ways that land politics are inseparable from shifting boundaries between insider and outsider.

Finally, I was also sometimes a friend. Prior to starting fieldwork, I spent three years doing research, translation, and campaign work with Stop the Wall in Ramallah. These relationships facilitated connections with activists, farmers, and lawyers who gave me a great deal of their time, and often introduced me to other people and places they thought would help me in my work. Our shared political commitments gave us a common language and the grounds for building trust. And more than helping me with fieldwork, my relationships with people in Stop the Wall have, without my always being aware of it, drawn me toward some land questions and away from others. But *Plots and Deeds* is not an activist ethnography. Instead, it is often a reflection on the limits of our political vocabularies, and an exploration of the struggles that have an ambivalent relationship to social movements.

These relationships inform the choices I have made to balance protecting the identities of those I interviewed with writing an ethnographic account about real places and people. The place names in this book are real. Some of the names are, too. I use the real names of public figures—the CEO of a company, a prominent lawyer, the head of an NGO—who have written or spoken on the public record about the issues they discuss with me. I also try to use the names of those whose expertise I rely on, and who often talked to me precisely because they wanted their specific struggles to reach a new audience. Sometimes, even if someone gave me permission to use their name, I have opted for a pseudonym if I judged that using their name could have adverse consequences, or could be potentially dangerous. Finally, I have tried to include a level of detail that will allow others to know how I've told their stories, to check my claims, or to delve deeper into the issues that I raise in the following pages.

This is a fraught moment for scholarship about Palestine and the Palestinians. In Gaza, Israel has destroyed archives, museums, and every single institution of higher education. It has killed university students, professors, presidents, and staff members. In the West Bank, Israel consistently closes universities, arrests students and staff, and prevents foreign scholars and students from working or studying in Palestine. The Israeli academy itself is deeply implicated in the subjugation of the Palestinians, while widespread racism and targeted repression have limited the possibility of dissent and made the position of the few Palestinians who teach at Israeli universities increasingly precarious. In the United States, student and faculty solidarity with the Palestinians is being met with increasingly severe repression. At the same time, however, critical knowledge production is flourishing. It is not just that there is a large body of scholarship about the place and its people in anthropology, history, geography, and other fields. It is also that the Palestinian condition is a crucial reference point—what the global studies scholar John Collins once called "Palestine's prophetic global significance"—for making sense of the troubling directions the world is headed in, and what decolonization and liberation might look like.[70] This scholarship nourishes the analysis of solidarity movements, and informs the ways that Palestine has become a truly international cause.[71] This is the paradoxical condition of Palestinian studies: at once under attack from all sides, while also more vibrant, and more important, than ever.

I offer *Plots and Deeds* as a critical engagement with Palestinian studies. This book is not addressed to those who question the humanity of the Palestinian people or their right to exist. Nor does it answer those who demand that we produce evidence, over and over again, of human rights violations. It is instead for those who are, or who might be, in solidarity with the Palestinian cause. By focusing on the different ways that land becomes meaningful to people and why they find it worth fighting for, I hope to challenge some of our assumptions about Palestinian life and to critique the frameworks that we often rely on to diagnose injustice. In doing so, my aim is not only to deepen our understanding of land in Palestine but also to provide a resource for imagining new forms of solidarity with the people who are refusing agrarian annihilation.

One

RUINING

THE LONG WAR ON
THE PALESTINIAN PEASANTRY

"THEY BURNED IT BEFORE THEY TOOK IT," ABU BILAL TOLD ME. IT was 2013 in Bruqin, and he was pointing to a hilltop, near an Israeli settlement, that had recently been bulldozed. "The army doesn't confiscate cultivated land," he explained, before continuing to tell me that he suspected that settlers had set fires to ease the legal expropriation.[1] This sort of dispossession is happening across the highlands. In 2019, Israeli forces razed a small Palestinian farm in the neighboring village of Farkha on the legal pretext that it was located on state property.[2] In the years that followed, the Israeli authorities took steps to facilitate the seizure of the entire area: military orders, paramilitary attacks, the construction of a new road and, finally, the creation of a new settler outpost in 2024. Similar events have taken place across the West Bank, where the interplay of settler colonial law and violence is one of the main drivers of agrarian dispossession.

But there are other ways that land can be ruined. One summer, I was discussing the work of the local olive oil cooperative with an older farmer in Farkha. He remarked that agriculture in the village was "in retreat." He explained how farming cannot support families, and how his children worked elsewhere, or had left Palestine altogether. People barely have the time to take care of their olive trees, he said, and even those who still farm only plow their land once or twice a year. From the porch where we were sitting, he gestured to the hills outside the village. It has become "wasteland [*bur*]," he sighed. "If our grandfathers came back from the grave and saw their land, they would die again."

Plots of land with overgrown trees, unruly vines, crumbling terraces, and wild thorn bushes are part of the agricultural landscape of the highlands. People called them "ruins" (*khirab*), a term that overlaps with "barren" (*jarda'*), "wasteland" (*bur*), "abandoned" (*matruka*), and "stripped" (*salikh*), and they had different explanations for why the land was in such a condition.[3] Everyone held Israel responsible to some degree. Some blamed those who left in the 1970s to work in Israel. Others blamed the young people who seemed to be more interested in their smartphones than in farming. A few noted that real estate development was making owners neglect agricultural land. During one interview in Qarawa, a man recalled how the soil used to be red, a result of regular plowing and grazing. "For the past two or three years," he continued, "when you go out to the land, you find that most of it isn't even touched." Talk of ruined land was always in reference to something lost or absent, and always prompted a comparison between what the landscape looked like in the past and the state that it is in today. In other words, "ruined land" is at once a description of a landscape and commentary on how it has changed.

Ruined lands provide an entry point for understanding agrarian annihilation in Palestine. When we ask how soils are degraded, trees are neglected, crops disappear, and ecologies change, we can better see the complex ways that organized state violence and coercive market forces have slowly destroyed the social and ecological relations underpinning peasant farming in the highlands.[4] We can also begin to see how annihilation is uneven and incomplete. What remains of peasant farming has helped families survive moments of crisis and has provided resources for theorizing and enacting agrarian self-determination. Ruined lands are the materialization of these contradictory processes, and by accounting for the different forces that have transformed the landscape, we can map out the terrain upon which struggles for land justice take place.

FIGURE 2. Ruined land, 2016.

Source: Author.

UNDERSTANDING PEASANT DISPOSSESSION

The Marxist tradition provides a generative framework for understanding peasant dispossession. Marx used the concept of "primitive accumulation" to foreground, contrary to the origin myths offered by the political economists of his day, the violent creation of capitalist social relations.[5] Primitive accumulation took a long time, with landlords and state authorities forcing peasants off their lands, and charitable organizations and carceral institutions transforming the dispossessed into complaint wage labor.[6] While the term "primitive accumulation" can give the impression that theft and plunder were only necessary to get the capitalist mode of production started, decades of scholarship have shown that violent dispossession is a recurring feature of capitalist accumulation and expansion.[7]

The imposition of private property is a fundamental aspect of primitive accumulation. For Marx, the enclosure of the English commons and their transformation into the private property of a new class of landlords was integral to the "classic form" of primitive accumulation.[8] The commons were a complex, highly regulated system of use and access rights that were inseparable from peasant social life.[9] Because enclosure was the effective dismemberment of peasant communities, it at times saw fierce resistance and required a great deal of ideological work to justify. Supporters of enclosure extolled the virtues of private property and condemned commoners as belonging to a "sordid race" akin to "barbarians," "Indians," or "spiders."[10] As European settlement exported enclosure across the colonized world, liberal philosophers and colonial administrators elaborated this racial ideology of property to legitimize the dispossession of Indigenous peoples.[11] Today, a round of "new enclosures" has demonstrated that enclosure and its racial ideologies are durable features of capitalism as well.[12]

Dispossession does not only produce workers, but surplus populations as well. "Surplus population" refers to people who require access to wage labor to survive but, for different reasons, have become redundant for capital; as the literary scholar Chris Chen puts it, surplus populations are those who are "deserted by the wage but still imprisoned in capitalist markets."[13] The geographer Ruth Wilson Gilmore has argued that this desertion should be seen as "organized abandonment" resulting from government "action and inaction," rather than some inescapable effect of economic forces.[14] And imprisonment is helpful for capital, creating a reserve army of labor that can keep wages down and employed workers compliant. Like capital and labor, surplus populations are also, to return to Marx, "a condition for the existence of the capitalist mode of production."[15]

The control of native land, labor, and surplus populations was a defining concern for colonial governance. Authorities sought to transfer land to white settlers and preserve peasant farms to keep labor costs low and control native populations.[16] "Whereas in England the essence of 'primitive accumulation' was the deprivation of the direct producers of the means of production," argued the sociologist and anti-apartheid activist Bernard Magubane, "in South Africa this process was distinctive in that the colonists sought through conquest to create a sufficient pool of labor and to push the rest into reservations, where they would continue to eke out some subsistence besides wage labor."[17] Where settlers required native land, and not native labor, enclosure was a means of land seizure and population confinement that took on increasingly violent, at times genocidal, forms.

Palestine is often seen as a modern laboratory of enclosure and confinement. More than two decades ago, the political theorist Achille Mbembe conceptualized the West Bank and Gaza Strip as "death worlds," arguing that "the most accomplished form of necropower is the contemporary colonial occupation of Palestine."[18] Others have also theorized Palestine as part a centuries-long process of enclosure, where a complex system of barriers, gates, cameras, drones, and biometric control shapes "high-tech" and "neoliberal enclosures" for the purpose of seizing land and "warehousing surplus people."[19] In these accounts, Palestine is the culmination of much earlier stages of racialized confinement of "unwanted populations" and an apocalyptic sign of a world to come.[20]

Enclosure and surplus population are vital for conceptualizing agrarian annihilation in Palestine, just as the endurance of peasant farming reveals something of the limits of their explanatory power. The dispossession of land, the transformation of peasants into workers, and the confinement of surplus populations help us understand the past century as a long war on the Palestinian peasantry. But this story cannot account for the enduring persistence of peasant agriculture and the changing ways it shapes rural politics. Israeli settler colonialism does not create a uniformly abject surplus population. Instead, it results in a range of different collective experiences for Palestinians that, in rural areas, are determined by the specifics of the "agrarian milieux" and the extent to which people still have access to land.[21]

COLONIAL DISPOSSESSION

During the later part of Ottoman rule, peasant farming was widespread in Palestine. In the 1800s, members of peasant households cultivated their own land, worked as tenants on large estates and, later, as wage labor on the citrus plantations on the coast. In the highlands, historians describe polycultures that included trees, field crops, and livestock adapted to diverse topographical and climatic zones. Farming was labor intensive, with coordination and cooperation organized through kin and clan.[22] The appropriation of agricultural surplus resulted in relations of trade, debt, and patronage that linked villages to urban centers and shifting regional arrangements of political power.[23]

Access to land was at the center of village life. Legally, agricultural land was primarily categorized as *miri* to which the sovereign maintained the "abstract right of ownership" (*raqaba*) and to which individuals enjoyed extensive use rights (*tassaruf*), provided they kept the land under cultivation.[24] Agricultural land might also be classified as *waqf*, meaning land endowed for families or religious institutions.[25] Property law shaped, but did not determine, how peasants accessed (and lost) land. In practice, agricultural land, even if it was legally *miri*, was inherited, mortgaged, or purchased outright. Different tenancy agreements allowed peasants to gain a portion of the harvest on land they cultivated, and sometimes permanent rights to land, trees, or both. Custom granted clans access to common land (*masha'* or *musha'*) and often distributed shares to this land according to the male labor power a household could provide.[26] These relations to land bound families and villages together, with conflicts over ownership and access indexing larger struggles around patriarchal power, the boundaries of peasant moral economies, and the extension of citizenship rights to rural people.

In the late 1800s, the Ottoman empire was increasingly integrated into circuits of global capital and spheres of European imperial control. Peasants, merchants, and landlords vied for control over olive oil, cotton, wheat, and other commodities that had become sources of wealth and power. Ottoman reforms facilitated the commodification of land and its acquisition by new, noncultivator owners.[27] The effects were the most drastic in the coastal plains, where absentee landlords began to acquire huge estates. But the highlands were also changing, with new property relations and opportunities for accumulation leading to the consolidation of land holdings and the rise of powerful rural families. These changes set the stage for agrarian dispossession under British rule.[28]

It was the British who brought Marx's "classic form" of primitive accumulation to Palestine. After the European powers divided up the Ottoman empire, Palestine became a British Mandate in 1920. Plans to institute liberal private property were informed by the ideology of improvement, which from its origins in the English enclosures had become the basis of a racial ideology of property that shaped land policies across the British empire.[29] As part of a larger goal to create free markets and turn Palestinian peasants into private property owners, British land titling began to liquidate the peasant commons.[30] High taxes and a rising demand for land driven by commercial agriculture and Zionist land purchases meant that British land reforms contributed to the dispossession and immiseration of the Palestinian peasantry.[31]

Dispossession fueled rural unrest and revolt. Before British rule, peasants, pastoralists, and tenant farmers were at the forefront of well-known fights against Jewish settlement. Resistance to Zionism became more pronounced under the British Mandate. Peasants also fought British attempts to restrict land access and enclose common lands, preventing surveyors from making much progress in the highlands.[32] Both those who remained in their villages and those who had been forced into the urban slums of Palestine's growing port cities played a leading role in the 1936 revolt. As historian Charles Anderson points out, "peasant activism sprung [*sic*] from a tradition of communal autonomism" and was part of a struggle "for the preservation of their patrimony and the multiple senses of community, attachment, and identity enfolded within it."[33] Even with overwhelming military power and the support of Zionist paramilitary forces, it took the colonial government three years of brutal counterinsurgency to finally crush the uprising.[34] Though they were ultimately defeated, peasant resistance galvanized wider Palestinian and Arab publics, becoming a core element of Palestinian identity that would inspire subsequent battles for land.[35]

THE CONSOLIDATION OF A SETTLER COLONIAL STATE

The Nakba set in motion a devastating process of agrarian dispossession that transformed Palestinian land politics. In 1948, the state of Israel was established in Mandatory Palestine. For Palestinians, this event is known as the Nakba, or "catastrophe." From 1947 to 1948, Zionist forces destroyed 531 villages and expelled their inhabitants. By 1949, an estimated 720,000–750,000 people of a population of 1.3 million, or about 80 percent of the Arab population that had once resided within the borders of the new Israeli state, had become refugees.[36] Those who remained became second-class citizens. The refugees in exile, through armed struggle, legal advocacy, and commemoration, fought to return to their homes and keep the memory of the land alive for generations born in the camps. Those who remained developed different ways to defend what they still had and recover what had been taken.

In the years following 1948, the Israeli state continued its war on Palestinian peasant farming. The new government went to work ensuring that rural areas could not be repopulated by peasant farmers, instructing soldiers to shoot those who tried to cross the border and harvest their crops, demolishing what remained of many villages, and uprooting "tens of thousands of dunums" of "abandoned olive groves" to replace with field crops.[37] It also established a legal framework to expropriate land from Palestinian refugees and citizens alike.[38] Emergency regulations enabled the state to expropriate "fallow" lands for Jewish farmers, while a seemingly innocuous land titling operation transferred extensive tracts of land from Palestinian to Israeli state ownership.[39] The dispossession of farmers facilitated their incorporation into the Israel economy as cheap labor, primarily in construction, while discriminatory state policies kept villages without basic infrastructure and services.[40] The Palestinians who remained inside Israel—urban residents of the few remaining Arab neighborhoods and towns, villagers in the central and northern parts of the country, and Bedouin in the south—all experienced the expropriation of their property and enclosure of their lands. For peasants, this was a process of annihilation that destroyed farms, eliminated legal ownership, and erased traces of their presence on the land.

This assault produced different battles over agrarian livelihoods and lands. Farmers who still had access to olive groves negotiated with state authorities and courts for the right to access their groves and the ability to not sell their oil at a loss.[41] The Galilee became a center of resistance to state expropriations, with Communist Party activists and lawyers helping to publicize the issue and contest dispossession in Israeli courts.[42] It was a planned expropriation that led to the pivotal Land Day protests of 1976, which subsequently became important for the political identity Palestinians in Israel, and are now commemorated across historic Palestine and the diaspora. This combination of legal tactics and popular organizing, and the expertise of the leading activists and lawyers, directly informed land defense in the West Bank years later.

While resistance slowed dispossession, there was little Palestinians could do to maintain a viable agrarian land base. From the 49 percent in 1955, by 1971 only 22 percent of Palestinian citizens of Israel were "engaged in agriculture."[43] In 2015, that number had fallen to around 2 percent, with 80 percent of the Palestinians working in agriculture "dependent on the Jewish sector."[44] Today agriculture is only a small part of the Israeli economy, and the Israeli state has effectively abandoned the remaining Palestinian farmers, using them instead as props to entice tourists to visit the "biblical landscape" of terraced hillsides and olive trees.[45]

PEASANTS IN AN AGRARIAN PERIPHERY

The fate of those who lived in the central highlands was different from the fate of those in Israel or the refugee camps. After the Nakba, in 1950 Jordan annexed the West Bank (the name of the territory comes from its location west of the Jordan River). In some ways, peasant agriculture continued as it had before.[46] Farmers in Farkha, Qarawa, and Bruqin managed a diverse agricultural economy, based primarily on rain-fed crops. Olives were the most important, followed by cereals like wheat and barley. Villagers also grew other fruit trees, such as figs and almonds; maintained home vegetable gardens; and raised poultry and livestock. Agriculture was labor intensive and required the energies of whole families, making its associated tasks integral to daily life.[47] Men socialized at the threshing floor or in the fields, women when foraging or bringing water from the village wells, and both together during harvests.[48] In the central highlands, agriculture was still an important part of the economic and social fabric of the village.

However, those in the central highlands experienced an economy reeling from war and government neglect. In the 1950s, the West Bank suffered from a postwar recession and then from a drought that hit rural areas especially hard.[49] The creation of Israel cut highland villages off from previous sources of employment and trade, while 280,000 refugees fled into the West Bank and increased its population by 60 percent, keeping wages down and unemployment high.[50] Throughout the 1950s and 1960s, debt remained a serious concern for the Jordanian authorities, and moneylenders reportedly charged exorbitant interest rates.[51] Jordanian government policy turned Palestinian villages into a source of agricultural commodities and a reserve of cheap labor for the East Bank and, after the oil boom, for the new petro-states of the Gulf as well.[52]

Fragmentary archival materials and interviews illustrate the difficulties that peasants faced in the highlands. In 1959, the village of Qarawa requested debt forgiveness on account of a poor olive harvest.[53] In the 1960s, according to one of my interviewees, loan defaults led to a powerful Nablus family seizing control of agricultural land in Farkha. Droughts, crop failures, and price fluctuations forced villages to demand aid from the Jordanian authorities. In 1960, for example, the local grain harvest was ruined by a fungus resulting from heavy May rains. As a result, in 1961 Qarawa received 21,000 kilos of grain from the Jordanian government (the number of "beneficiaries" was listed as 700 people, from a village with a population of 921) and the land tax was reduced by 50 percent.[54] The next year, in 1962, the price for grain in Ramallah jumped by 38 percent. "Please tell your commanders in the stations in this area," wrote the sub-governor of Ramallah to the police commander of the area, "to inform farmers that the Minister of Agriculture is seriously working to safeguard grain seeds for the farmers this year and that issue is currently under urgent study, and that appropriate steps will be taken to safeguard the seed requirements of the country by the relevant authorities."[55] In 1963, another drought pushed villages in the Ramallah district to request aid and tax forgiveness.[56]

These conditions led to the economic and social devaluation of peasant labor in the highlands. Studies of the villages in the central highlands all note increasing levels of immigration in the 1950s and 1960s, and those with the means to do so sent their sons to study abroad.[57] According to one account, "some villages in the Jerusalem-Ramallah region, such as Baytin and Bitunia, were literally emptied of young men who were the sons of landowners."[58] Those who remained struggled to get by, and could find themselves becoming tenants on the holdings of village elites who were building up larger estates. Remittances fueled the purchase of land back home, creating an emerging class divide between those who received remittances, and those who did not.

Under Jordanian rule, the West Bank became an agrarian periphery. Peasant agriculture was important to the West Bank's economy and shaped the rhythms of life in highland villages in the 1950s and 1960s. But the highlands were also effectively a "periphery of the Jordanian economy," a source of agricultural commodities and cheap labor, rather than the destination of investment.[59] These conditions set the stage for Israeli rule.

PEASANT WORKERS UNDER ISRAELI OCCUPATION

In 1967, Israel occupied the West Bank and the Gaza Strip. While the government never declared formal sovereignty, it set about integrating these territories into Israel legally, economically, and administratively, while separating the Palestinian population from the new population of Jewish settlers.[60] Using the same legal tools and administrative techniques that the state had refined in the 1950s and 1960s on the Palestinians within Israel, the military authorities of the West Bank oversaw a new cycle of primitive accumulation driven by the territorial logic of colonial expansion that also served the economic interests of Israeli capital.

Military rule transformed the occupied territories into a captive market and a source of cheap labor. Early Israeli experiments with agricultural development gave way to a series of policies that were devastating for Palestinian growers: restrictions on the cultivation and marketing of certain crops, little access to credit, and open competition with subsidized Israeli growers and cheap imports.[61] Wages were far higher in Israel, and like thousands of others from Palestine's refugee camps and villages, Palestinian men from the highlands found jobs in construction sites, farms, factories, hotels, and restaurants.[62] These wages allowed for higher levels of consumption that were fueled by consumer goods produced or sold by Israeli companies.[63] Labor and consumption were a vicious circle, each extending and entrenching Palestinian dependence on the occupying power.

Israel also began to take over Palestinian land for Jewish settlements. It followed established colonial practice, with the judiciary and military conspiring to legalize massive land seizures and transfer property to settler control. One of the most consequential legal mechanisms was "state lands," in which Israel asserted legal control over uncultivated, untitled land in the West Bank.[64] This doctrine was designed to provide a legal basis for colonization, a purpose that was discussed openly by representatives of the Israeli government and settler organizations at the time.[65] To accomplish the desired seizures of Palestinian land, the authorities had to ignore the original intent of the Land Code; more than a century of Ottoman, British, and Jordanian jurisprudence; and the basic requirements of international law.[66]

The colonization of the highlands began in the late 1970s, driven by a potent mix of messianic ideology and economic crisis.[67] Ariel, one of the first settlements to be constructed in the central highlands, was established just north of Salfit in 1978. More would follow. To encourage Israelis to live in the West Bank, the state offered subsidies and low-interest mortgages, with developers selling the promise of secure ownership, a beautiful setting, and easy access to urban jobs and amenities just across the Green Line.[68] While ideological settlers were often the vanguard, it was the lure of affordable housing that brought thousands more into the West Bank, gradually turning the highlands into residential satellites of Jerusalem, Tel Aviv, and other large Israeli cities.

In the 1970s and 1980s, trade policies and labor migration had more of an effect on peasant agriculture in the highlands than land confiscation. The Israeli authorities had no interest in Palestinians relocating to Israeli cities, and proximity to worksites—combined with a system of contractors, brokers, permits (although most worked illegally), and transportation—ensured that men maintained residence in their villages.[69] Employment outside the village meant that people spent far less time in the fields. In the early 1980s, sociologist Salim Tamari found that "in the hilly region of the West Bank very few households live exclusively from their family farm"; in one of the villages he studied in the central highlands, only eight families (5 percent of the households) worked a "substantial portion of the year in their family land."[70]

While labor intensive, rain-fed farming remained the main form of village agriculture, higher wages and cheaper food made many kinds of crops less important to household subsistence. Those I interviewed recalled how people no longer had the time or incentive to cultivate wheat or barley, replant unproductive fruit trees, or care for large herds of goats and sheep. Pointing to the hills above the village, Abu Ashraf, a resident of Qarawa and operator of an olive press, told me that "all the hills were planted. If you look at the barren parts [al-jirda'], it was planted [...] even the rocky places." Farmers replaced field crops and fruit trees with shorter lifespans with olive trees, whose resilience could mask the abandonment of orchards.[71] "Many peasants [fallahin] went and took work in the city, and in Tel Aviv," and others left for Jordan or the United States. As a result, he said, they "neglected the land [ihmal al-ard]" and their "connection [irtibat] to it weakened." The decline in crop diversity meant that an increasing number of tasks, and the skills and social relationships required to get them done, became irrelevant to rural livelihoods.[72] The effect was a slow enervation of the power of peasant labor to generate a sense of social belonging and shared purpose.

Israel often dispossessed rural Palestinians without expelling them. Surveying the transformation of Palestinian life after two decades of occupation, the economist Yusif Sayigh detailed how an "effective and comprehensive web" of Israeli policies, laws, and court rulings had achieved the "uprooting, dispossession and displacement of the national population with the imposition of a stunting state of dependence on those who remain in the country." Sayigh conceived of primitive accumulation as a "continuous process" that extended far beyond "economic dispossession" into the domain of "collective and individual political, social and cultural rights and freedoms." Dependency, he concluded, was not the result of the "invisible hand of market forces," but "the visible hand of the occupying power."[73] But wages and commodity prices worked alongside this visible hand, with Israeli settler colonialism preserving the peasant farm while reducing the economic power and social importance of peasant labor.

And yet, peasant agriculture did not disappear. Some farming labor was taken up by those who remained in the village—women, children, and elderly members of the household. Men who worked in Israel were still able to cultivate their land on weekends and holidays, with some sectors (like construction) allowing for workers to be absent for weeks during the olive harvest.[74] Peasants replaced field crops with olive trees; lawyers, surveyors, and agronomists assisted peasants in making land claims; and various organizations emerged to deal with interrelated problems of agricultural development, labor migration, and land defense. After the First Intifada began in 1987, many Palestinian workers lost or could no longer reach their jobs in Israel and returned to farming. Building on a decade of rural activism, which I will discuss in more detail in subsequent chapters, peasant farming inspired projects for self-sufficiency and land defense. Throughout the 1970s and 1980s, peasant farming remained a safety net in times of crisis, and a political resource in times of revolt.

DISPOSABLE PEASANTRIES

The 1990s saw the end of the uprising. Talks between the Palestinian leadership and Israel led to a series of agreements, known as the Oslo Accords, that divided the jurisdiction of the occupied territories between Israel and a newly created Palestinian governing body, the PA. Over the decade, Israel expanded settlements in rural areas and maintained control over trade, ensuring that the West Bank remained both a land reserve for colonization and a captive market for Israeli capital. The PA, for its part, embraced liberalization while never developing an agricultural development strategy to keep farmers on the land. For the remaining peasant farmers, the so-called peace process represented further marginalization and dispossession.

During this period, Israel began to reduce its vulnerability to Palestinian labor while deepening its control over Palestinian land. In response to the strikes and boycotts of the First Intifada, Israel replaced Palestinians with workers from Eastern Europe and Asia, and instituted a new permit and checkpoint system to better control those who continued to work in Israel.[75] It also sought to relocate Palestinian labor out of Israel proper, and into more easily contained settlements in the West Bank.[76] In the central highlands the Ariel settlement grew rapidly, absorbing immigrants from the former Soviet Union. In 1999, Israeli authorities established a new settlement called Brukhin. Construction of this settlement saw the gradual dispossession of landowners in Bruqin and the surrounding villages, while operators of the settlement industrial zones began to employ them as workers. In 2013, showing me the permit that enabled him to access a factory in the industrial zone of Burkan, one young college graduate from Farkha explained that while he hated working in a settlement, it was the best paying job in the area.

The division of the West Bank into Areas A, B, and C provided Israel with a justification for restricting Palestinian access to agricultural areas. Recall that the interim agreements gave Israel total control over the land of Area C, about 60 percent of the West Bank. This new distribution of jurisdiction was layered on top of state lands, military zones, and protected natural areas, providing Israel additional tools to consolidate settler control in the West Bank. In Bruqin, where much agricultural land was designed Area C, Israel has effectively made investments in irrigation, greenhouses, and even terracing illegal. In 2013, for example, the authorities ordered farmers to remove basic improvements they had built on their lands; otherwise, the state would demolish them, and the farmers would be fined for the expense.[77] The expansion of settlement infrastructure and the route of the Separation Wall creates additional barriers to access, while proximity to settlements means that farmers risk harassment, arrest, and bodily harm from both settlers and soldiers when they attempt to reach their lands. In Bruqin, these various enclosures have dispossessed, to varying degrees, residents of more than half of the village's 12,285 dunums of land.[78] The same process is underway in Farkha, where in 2019 settler paramilitaries and soldiers began to take over an area of 1,250 dunums that the government claims was declared state property in 1982.

Colonization also destroys agricultural land. Bulldozing land and uprooting trees is a common practice, both to clear the way for settler housing and infrastructure, and to exact revenge or collectively punish Palestinian communities. Israel has also turned the West Bank into a dumping zone, creating a condition that anthropologist Sophia Stamatopoulou-Robbins aptly calls a "waste siege."[79] In the central highlands, flows of raw sewage and chemical waste from hilltop settlement housing and industrial zones have damaged crops and soil since the 1990s.[80] In al-Matwi, located between Bruqin and Farkha, pollution has also made entire areas less accessible, removing both agricultural land and recreational space.[81] Farmers have complained that it is difficult to market their produce, as the area has developed a reputation among Palestinian consumers who are concerned that anything grown or pastured in the area may be contaminated.[82] In other words, destruction of agricultural land to expand settlements increases the likelihood that places that Palestinians still have access to will be polluted and degraded.

Environmental changes can produce hostile ecologies. In the central highlands, the combination of urbanization and pollution has created a welcoming habitat for wild boars and made the area around Salfit the wellspring of reporting, rumor, and debate about the role of Israel in the wild boar problem.[83] Wild boars have a devastating effect on agriculture. Political ecologist Saad Amira observes that boars act as "mini bulldozers" that complement Israeli colonization, and in all the interviews I did in Farkha, Bruqin, Kafr 'Ein, and Qarawa, I would be hard pressed to find a single farmer who did not mention them.[84] Farmers reported that these animals generally avoid olive trees, instead feasting on whatever is closer to the ground, rooting up seeds, and trampling new saplings. In Farkha, it was the boars that finally put an end to the cultivation of wheat, which people had managed to continue growing into the 1990s. Environmental damage and ecological change have adversely affected agriculture on the land that farmers can still reach and further circumscribed the diversity of crops that they can cultivate.

For those who can still cultivate their land, Israeli movement restrictions and trade barriers—what political scientist Caroline Abu-Sada calls "silent processes and mechanisms"—make it very difficult for farmers to access markets or offer competitive prices.[85] Since the 1990s, Israeli authorities have restricted the movement of Palestinian products into Israel, undercut Palestinian producers by importing cheaper goods, and allowed Israeli growers unfettered access to Palestinian markets.[86] Closures and security inspections have increased import and export costs considerably for Palestinians, creating all sorts of problems for farmers who produce enough surplus olive oil to sell on the market. Farmers find little help from the PA, which lacks the sovereign means and political will to protect small farmers. These mechanisms are less visible than bulldozed lands and uprooted groves, but just as harmful to Palestinian agriculture.

The 1990s marked a change in how Israel treated rural Palestinians. This shift was part of a new phase of Israeli rule, one that political scientist Neve Gordon argued operates according to a "politics of death."[87] Previous practices of enclosure and dispossession continued, of course. The difference is that Palestinian labor has been increasingly discarded, and the expansion of the settlement enterprise has degraded the capacity of the land to support peasant farming. Peasants, like the wider population that they are a part of, are increasingly treated as a disposable.

In these conditions, peasant farming constitutes a shifting part of village livelihoods and has inspired new economic and political projects. While agriculture's contribution to GDP dropped by about half between 1993 and 2006, employment in agriculture doubled.[88] Peasant farming and home gardens were vital for family survival during the Second Intifada (2000–2005), when closures and curfews often prevented Palestinians from leaving their villages, and even their homes.[89] In the central highlands, peasant farmers created new cooperatives to deal with collapsing olive oil prices. This period also saw the beginnings of renewed agronomic interest in rain-fed farming and its related system of knowledge. Ismail Daiq, one of the founders of the Palestinian Agricultural Relief Committees (PARC), led a research team that carried out extensive fieldwork in the West Bank, cataloging peasant farming techniques (what he alternately called "local knowledge," "indigenous knowledge," and "rural people's knowledge") in hopes of integrating them into a broader program of agricultural development.[90] As in previous eras, peasant farming supported livelihoods during crisis, and represented a social and epistemological resource for those hoping to keep Palestinians on the land.

Rural land struggles continued. While most attention has been given to the urban warfare and suicide bombings of the Second Intifada, there were important agrarian aspects to the uprising as well. In response to Israel's construction of the Separation Barrier in 2002—which, under the pretext of security, sought to effectively annex 10 percent of the West Bank—villagers mobilized to protect their lands. Across the West Bank, villagers reactivated or assembled land defense committees (also called popular committees), filed court cases, and organized demonstrations and direct actions.[91] These defensive struggles continued long after the Second Intifada ended in 2005, with regular Friday marches in small villages in the central highlands like Nabi Saleh and Bil'in becoming global symbols of resistance.

SELLERS OF LAND

The defeat of the uprising led to the emergence of neoliberal state-building in the West Bank.[92] Under the premiership of former International Monetary Fund economist Salam Fayyad, the PA embarked on economic liberalization and normalization with Israel, and was rewarded with massive infusions of donor funding.[93] Real estate and finance were an important part of the PA's development strategy. The rural land between Ramallah and Salfit is one of the largest contiguous zones of A and B in the West Bank, and Palestinian government and private interests channeled infrastructure and investment into this area, where Palestinian planning is potentially feasible and ownership more secure. The new city of Rawabi was the flagship project of the Fayyad years and the symbol of a new liberal, market-friendly Palestine.[94] Due to the expropriation of village land, the architectural resemblance to

Israeli settlements, and high prices of apartments, the project received a great deal of academic attention and political criticism.[95] But while Rawabi was the biggest and loudest, there were many other commercial and housing projects that were slowly increasing the demand for rural land.

It was not long until other developers made their way into the central highlands, buying land in Farkha, Qarawa, Bruqin, and other villages in the area. The Ramallah-based Union Construction and Investment (UCI) was the largest company, and it purchased hundreds of dunums of land for its TABO real estate project. Smaller companies like Manazel followed suit, as well as individual investors and speculators. Rising prices did not seem to deter other buyers from moving in later. In 2022, signs had appeared announcing another new residential project, and I heard rumors that large Palestinian companies had been buying up more land in the area.

Buyers initially came to the highlands in search of cheap land. According to village councils, sellers, and officials at the land registry, in the late 2000s, a dunum was going for JD 2,000 up to JD 3,000 (about $2,800 to $5,200). After the public announcement of development projects and the beginning of the land boom in the early 2010s, these same parcels could be sold for many times their initial purchase price. Village residents often mentioned that outsiders were buying formerly agricultural land that had fallen into disuse and disrepair. In contrast, far less of the prime agricultural land and well-cared-for olive orchards in Farkha seem to have been sold.

The same forces that dispossessed peasants and pulled them out of agriculture also made land cheap and, importantly, made people willing to sell it. Abu Dawood, a farmer and former teacher said that before the 1967 occupation everyone worked in agriculture. Afterward, Israel "attracted them with money," but "in exchange, they lost their land." The landscape changed, becoming "ruined [*khirab*]" and no longer "clean or taken care of." This account resonated with other stories farmers had told me: about the military confiscating land for the construction of settlements, about the abandonment of grapevines and fig trees during years of working in Israel, about the wild boars that devoured wheat and crushed saplings. "Most people left their land," Abu Dawood explained, and when a person leaves his land, "it becomes cheap to him." After decades of de-agrarianization, selling their devalued assets was the best that many villagers could hope for.

While land sales are linked to dispossession, they are experienced in qualitatively different ways. Farmers talk about the confiscation of land for settlements, or its isolation behind walls and gates, as theft. But the loss of land to Palestinian developers is different. "It makes no difference to me whether a Jew or a Palestinian takes my land," Abu Dawood told me, since "the result is that my land is gone." But for many, the act of sale shifted the responsibility of loss to the seller, just as the devaluation of land made it difficult to argue that anyone should abstain from the market. "Who is better off," Abu Ashraf asked, "the one who remains on the land, with all its troubles and difficulties, running behind the sheep in the hills, or the person who goes to the city and makes some money?" Due to the diminishing prospects farming offered, it was hard to blame people for abandoning the land.

The transformation of agricultural land into real estate puts two pressures on peasant farming. First, the transformation of farmland into real estate permanently takes areas out of agricultural use. The land registry is not public, and therefore it is hard to know exactly how much land has been sold. In 2016, current and former village council representatives estimated that UCI owned around 1,000 dunams in Farkha and 650 in Qarawa (one-sixth and one-tenth of total village lands, respectively). Since that time other projects have appeared, likely making the amount of land owned by companies or nonresident investors much larger. Second, the detachment of ground rent from agriculture encourages farmers to treat their land as potential real estate, creating the conditions for "anticipatory disinvestment," or the calculation that since it is likely that land will be converted to suburban real estate in the future, agricultural investment is a poor choice.[96] Palestinian developers and speculators are not analogous to Israeli settlers and state forces; indeed, as we will see in the next chapter, some developers frame their efforts as land defense. But they do take advantage of a history of peasant dispossession and, by slowly transforming the political economy of land, contribute further to the destruction of peasant farming.

Rising land prices may create new difficulties for efforts to revive peasant agriculture in the highlands. Access to farms and home gardens is still important during times of crisis, and several farmers remarked to me in 2022 that during the COVID-19 lockdowns, people spent considerably more time in the fields. The cooperative movement has been scaling up its efforts, and Farkha saw the reclamation of unused land and its conversion into an experimental farm. But farmers and activists are not only struggling here against Israeli confiscations. They are also fighting to convince others that it is worth their time and effort to hold onto their land and return to farming.

THE LONG WAR ON THE PEASANTRY

One summer evening, at the end of my fieldwork, I interviewed three farmers in Farkha. These men were in their fifties and sixties, and all of them were active members of the village's olive oil cooperative. I asked them to tell me about the main challenges facing agriculture in the highlands. They explained how Israeli and international companies dumped cheap products, from watermelons to potatoes, on the Palestinian market. They pointed out that the lack of access to water meant that they could not diversify their crops. They worried about how Israel confiscated uncultivated land. The talked about how their children preferred nonagricultural work, and that even those who did want to farm would be left with little land to do it on. One farmer recalled that, in the past, money from olive oil could pay for a university education. In a few decades, he mused, you might not be able to find any more olive oil for sale in the village.

These conditions represent the latest phase of a war on peasant farmers in Palestine. This war began more than a century ago. It has been carried out by legal and extralegal means, and by military force and economic domination. It affects people, plants, animals, and environments in different ways, and over different timescales, such that some kinds of loss, such as the selling of devalued farmland to developers, can seem entirely disconnected from the more violent aspects of settler colonialism. But together, these forces have sapped the capacity of peasant labor to create the stable livelihoods and strong social relationships that can anchor collective attachments to the land.

The situation in the central highlands is not unique. Israel has robbed Palestinians of their land base and severely weakened peasant agriculture across the West Bank. Outside of large city centers like Ramallah, Tulkarm, Nablus, Bethlehem, and Jericho, colonization has shaped patterns of Palestinian urbanization, and opened new real estate frontiers for Palestinian capital.[97] These processes take different forms, from the dense agglomerations that blend city, village, and camp, to exclusive villas and commercial spaces in which "concentrated inequality" puts Palestinian class disparities on stark display.[98] What they all have in common is that they are built on the ruins of agriculture.

While most rural populations are not facing a military assault from a colonial power, many are facing annihilation. Just around the time that Israel's military occupation was being established, elsewhere in the world economic restructuring and abandonment of agrarian reform resulted in the exodus of peasants from the countryside across the Global South.[99] Subsequent cycles of dispossession and "new enclosures" have produced more "surplus peoples," especially as capital moves into the countryside in search of land, but has little use for the people who live there.[100] From the central highlands of the West Bank to contested rural spaces across the planet, new struggles for land, and new visions of land justice, are emerging. It is to that part of the story that we now turn.

Two

OWNING

LAND DEFENSE AND PROPERTY

IN THE WINTER OF 2009, ISRAELI SETTLERS TOOK OVER A SPRING BE-longing to the Palestinian village of Nabi Saleh. For years after, the village was the site of regular marches, creative protest tactics, and fierce clashes with Israeli forces. The tenacity of the people living there; the way that the protests drew in Palestinian, Israeli, and international activists; and the charismatic presence of the Tamimi family, especially the then teenage Ahed Tamimi (who was arrested after she slapped a soldier in the face): all these factors contributed to extensive media coverage and an outpouring of solidarity across the globe. For a time, this tiny village in the highlands was emblematic of the struggle for land in Palestine.

Along the road at the entrance to Nabi Saleh, where protesters often confronted soldiers and jeeps, stands a line of bullet-scarred billboards. On one, a young husband and wife look out across the landscape. In the second, the same couple is accompanied by two children. They stand in the shade of an olive grove. In a third, the husband stands alone next to an old olive tree. He looks out to meet our gaze, a smile beaming across his face, and proudly holds a document. "With monthly payments," the caption above him reads, "you'll have land with a title deed."

FIGURE 3. Real estate advertisement, "With monthly payments, you'll have land with a title deed," 2016.

Source: Author.

These billboards are advertisements for TABO, a real estate project run by Union Construction and Investment (UCI). This company is selling not only real estate, but also land defense. Israeli land confiscations "occur because there are no title deeds to prove the original owners," explain company advertising materials. When you buy property from the company, the story goes, your financial investment is also a political one, legally protecting land from colonial encroachment. Along the main route leading out of Nabi Saleh toward the town of Salfit, narrow roads branch off and wind upward to UCI's new hilltop properties in the neighboring villages, which include Qarawa, Farkha, and Bruqin. Fluttering from the electricity poles, company banners proclaim: "The Homeland, We Are Its Owners."

What are we to make of all this? Following critical scholarship about

Palestinian capitalism, we might see the creation of private property, the financialization of land, and the celebration of investment as alien to the ways that rural Palestinians relate to land, and as a rupture with the sorts of resistance they practice in places like Nabi Saleh. It is true that the market-friendly reforms and institution-building that happened in the West Bank after 2007—what many have called "neoliberal Palestine"—created the conditions for something like TABO to emerge, but it is also true this project is part of a much longer tradition of land defense.[1] In the following pages, I tell one part of this story by exploring how private property became a part of land defense in the highlands. Israeli settler colonialism is premised on the juridical elimination of Palestinians as owners. Since 1967, the creation of so-called "state land" and attempts by private settler companies to register Palestinian property have played a decisive role in shaping the legal, social, and political dimensions of ownership for Palestinians. This history helps us understand both the politics of Palestinian land titling in the present moment, and the critiques rural Palestinians make of what is happening to the land, and to land defense, in the highlands. Today, justice is unimaginable without property ownership, even as property ownership continues to fail those who need it most.

LAND, PROPERTY, AND SETTLER COLONIALISM

Property is a means of conquest, and across settler colonies it has provided both the ideological justification and the legal architecture for native dispossession.[2] The spread of legal property ownership granted merchants, speculators, investors, squatters, and other agents of frontier expansion the privilege of state protection and the ability to commodify land and incorporate it into settler political economies. It was a process that, over centuries, transformed land into property for European owners and their descendants.

That being said, it would be a mistake to think that natives had land, and settlers had property. "The popular idea that Europeans had private property, while the [Native American] Indians did not," writes environmental historian William Cronon, "distorts European notions of property as much as it does Indian ones."[3] Both settlers and Indigenous peoples made distinctions between "land tenure" and "sovereignty," or the rights to land they had in relation one another as members of a political community, and rights they had to land in relation to other political communities.[4] Conflicts over land cannot be explained by snowballing misunderstandings; indeed, both settlers and natives were quick to learn about each other's property systems. Instead, at issue was the question of which authority would determine the rights and responsibilities people had to one another, and to the land, in a territory.

Different property regimes have played a role in colonial conquest. Private property is the signature legal form of settler power, a means of "bounding the land" into a set of discrete resources that could be appropriated and sold.[5] Later, settler authorities imposed private ownership on subjugated Indigenous nations in the hopes of dissolving collective political identities; "elimination turned inwards" was how historian Patrick Wolfe described this process in his foundational article on settler colonialism, pointing out that in the United States, it was "a faster method of land transference than the US Cavalry had previously provided."[6] But settlers have turned to other forms of ownership to secure control over territory. As historian Allan Greer points out, "settler commons" were far more important to early colonial empires than private property.[7] Various forms of state property, public lands, and natural reserves also have a long history, and remain important means of dispossession to this day. It is the interplay of these various property regimes that determines the operations, and contradictions, of settler colonial power.

These different property regimes also transformed Indigenous social formations. In their confrontations with settlers, some Indigenous peoples refused European property systems entirely, and others attempted to adapt to them to hold onto their land base.[8] Such double binds are at the heart of contemporary land claims, with efforts to gain state recognition of traditional territories often forcing Indigenous peoples to make their forms of land tenure legible to settler law, and losing a great deal in the process. Property may be a means of elimination, but it does far more than erase Indigenous relationships to land. Instead, different regimes of property produce different forms of Indigenous land defense, often with serious, long-term consequences for Indigenous societies.

SETTLER COLONIALISM AND LAND ACQUISITION IN PALESTINE

When Jewish settlers arrived in Palestine in the early 1880s, they encountered complex arrangements of property under the sovereignty of the Ottoman empire. Whether attempting to buy shares of common land (*masha'*), or obtaining title to large holdings through absentee landlords, early settlers depended on market transactions to acquire property. The final years of Ottoman rule in Palestine were a time of trial and error, giving rise to important ideologies of "pure settlement" and "national capitalism," and creating the knowledge, skills, and institutions—most importantly, the Jewish National Fund (JNF), which was chartered in 1897—needed to build a territorial base for Jewish settlement.[9]

Under British rule during the 1920s and 1930s, settlers transformed the legal architecture of the land market to their advantage. From the creation of the colonial government itself to the formulation of ordinances and policies and the implementation of laws and regulations, Zionist advisers, leaders, lobbyists, and lawyers sought to shape land policy such that no fetters were placed on the private acquisition of land.[10] The Zionist movement was greatly helped by the British land reforms that attempted to expand the reach of absolute private property and encourage commodification, and when policies emerged that might restrict purchases—for example, protections for tenant farmers or size restrictions on purchases—it was adept at weakening or scuttling them. Zionist land buyers also developed tools for getting past legal and social barriers: disguising sales as defaults on loans to hide the voluntary nature of a transaction, using irrevocable power of attorney to circumvent restrictions on the direct sale of property, employing brokers and frontmen to disguise the identity of the buyer, and conducting transactions outside of the official land registry to avoid detection.[11] "The market," in other words, was not some preexisting space that settlers entered into, but a set of legal and political structures that the Zionist movement helped create, with the explicit goal of extending settler control over as much land as possible.

Palestinians took different approaches to defending land. Palestinian peasants and tenant farmers were the main obstacle to the creation of a Zionist land base, and it was their resistance that galvanized national opposition to colonization. On the one hand, they fought Zionist land claims and British rule, refusing to cede use rights, cooperate with surveyors, accept British legal reforms, or obey eviction orders.[12] On the other, they demanded recognition of customary rights and tenancy arrangements in colonial courts.[13] The emerging Palestinian bourgeoise—or the liberal intellectuals and businessmen historian Sherene Seikaly calls "men of capital"—came up with a different approach to land defense, one that embraced private property and capitalist development.[14] The Arab Bank, the Arab Company for Saving Land in Palestine, and Arab Nation Fund were all founded in the early 1930s and engaged in what we might call financial land defense, either by pressuring landowners not to sell, or to purchase land that might be otherwise acquired by the Zionist movement.[15] Palestinian capitalists also sought, as historian Munir Fakher Eldin has shown, to protect territory by purchasing land themselves and converting it into plantation agriculture.[16] The struggles of the peasantry became the symbol of the Palestinian national movement, while the liberal defense of private property would remain an uncelebrated aspect of land defense that, since the 2000s, has become increasingly prominent in the West Bank.

War accomplished what the market never could provide. Of the 20.6 million dunums of land under Israeli sovereignty after 1948, only 2.8 million were under "formal state or Jewish ownership."[17] In the 1950s and 1960s, Israel developed a variety of legal and administrative tactics to extinguish refugee property rights and attack the land base of the Palestinians who had managed to remain. By 1960, 92 percent of the land was effectively held as "inalienable Jewish-Israeli national land."[18] Thus, we should be cautious about drawing too sharp a distinction between the illegitimacy of violent dispossession and the legitimacy of legal transactions. Instead, we should see both as part of a project of destroying Palestinian political authority over the land, with the war on Palestinian ownership continuing through the rule of law.

THE WEST BANK LAND GRAB

After 1967, Israel became the effective sovereign in the West Bank and Gaza Strip.[19] Soon thereafter, the state began to seize control of Palestinian land for military bases, buffer zones, agriculture (especially in the Jordan Valley), and, beginning in the late 1970s, the huge project of residential housing. Taking advantage of the fact that the Jordanian land registration had only finished the settlement of title in 28 percent of the West Bank, both the military authorities and private settler companies sought to gain control of land.

The creation of state lands is one of the most important legal mechanisms that Israel has used to dispossess Palestinians in the West Bank. The idea is simple: according to Israel, any land that is untitled and uncultivated is the property of the state.[20] In the mid-1980s, Israel had already seized "direct possession" or placed signification restrictions on Palestinian land use in half of the West Bank, leading researchers to conclude that land dispossession was part of a political project that sought to create "interconnection" between Jewish colonies and "fragmentation" of Palestinian space.[21] From 1980 to 1984, the Israeli government declared 800,000 dunums property of the state. By 1992, it was 900,000. Today, land classified as Israeli state land amounts to around 1.2 million dunums, or 22 percent of the West Bank.[22]

State land confiscations are an important part of the legal basis for colonization in the highlands. The Ariel settlement, one of the first in the central highlands, was established just north of Salfit in 1978 on land claimed as Israeli state property. In 1999, Israeli authorities established Bruchin, dispossessing owners in the village of Bruqin. The development of housing and infrastructure slowly materialized the state's legal claims in banal ways. In June 2013, for instance, residents of Bruqin received notice that the Israeli authorities had decided to build 550 new housing units in the settlement of Bruchin. The announcement, translated into Arabic and printed in the Palestinian newspaper *al-Quds*, specified that Khirbat al-Fakhakhir and al-Balata, two areas part of "the lands of Bruqin," would be incorporated into the settlement's new master plan and rezoned from agricultural to residential use. In 2021, the Israeli authorities announced their intention to expand Ariel and build a road from the settlement through the al-Batin area of Farkha, which had been declared state land in 1982. Construction of a settler road began in the fall of 2023. A few weeks after it was finally paved in 2024, settlers built a new outpost in al-Batin.

A second mechanism of land grabbing is through private transfers. The same institutions and ideologies that developed under late Ottoman and British colonial rule informed land-buying activities in the West Bank. Shortly after the occupation began, both quasi-state institutions and private companies began to try to buy land from Palestinians.[23] In the late 1970s, companies espousing "private settlement"—mixing the national capitalism of early Zionist settlement with a new resistance to centralized planning that characterized the ascendent free-market ideology—sought to acquire land in the West Bank.[24]

Private transfers required legal manipulation. In the 1970s and 1980s, Israeli military orders created the legal basis for these transactions by modifying Jordanian law, legalizing private land sales, extending the operative period of irrevocable power of attorney from five to fifteen years, and transferring registration disputes from civil to military jurisdiction.[25] Many of these transactions were fraudulent, and private settlement companies attempted to launder their property claims through first registration (*tasjil mujjadid*), a legal process that allowed individual owners to initiate land registration privately.[26] Buyers exploited the tax registries, which contained an estimate of surface area and no cadastral maps, by drastically inflating the size of the plot that they claimed to be buying.[27] Notaries public, government officials, and land registry employees all aided this process by providing documents, overlooking obvious irregularities, and allowing both companies and land dealers to act with impunity.[28] Brokers and irrevocable powers of attorney kept transactions secret for years, while intimidation, assault, blackmail, and kidnapping were all used to create the semblance of a legal transaction or, at least, to keep people quiet. As had been the case under British rule, settlers were not only trying to buy land; they were making the rules of the game and, when these rules did not work in their favor, violently breaking them.

Palestinians call this combination of secret transactions, fraud, and violence *tasrib* (leakage). While more limited in the 1970s, cases of *tasrib* exploded in the 1980s.[29] Journalists were speaking of a "gold rush" that was drawing in ideological settlers, opportunistic speculators, and buyers hoping for an affordable apartment or a private villa.[30] By the end of the 1980s, mounting scandals, stories of corruption, government cover-ups, and the suicide of an Israeli real estate developer (who sold some $10 million worth of property to Israeli buyers that he did not legally own) resulted in the collapse of several real estate projects and warnings by senior Israeli figures steering investors away from buying land in the West Bank.[31] Private settlement slowed in the late 1980s, but in the 1990s began again. According to Mohammad Nazal, a lawyer who has been following *tasrib* for years, there was a renewed burst of fraudulent land claims in the mid-2000s.[32] In 2019, the office of the legal adviser in Judea and Samaria circulated a legal opinion about the possibility of removing restrictions created by Jordanian law on settler land purchases in the West Bank, and in 2020 the settler NGO Regavim brought the issue to the Israeli Supreme Court.[33] In 2021, there were reports that the JNF would begin buying land in isolated settlements and return to its archives in search of incomplete and unregistered land deals.[34] The same ethnonationalist settler movement is also, at least when it suits their territorial agenda, a cheerleader for the selective liberalization of property law in the West Bank.[35]

The existence of both state and private land grabbing creates opportunities for collusion and manipulation. State authorities have been known to declare property that settlers claimed to have purchased as state land to shield the purchasers from scrutiny and resolve legal complications. Settlers also use the possibility of state confiscation to pressure Palestinians to sell their land. One activist from Farkha told me how, in the 1980s, brokers would approach landowners and tell them that their land was going to be confiscated. The confiscations were not actually planned, and the idea was to trick people to think, as he put it, "the land is going, I might as well sell it and get a little money for it." In 2015 and 2016, I interviewed several lawyers who had noticed that the Israeli authorities were paying much closer attention to first land registration cases, making claims on contested properties against settlers and Palestinians. One lawyer, who was working on a case in the highlands that had been dragging on for years, told me how the owner of a settler real estate company approached him to make a deal before the state confiscated the land from both sides. But whether the state is colluding with settlers or trying to exercise some control over them, the loss for Palestinian owners is always the same.

Israeli rule amounts to the elimination of Palestinian property rights. The creation of state lands, which refuses to recognize evidence of Palestinian ownership, does so categorically. Private transfers work differently, recognizing Palestinians as rights-bearing subjects only when they act as *sellers* of land.[36] Erasure and partial recognition go together, each serving to extend settler sovereignty over territory by eliminating the juridical existence of Palestinians as property owners.

PROPERTY OWNERSHIP AND LAND DEFENSE

The drive to eliminate Palestinians as owners forced Palestinians to protect their land through recourse to property ownership. As Palestinian intellectual Abdulrahman Abu Arafeh noted during one of the 1981 meetings of the Conference on Steadfastness for Development, when land is lost, "it is not only the loss of the owner, but in the end is a loss for all of us."[37] State lands and private transfers created different sites of contestation. For the former, Palestinians could object before a special military tribunal. For the latter, which were treated as land registration procedures, Palestinians could object during first registration proceedings, which were adjudicated in Palestinian civil courts until a military order transferred them to a special military court in 1984. New legal aid organizations, such as the American Friends Service Committee (founded in 1974), al-Haq (in 1979), and the Committee of Arab Lawyers (in 1980), worked with individuals, land defense committees, village councils, and municipalities to provide legal advice and representation.[38] Such efforts linked village land struggles to growing mass organizations and professional networks, which connected Palestinians to international organizations and experienced lawyers in Israel.[39] These relationships, which began to take shape in the 1970s and 1980s, informed a legal approach to land defense that continues to this day.

Objecting to state confiscations required evidence of prior ownership and continuous cultivation.[40] Providing this evidence so was not straightforward. During an interview, one prominent Palestinian lawyer told me how, in the 1980s, farmers knew how long it took to plow a plot, but were often hard pressed to provide him with an exact measurement of surface area. Lawyers and activists, then, had to establish proof of private ownership and instruct owners how to make their claims legible to the Israeli state. In 1982, al-Haq published *Land and the Legal Means to Preserve It*, a pamphlet that explains to the "ordinary citizen" how to object to state land declaration. In walking an owner through the steps of making an objection, it suggests that an owner try to find "experts [*ahl al-khibra*]" such as "an engineer, a surveyor, or a member of the valuation committee" to attest to their ownership claims.[41] Across the West Bank, surveyors, lawyers, and agronomists interpreted documents, crops, and landscapes to strengthen ownership claims and to teach rural owners how to make their claims legible to the state.[42]

Fighting land sales was similar, but there were some important differences. First, lawyers had to learn where, exactly, an Israeli company claimed
to have bought land.[43] Next, making a successful legal objection relied on establishing the fraudulent nature of the Israeli company's claim. The quality
of forgeries varied wildly. Sometimes they were sloppy, revealing a bizarre
level of negligence. One company, for example, presented a bill of sale in
court carrying the signature of a deceased landowner. Oblivious to how the
old the man had been, the date on the document meant that the purported
seller would have signed the contract when he was only a small child. Others
were sophisticated, holding more closely to the social lives of those they tried
to implicate, or even basing their claim on a legal transaction. Raising objections required a great deal of detective work, gathering shards of information
and piecing them together to prove, hopefully, that a sale never occurred.

Legal objections were one front in a larger battle against fraudulent
transfers. Landowners published notices in the press about suspicious offers,
warned others not to buy and sell land in certain areas, and named those who
were collaborating with Israeli companies. Activists acquired documents establishing the identity of land dealers, which they circulated around town
and read aloud in places of worship. Nationalist militants ostracized, intim-
idated, and sometimes killed the brokers, mukhtars, and others involved in
the transfer of land to Israeli companies.[44] In the central highlands in 1983,
for example, a mukhtar from Farkha was found dead in his car near Salfit;
according to *Al-Fajr Weekly*, he had been murdered in retaliation for his role
in land deals.[45] In widely circulating Palestinian newspapers like *al-Fajr*, *al-
Sha'ab*, and *al-Tali'ya*, Palestinian journalists published exposes of fraudulent activities; revealed the connections between land dealers, companies,
and the military government; and perhaps most dangerously, published the
names of land dealers. As these cases received more publicity and scrutiny,
mysterious fires broke out in the courts of Nablus, Jenin, and Bethlehem,
destroying files pertaining to fraud cases, while a break-in at the Ramallah
court had the same result.[46] In 1985, the journalist Hassan Abdulhalim was
murdered, his headless body dumped in the hills outside of Ramallah.[47] By
spreading these stories across the West Bank, often at great risk, owners, activists, and journalists sought to reveal what companies and brokers hoped
to keep secret.

Defending land in this manner had different effects. First, few objections to state land confiscations succeeded. Those that did only won temporary reprieve. If their land was desired by settlers, they would face further confiscation orders and invasions. Objections to fraudulent first registration claims were initially more successful, but winning these cases also only offered temporary respite. Cases that I have seen can drag on for years in a legal system that entertains even the most thinly documented settler claims, and in which companies can disappear, change names, and try again and again. At best, legal victory for Palestinians is deferral.

But objections were not only about winning in court. In cases purportedly involving a sale, objecting was about both *preventing* loss and *proving* innocence. Owners went (and still go) to court not only to challenge these claims, but to publicly demonstrate that they had not colluded with Israel. Nidal Taha, a lawyer who worked on these cases in the 1980s, argued that forgery not only robs owners of land and property rights, but also sows doubt.[48] Claims of complicity in *tasrib* isolated property owners and threatened to hold them politically and morally responsible for the potential loss of land. Land defense, to recast Taha's formulation, sought to ensure that violations of "private rights" were transformed into a "public issue," and also to ensure that fraudulent land sales were not reduced to a painful personal burden, but instead became part of a shared anticolonial struggle.[49]

Finally, property claims had important political uses. Similar to the antiapartheid struggle in South Africa, lawyers and NGOs used property claims as part of an advocacy strategy that drew attention to violations of human rights and international law.[50] Law might not prevent the land from being taken, but by showing that the land was illegally stolen rather than legally surrendered, advocates sought to pierce Israel's claims to be a law-abiding state and to undermine its international standing. Property ownership allowed for a claim to territory that operated very much within the liberal order, offering evidence that Palestinian presence on the land predated settlement *and* that Palestinians owners were more law-abiding than their colonizers.

PALESTINIAN LAND TITLING

More than a decade after it was created, the PA began to title the land of the West Bank. In 2002, the PA established the Palestinian Land Authority (PLA) to consolidate the responsibilities of property creation and administration. In 2005, the PLA, the World Bank, and the Finnish Ministry of Foreign Affairs launched the West Bank and Gaza Land Administration Project (LAP-1). The purpose of LAP-1 was to formalize ownership, not to create a new regime of private property where one did not previously exist.[51] The first rural site was in the central highlands, in the village of Qarawat Bani Zeid.

Titling incorporates land defense into the new imperatives of neoliberal state-building. Land defense was an implicit part of early titling projects.[52] With the creation of the Land and Water Settlement Commission (LWSC) in 2016, it became explicit. "Territory is the main element for constructing a state [and] the core of the conflict," reads the opening line of an early, internal concept paper, which argues that the settlement of title can prevent both Israeli land confiscation and "leakage" (*tasrib*). Titling operates on "the castle metaphor" of property, which, as legal geographer Nicholas Blomley explains, "relies upon a spatial logic of defensive boundaries, with a sharp divide between a secure inside and a threatening outside [that] invokes notions of lordship, dominion and sovereignty."[53] As a part of neoliberal state-building, land titling was about asserting government control over territory and encouraging economic development through the creation of land markets.[54] Property aligns these contradictory logics, allowing the PA to create the conditions for land commodification while pursing land defense at a national scale.[55]

PA titling has created a new legal space in the West Bank. At first, titling was confined to Areas A and B, where the PA has full civil control. But under the LWSC, the PA began to survey land in Area C as well.[56] The result is two land registries. First, there is the Israeli registry, which covers the entirety of the West Bank. It is based on the Jordanian settlement of title, which was frozen in 1967, and likely any first registration procedures that occurred since. While Israel does not interfere in the PA's administration of property in Areas A and B, it does not recognize PA authority in Area C. As a result, in 60 percent of the West Bank, Israeli police and courts govern property. Second, there is a new Palestinian registry. This registry is also based on the

Jordanian settlement of title, but is being updated and expanded by PA land titling. In Areas A and B, PA police and courts regulate property. In Area C, whatever areas the PA is able to survey creates a potential shadow registry without immediate legal power.

In practice, PA titling can do little to prevent colonial encroachment. Since the Israeli authorities do not recognize PA authority in Area C, any attempt to use PA titles to contest state land declarations is futile. As far as private transfers are concerned, the creation of a registry may allow PA police and intelligence to more effectively track property transfers, especially in Area B. But without the power to prosecute the Israeli buyers, their power is limited to punishing Palestinians suspected of involvement in such deals. The West Bank under the PA is akin to a native reservation, where property rights do not align neatly with territorial sovereignty.[57]

While PA property titling does not provide legal protection now, surveys and registries may be the basis for building international support for Palestinian land claims in the future. If this turns out to be the ultimate use of these new registries, then PA titling will be the latest in a long series of efforts to use liberal property claims to make Palestinian presence and political collectivity legible to the international community. It is this prospect that fuels settler opposition to the project, which they claim is establishing a "fake Palestinian land registry in Judea and Samaria."[58] The Israeli settler NGO Regavim, pointing to the "hundreds of people" employed by the PA to register land in Area C, has denounced the Israeli government for its "shameful inaction" in not doing more to exercise Israeli sovereignty over the West Bank.[59] In 2020, the Israeli government began to discuss (publicly) the idea of titling the land in Area C.[60] A 2021 report by the Israeli Ministry of Intelligence articulates the future implications of allowing the Palestinian settlement of title to go unchallenged. "[Palestinian land titling] embodies [sic] the Palestinian Authority as being a sovereign authority," explains the report, and as a result "strengthens its control over its citizens and provides the Palestinians with an important tool in its legal campaign. It must be emphasized that in the absence of an alternative registration arrangement, it is quite likely that at one time or another, the legal authorities in Israel and/or worldwide will endorse the Palestinian registration."[61]

While land defense may be one aspiration of land titling, land commodification is its actual result. Land titling raised land prices and increased property transactions.[62] It did not, however, create a neutral market where every kind of transaction is possible. Instead, land titling created the legal and administrative infrastructure that facilitated the operation of dominant economic interests, helping transnational companies, banks, and investors interested in real estate development acquire control over land in the West Bank.

PRIVATIZING LAND DEFENSE

In the central highlands, real estate developers are buying up land for housing projects and speculative investments. There have been smaller ventures, like Manazel's ill-fated al-Direh villa development, and purchases by more well-established developers. UCI has been the most important company operating in the area and, as noted in the previous chapter, became the largest single landowner in the mid-2010s in Farkha and Qarawa, and likely Bruqin as well. In the mid-2000s, UCI was indistinguishable from the other developers that were rebuilding Ramallah, serving the city's professional classes with luxury apartments and villas.[63] In 2007, brokers working for the company (or perhaps hoping to sell to the company) began to buy up formerly agricultural land in the central highlands. Years later, these purchases became the basis of a very different kind of real estate venture.

In 2011, the company launched TABO. The project takes its name from *tabu*, one of the Palestinian Arabic words for "land title," and offers titled land for sale. Primarily through first registration, but also through PA-run titling, the company divided its holdings into 1 dunam parcels, built roads and utility networks, and offered the parcels for sale to Palestinian buyers. An easily accessible website and in-house financing make land easy to buy. UCI encourages new buyers to build homes, offering services for the construction of single-family villas. During the period of my research, the hoped-for suburban communities never materialized in the hills. Instead, land was purchased as an investment. The shortage of land created by Israel's military occupation, land purchases from other large companies, and various private and public developments have pushed land prices even higher. A decade after launch, UCI could advertise "annual returns of up to 10.5%" for those who bought land through TABO.

TABO is also a land defense project. Buying land through TABO, the company claims, is an "ethical investment," since "registering a title deed in your name puts Palestine's land in the hands of its rightful owners, helping prevent illegal land confiscation in Palestine."[64] For its legal claims, TABO explicitly builds on the work of human rights organizations, and the history of struggle is a cornerstone of TABO's advertising. Company billboards recall a much larger repertoire of images that would likely be familiar to passers-by in which Palestinians face the viewer, displaying title deeds to their land.[65] But unlike displaced refugees or dispossessed peasants, TABO's customers display them to celebrate the land they now own, rather than as evidence of the land that they have lost. In the beginning, online advertisements were replete with the poetry of Mahmoud Darwish, annual Land Day commemorations, and land-centered photography contests. In one "special deal for Land Day," customers were offered free landscaping services. "Own land," said the advertisement, "and planting is on us." In the mid-1980s, researchers Osama Halabi and Meron Benvenisti opened their important study on Israel's land policies in the West Bank by noting that land "is valued as national patrimony, not a piece of commercial real-estate."[66] In the new political economy of the West Bank, developers and investors wagered that it could be both.

But the defense of the land through private initiative also has precedents, even if they are never acknowledged, or even are disavowed. The first comes from Palestinian liberalism, especially the Mandate-era men of capital who sought to protect land through private ownership and development. The second is from Zionist colonization. TABO is a mirror of the private settlement movement of the 1980s: expressing hostility to red tape and bureaucratic inefficiency, employing brokers to acquire land and first registration to title property, and championing the private market and homeownership as the vehicle for national territorial aspirations. The legal and economic conditions of the post-Oslo West Bank, where real estate is one of the few secure investments in the shrinking Palestinian cantons, create the possibility for real estate developers to claim that the land market can serve the national interest.

What is novel about TABO is that it is land defense *in* the village, but not *for* the village. It advertises olive groves, terraced hillsides, and ancient ruins as the backdrop to country living. The Israeli developers that began to build the settlements in the 1970s and the Palestinian developers that broke ground for suburbs, villas, and a planned city in the 2000s share a vision of the highlands as idyllic and unspoiled. Through markets and mortgages, they promise relief from the prices and pollution of the city and return to the beauty of the land. This juxtaposition may well be a universal aspect of planetary suburbanization; what is specific are the politics of place. TABO's innovation is a rural land defense project that, for the first time, has nothing to do with agriculture. In this vision, the nonresident landowner replaces the resident villager, and investment replaces cultivation, as the respective agent and action of land defense.

A MORAL ECONOMY OF PRIVATE PROPERTY

"I don't want to say their names, but their names are known." It was evening, in the summer of 2013. I was in the sitting room of my companion's sister-in-law, joined by several of his relatives. One man had been talking about one of the hills that had been purchased by a real estate company in Bruqin. He suspected that, somehow, the PA was benefiting from the sales. He had heard that two land brokers (*simasara*), one from Farkha and one from Kufr al-Dik (another village nearby), had bought the land cheaply and then sold it to UCI. He did not want to say, exactly, who they were. There is a lot of fear about selling land, he told me, and recent news about fraud in Salfit has made people worry that Israeli settlers might be trying to purchase land. Even people from neighboring villages can raise suspicions. "You should only sell to someone local [*ibn al-balad*] that, through connections of family or reputation, you know you can trust."

This conversation happened in 2013, and I would come to have many more that expressed similar fears and understandings of land sales in the 2010s. Palestinian titling projects and corporate real estate hoped to use private property to pursue land defense. But in interviews with me as well as in conversations people had with one another during land titling, the increase in land sales also created fears about *tasrib*.

The whole process is one in which outside forces appear without much warning. Billboards for new developments, roads carved into the mountains, signs indicating land for sale, and announcements posted in village councils: all of these come later, after the land has been sold. Rumors about companies, titling projects, and government plans circulate to both explain and predict price increases, which village residents described as "crazy," "fantastic," and "unnatural." For ordinary people, the determinations of price on the real estate market are beyond any kind of immediate control, producing an experience that is both banal and bewildering.

Real estate deals made the broker into a singularly visible, and rather despised, figure.[67] People called them *simasara* (sing.: *simsar*) to describe and condemn their work, which involved obtaining privileged information, exploiting knowledge disparities, keeping secrets, and trying to leverage local knowledge as best they could. Brokers would call people out of the blue to make offers on property. Their names would appear on publicly posted first registration announcements. Many people I spoke with assumed they were driven by money, not concern for the well-being of their neighbors or the village, and noted how they exploited distress and desperation for profit. Since landowners will often only interact with brokers when they sell their land, the latter has become a figure to represent a much larger process of land acquisition and development that is largely hidden from view.

Real estate companies used brokers to obtain land, and residents believed that they also used them as fronts to disguise the extent of projects. They shared stories of brokers taking advantage of those who lacked an understanding of the market and trying to convince people that their land was worthless. Brokers purchased land through irrevocable power of attorney, which shielded what people believed to be large real estate companies. One man in Qarawa, for instance, shared with me how he sold land to a broker, learning months later through a newspaper announcement that it had been acquired by a developer. In Farkha, a first registration announcement posted on the wall of the village council showed a complicated transfer in which the rights of multiple people moved through a series of mediators, including one well-known land broker in Ramallah, to UCI. The transfer began in 2008 and was only posted publicly in 2013. In Qarawa, people told me, brokers from the village purchased land before the settlement of title commenced as part of a plan; "a half hour after the objection period [of forty days] ended," one man surmised, "they all went and sold their land to the company." Whether this was on purpose or not, what brokers effectively helped to do was keep the scope of the project hidden, and keep prices down, at least while initial purchasing was happening. From this perspective, the real estate market was an act of coordinated deception.

Settlers used the same tactics. Legal instruments like irrevocable power of attorney, brokers, and frontmen all played a leading role in Zionist land purchases during the British Mandate, and in the early years of the occupation of the West Bank. Unsurprisingly, people drew associations between the activities of the brokers and the problem of *tasrib*. They called brokers "collaborators" and recalled news stories or histories of fraudulent deals. Men from Qarawa told me about a nearby hill where they used to go for walks. In the 1960s, surveyors appeared and mapped the area. When they asked what was going on, they were told that a Kuwaiti company had purchased the whole mountain. Years later, settlers moved in. These companies, they told me, they're all the same: they're run by capitalists, "capital is a coward," and they'll sell to the Israeli companies. Unsurprisingly, most of those I spoke to were less sanguine about the prospects of new investment properties serving the cause of land defense. During one of my conversations with Abu Ashraf, the olive press operator introduced in chapter 1, he remarked that the buying and selling of land in the area was happening in a "crazy way, without rationality." He worried that land would "leak [*itsarrab*]" to Israeli companies and the make the occupation a "legal occupation."

Palestinian government corruption contributed to these fears. The larger critique of the PA, aptly summarized by one Qarawa resident's quip—"we don't have a government, we have a company"—played out in specific ways in the titling process, often due to rumors that powerful figures connected to the government were illegally acquiring land and gossip about the PA's perceived relationships with brokers. These accusations dogged the land titling in Dura, while an unpublished assessment commissioned by the World Bank of PA titling in Bethlehem noted that residents were suspicious of the project because of the widely held perception that municipal employees had dealings with land brokers, or were in the business themselves. Such fears played out in the central highlands in stories about relationships between officials and brokers, or rumors of PA involvement in real estate projects. The point here is not that all these claims are true; indeed, part of the problem is how difficult they are to verify. What is clear, however, is that land markets activated fears that corrupt officials, greedy businessmen, and unscrupulous brokers colluded to take advantage of rural landowners.

It is a fitting end to this account that, in 2022, I found myself the object of suspicion. It was, I had decided, my last day of research. Driving back from Salfit to Ramallah, I passed through Farkha and decided to visit the hilltops of Qarawa to walk and take some photographs. I parked my rental car, which had yellow Israeli plates, on the top of the hill. As I was taking pictures of the view, a passing car stopped. A group of men emerged, and an older man addressed me in Hebrew. We spoke in Arabic. They invited me to come with them—the older man was a contractor—and see one of the properties he was working on. The two younger men were convinced I was a land broker and, likely, an Israeli. One asked to see my passport, while the other introduced me as a broker (even though I thought I had convinced them otherwise) to someone who stopped by. Eventually we seemed to smooth things over and I was invited to dinner. "You were scared when we turned around and drove up the hill," my interrogator-turned-host told me, "but you're not scared anymore." But I was still unsettled. Long after the land boom of the early 2010s, fears about brokers, and outsiders more generally, had not disappeared.

In his classic account of peasant moral economy, political scientist James Scott pointed out that agrarian norms and rights gave rise to a formulation of justice that differed from both liberal and Marxist accounts. According to Scott, this peasant concept of justice was based on the "norm of reciprocity" and the "right to subsistence" that together determined the expectations peasants had of one another, of elites, and of political rulers.[68] We might see property as part of a Palestinian moral economy, one whose elements include the proper treatment of the village community, practices of anticolonial land defense, and expectations for transparency and fairness in the buying and selling of land. This moral economy draws on peasant traditions and is deeply rooted in the highlands. But unlike Scott's formulation, it does not stand in stark opposition to the liberal order; instead, it is deeply enmeshed with the values and practices of private ownership.

THE POWER OF OWNERSHIP

In 1970, the Palestine Liberation Organization (PLO) published a pamphlet entitled "Village Statistics 1945: A Classification of Land and Area Ownership in Palestine." This pamphlet was a reprint of British government data with commentary by Sami Hadawi, who had worked in tax assessment and land valuation for the Mandate government and who, after 1948, became a tireless advocate for the rights of Palestinian refugees. In his introduction, Hadawi explained that the purpose of publishing these rather dry colonial statistics was to counter "allegations that Palestine was a Jewish country and that the Arab inhabitants constituted an insignificant minority of nomads who roamed the countryside."[69] In Hadawi's text, property ownership combines historical, legal, and political claims that disprove the colonial narrative and make a case for Palestinian rights, addressed to the world.[70]

After 1967, private ownership became a way to highlight the illegality of Israeli land policy in the West Bank. In 1985, in his landmark study *Occupier's Law*, lawyer and writer Raja Shehadeh explained how "by ruling that international law prohibits the taking of private property, the [Israeli] court suggested to the government that it would hold differently if the property seized were not private property," creating the legal framework for dispossessing Palestinians through state land procedures.[71] Countless studies have been produced since documenting Israel's violations of private property rights, from defining Israeli land policy in 1986 as "interference with private land ownership" to revealing in 2007 that "the majority of settlements have been constructed either entirely or partially on private Palestinian land."[72] The Associated Press, reporting in 2024 on "Israeli land seizure in the West Bank," explained that "by declaring them [the land] state lands, the government opens them up to being leased to Israelis and prohibits private Palestinian ownership."[73] Today, we largely take property ownership for granted when discussing Palestinian rights.

Scholars and activists have almost exclusively focused on how Israel dispossesses Palestinians, sharing a forensic commitment to documenting the techniques that Israel uses and the lands that have been lost. Early scholarship examined in detail Israel's use of law to dispossess Palestinians in the West Bank and Gaza Strip, often situating this legal regime within the longer history of colonization.[74] While more recent scholarship has expanded the historical and theoretical scope of this discussion, the primary concern remains with understanding what colonial power takes away.[75] How (and why) Palestinians might turn to property to make land claims, and the consequences of doing so, is often an afterthought. Most of the time, it is not considered at all.

Property is powerful because it offers the possibility of making Palestinian rights legible at multiple scales, and to different authorities and publics. In contrast to many other settler states, where Indigenous people need to demonstrate continuity with a precolonial culture that is fundamentally different from the liberal order, Palestinians demand rights from within it. Statistics on land ownership circulate in international institutions and national governments, activists deploy images of refugees and peasants displaying title deeds in presentations and on social media, and the PA registers property to demonstrate its sovereign capacity and make territorial claims to land. But property is not somehow just there, ready to be used. Surveyors and lawyers must translate documents, owners must modulate their behaviors to fit into legal norms, and governments must create new maps and archives. The cumulative effect has been the suturing of the land struggle to liberal legal rights, effectively conscripting Palestinians as owners and defenders, not only of land, but of property itself.

The result is that we can find the defense of property within different, and often bitterly opposed, Palestinian political projects. The activists and lawyers who began to work with rural landowners in the 1970s were not only defending their legal rights; they were also contributing to the creation of a Palestinian society based on human rights, the rule of law, and respect for private property. This liberal vision was taken in different directions in the 2000s, and in the central highlands we can see early experiments with the fusion of land markets, sovereignty, and land defense. It would be a mistake to dismiss the claims of PA officials or private developers as nothing more than a legitimation or marketing strategy; instead, we should see them as fitting neoliberal governance and private capital accumulation within an existing Palestinian legal tradition. Even those who have been cheated by these new projects are not calling for the abolition of "the market" or "private property." On the contrary, their critiques of deception and corruption rest on the sanctity of ownership. Property's power lies in its ability to be taken for granted. It is not a neutral tool that can be used as part of a movement toward liberation. Instead, it is an arrangement of power that transforms Palestinian society along the way.

Three

SELLING

LAND COMMODIFICATION AND
THE LOSS OF VILLAGE CONTROL

IN RAMALLAH I SPENT A GOOD DEAL OF TIME WITH A LAWYER WHO
had frequent dealings with land. One of his clients had run into a disagreement with a neighbor over the exact path of an access road, so one summer
afternoon I joined this lawyer and his cousin, who was visiting from Florida
and, like me, seemed to just be along for the ride, on a trip to a village north
of the city. When we arrived, we did not immediately deal with the road problem. Instead, we met up with a man who was trying to sell property. He listed
its qualities: classified as Area A (and therefore out of danger of Israeli demolition or confiscation), productive olive trees, and high, flat areas with a good
breeze and a nice view, perfect for building a house. "A dunum goes for around
twenty thousand Jordanian dinar, but they'd probably take fifteen," he said,
before inviting us to walk around the plot to get a sense of it. The man, who I
realized was the lawyer's client, then rode with us to the edge of the village.
We chatted about who was buying and selling property, and he remarked that
UCI had bought up several hills in the area. We waited awhile for the other
parties to arrive, and when they finally did, everyone got down to business.
Maps in hand, they discussed where the new access road could go.

This most minor of disputes caused those present to reflect on the past. It turned out that the visiting cousin had grown up in a village like this one. There's plenty of land, he observed, what is there even to fight about? He then shared a childhood memory. Before dinner, he recalled, his mother used to send him out to the neighbors to see if anyone wanted to eat with them. This sort of thing doesn't happen anymore, he said. Instead of taking care of one another, everyone only thinks of themselves. One of the other men agreed, commenting that "our ancestors were better." He explained further so that I would understand: in the past, he said, people were content with the blessings (*barakat*) that came from being generous, and did not waste their time arguing over three meters of road. This feeling that new sources of wealth and the pursuit of profit were eroding communal values was something I encountered often during my fieldwork, especially when people discussed conflicts over land.

This discourse has the hallmarks of a story that is often told about capitalism and community. The antagonists in this narrative are predatory capitalists, usually aided by state functionaries and agents of international financial institutions. They are outsiders, and their understanding of the world is at odds with the local communities that live in the places they seek to plunder (or, as they prefer to put it, "develop"). As a result, resistance emerges "from below" against the forces arriving "from outside" or "from above," making local struggles visible to global progressive movements and deserving of international solidarity.

This is not quite what happened in the central highlands. Instead, as agricultural areas were incorporated into urban real estate markets, village landowners either sold land or became owners of valuable financial assets. Those who were dissatisfied with these changes proffered critiques of land commodification that drew moral boundaries between the village community and outside forces, with daily struggles and complaints outlining what village control over village land would look like. But the commodification of land made such distinctions unstable, not only eroding social relations from within, but also revealing the ways that the village might never have been a just place to begin with.

THE QUESTION OF PEASANT RESISTANCE

The study of peasants is inseparable from the study of resistance. Understanding the revolutionary potential of the peasantry was a central concern for anticolonial intellectuals, and the peasant wars of national liberation animated early scholarship in peasant studies.[1] With the end of formal colonialism and the agrarian transformations wrought by the Green Revolution, researchers turned to social movements or practices of "everyday resistance."[2] "If there is any hegemony today," anthropologist Michael Brown quipped in the mid-1990s, "it is the theoretical hegemony of resistance."[3] And when governments and large corporations began to acquire huge tracts of farmland after the 2008 financial crisis, there was an outpouring of writing about a new global land grab and a renewed interest in those resisting dispossession.[4] While the reasons for resistance have changed over time, the theoretical frameworks and political commitments of those studying peasants has ensured that it has remained a defining concern of the field.

Resistance is also a perennial subject of critique. Scholars have long pointed out that studies of resistance tended to simplify the workings of power and romanticize the oppressed.[5] They have worried that a focus on resistance fails to account for actual motivations of those resisting, and ignores instances of complicity and collaboration.[6] Indeed, these concerns tend to resurface each time we turn our attention to new sites of social and political conflict. The most recent scholarship on land grabbing, for example, quickly pivoted to explore "acquiescence" and "incorporation," and offered a critique of the ways that resistance "suffers from simplification" and led to the "idealisation of the peasantry."[7] But even those who wish to dethrone resistance still are in its grip; these other responses to land grabbing, after all, seem to matter conceptually and politically only in relation to resistance (and its absence). Indeed, the search for resistance is so deeply ingrained in scholarly discourse that it may be impossible to escape.

Of all the writing about resistance, anthropologist Sherry Ortner's critique remains the most incisive. She makes three important points about studies of resistance. First, they often ignore the internal complexity of oppressed groups as a result of the "impulse to sanitize the internal politics of the dominated."[8] Second, they engage in what she calls a "thinning of culture," or a tendency to ignore the values and frameworks that dominated

groups draw on to understand the world.⁹ Third, they struggle to provide
an account of subjectivity that is adequate to understanding the "projects
that [dominated groups] construct and enact."¹⁰ The result, she concludes,
is a scholarship that often displays "a kind of bizarre refusal to know and
speak and write of the lived worlds inhabited by those who resist (or do not,
as the case may be)."¹¹ The point here is not to replace resistance with something else, but instead to provide a richer account of political struggle that
includes, but is not oriented around or authorized by, resistance.

The "commons" is one of the idioms through which a resistance/domina-
tion framework shapes our understanding of rural Palestine. To clarify, I do
not mean that scholars are studying the systems through which rural producers organize land access or use rights. Instead, I mean that when scholars
invoke a bundle of qualities—common land, reciprocity, cooperation—
they intend to signal some essential quality of rural Palestine that stands
in opposition to settler colonial and capitalist encroachment.¹² For the geographer Gary Fields, cooperative agriculture, open fields, and a "culture of
reciprocity" are the defining features of "Palestinian agrarian life."¹³ Political
economists Linda Tabar and Samia al-Botmeh claim that "the peasant communities have their own communal relations to land, in which access and
utilization of the natural habitat and resources are shared in common" that
stands in contrast to the "private property lines" of Rawabi, a large Palestinian real estate developer.¹⁴ Architect and anthropologist Khaldun Bshara sees
both Rawabi and TABO as part of the "elimination of the 'common' and [the]
subsequent conversion of land into [an] easily defined and therefore easily
traded commodity."¹⁵ Such framings set up a dichotomy between inside and
outside, seeing settler colonial and/or capitalist domination coming from
outside the village, and resistance (potentially) emerging from within.

There are two problems here. The first is what is left out in this framing: an account of the complexity of land politics among rural Palestinians,
which simply cannot be boiled down to a conflict between private and commons, or a struggle against outside forces. The second is what we are left
with. To borrow language from Ortner, these accounts, whether they look
at "individual acts of resistance" or "large-scale resistance movements," pass
over how those who resist "are often themselves conflicted, internally contradictory, and affectively ambivalent."¹⁶ The result in Palestinian studies is

a framework that, while drawing our attention to a very important problem, offers a foreshortened perspective on rural struggles for land.

How then might we account for dispossession without inadvertently sanitizing village politics? One way to do so is to dwell on *how* people both idealize and critique the village community. In the conflicts that have emerged around land commodification, villagers "draw on," as anthropologist Marc Edelman put it in his reappraisal of the moral economy framework, a "deep, historical reservoir of moral economic sensibilities as well as on old protest repertoires and agrarian discourses."[17] In doing so, they both evoke a moral boundary between the community and outside forces, and grapple with the ways that land commodification exposes the village's social fractures. These daily land struggles and complaints allow us to see how the desire for village control of land becomes an important, albeit ambiguous, element of land justice.

MAKING VILLAGE LAND INTO A COMMODITY

Family land is a widespread form of land tenure in highland villages. It is not a legal category, and it includes *mulk* (in built-up areas) and *miri* (in agricultural areas).[18] While family land was not formally titled, those familiar with the landscape knew the boundaries, which were marked by terraces, trees, or other landscape features. Heirs often each have shares in an undivided family plot. Cultivating the land required cooperation, and selling it required an agreement between all heirs, or partition and sale of a smaller part of the family land (which also required agreement). After 1967, Palestinians generally avoided the Israeli land registry, choosing instead to buy and sell land outside of official channels. While these transactions are often called "informal," they had their own system of contracts, witnesses, and even means of insurance that, while not perfect by any means, allowed some semblance of security for buyers and sellers.[19] But before the mid-2000s, buying and selling of land was predominantly a local affair; land was inexpensive, farmers told me, and there was not much interest from outside parties.

Rural arrangements and norms impeded the ability of developers and urban investors to acquire family land. First, the lack of formal private property was a serious problem for those who needed clear legal title to secure their investments. Second, the historical importance of land to rural livelihoods and of its inheritance to the maintenance of familial bonds created a culture that did not celebrate land sales. Third, the need for consent of all shareholders made it difficult to buy land, while fragmented plots required consolidation to take advantage of economies of scale. Thus, while family land could be bought and sold, it could not easily be bought from and sold to anyone or put to any use. As anthropologist Eric Wolf put it long ago, even when "private property in land is the rule in the community," land is not always a "complete commodity."[20]

New arrangements of government power allowed Palestinian developers and speculators increased access to rural lands. As mentioned previously, the PA created a dedicated government ministry, the Palestinian Land Authority (PLA), in 2002 to streamline the titling, buying, and selling of property. In 2016, it transferred responsibility for titling to the Land and Water Settlement Commission (LWSC). For the past two decades, Palestinian land registration teams have been hard at work, doing their best to formalize property ownership and assign a single owner to a single plot of land. By moving governance of property transactions into a state authority and clarifying ownership rights, land titling made it easier for nonresidents to acquire land in West Bank villages.

The process that made land available to capital was incremental and happened without much fanfare in the central highlands. It looked something like this in the mid-2010s: Each morning, the surveyors assembled in the office of the PLA in Salfit. After tea and cigarettes, they would divide into teams, pile into a truck, and drive out to the villages where the settlement of title was underway. On good days, they arrived at the village council building to find local guides awaiting them. Each team had a list of plots. The village council would have coordinated with village landowners, and they took turns walking the land with the survey team. The owner, often with the help of the local guide, indicated the borders. One surveyor marked walls and rocks with red paint. Another registered coordinates in a GPS device. After the plot had been demarcated, the head of the survey team explained to the owner when they were to appear at the PLA, and what documents were required to finalize the claim. Then it was on to the next one. Scenes like this one have played out thousands of times across the West Bank, as it takes months to finish mapping, and years to resolve conflicts and finish the

settlement of title in a single village. But over the past two decades, significant progress has been made.

Land titling has been an important driver of land sales over the past
decade in the central highlands. While it is difficult to say how much land has
changed hands, extensive interviews with residents and PLA officials suggest that the land market has expanded significantly. Since the mid-2000s
many landowners have sold small plots of land to developers and speculators. Nearly every landowner I spoke to could tell stories of fantastic gains, of
people who were too foolish to take advantage of the opportunity, or of those
who were savvy enough not to agree to the first offer. A 2019 assessment,
carried out by the Palestine Economic Policy Research Institute in cooperation with the PLA, concluded that land titling increased the number of property transactions.[21] These findings confirmed what was common knowledge
among those involved; when the PA began the settlement of title in Farkha in
2016, during the initial community meeting a PLA representative listed the
benefits of participation, ending with the most obvious: "you all know what
happens to prices." With the expectation that titled land will fetch a better
price, even rumors of titling are said to push up property values.

These new legal arrangements have allowed nonresidents to acquire
village land. Larger tracts of land held by Palestinian real estate companies
are sold to Palestinian buyers, and individual brokers and investors are also
known to buy land unconnected to any large development project. Interviews and newspaper reports mention Palestinian buyers from Ramallah,
Hebron, Jerusalem, and perhaps from other cities in Israel. Residents mention seeing strangers visiting, often driving Israeli vehicles (a privilege enjoyed by Palestinians with some form of Israeli ID), distinguished by their
yellow license plates. Projects like TABO explicitly market to Palestinians
in the diaspora, and the company claims that 30 percent of its buyers live
abroad.[22] While it is impossible to provide exact figures without access to the
land registry, it seems that a significant amount of village land is under the
legal control of people who do not live in the central highlands.

These new owners have transformed the landscape. In addition to constructing a housing project overlooking Qarawa and several model homes
spread out across the rest of the villages, the real estate companies have built
new roads across the hills and connected plots of formerly agricultural land

to water and electrical infrastructure. Real estate developments like TABO encourage the creation of separate enclaves, connected by roads and boasting their own maps and street signs. New owners have also made land more amenable to recreational use. Village residents call this type of a development a "park" (*muntaza*). These are landscaped for the purposes of sitting, cooking, and enjoying the view. A few buyers have also constructed vacation homes, which village residents call "villas" or "chalets," and which seem to be used for temporary escapes from the city. These properties are also gated, and a few have impressive gardens. Upon one gate was a bold sign prohibiting entrance and promising legal charges against trespassers. Another sign, in the middle of a rocky field, announced land for sale. When I last visited, in 2022, these areas were often fenced off, with homes gated and secured by cameras. A growing patchwork of exclusive spaces is taking shape in these hills that is slowly making land inaccessible to those who live there.

These legal and material transformations are making land valuable in new ways. First, the increases in prices are often quite drastic: for example,

FIGURE 4. Gated property, 2022.

Source: Author.

14 dunums of rural land priced at JD 6,000 in the early 1990s had increased to JD 20,000; a 20 dunum plot in the mountains between Bruqin and Farkha that was sold for JD 1,000 had increased to JD 10,000. Second, new kinds of land are now valuable. When land was used for agriculture, rocky hilltops were far less sought after than terraced hillsides. Now it is the hilltops, which are the hardest to reach and least remunerative to farm, that are prized for their flat topography and breathtaking views. Prices have doubled, tripled, and in some cases, quadrupled, as devalued agricultural land is reimagined as tomorrow's valuable real estate. As someone once joked to me, it meant that owning rocks was worth more than owning trees.

These changes in property value and land use exceed any single real estate project, and now simply owning land can be the source of newfound wealth. Sometimes, this can allow some strategic maneuvering. One man I interviewed explained how his neighbor had sold nearly 50 dunums to a developer. The developer then offered this man JD 9,000 for his land. He refused. The developer tried later with a higher offer of JD 17,000. Again, he refused. "When they run electricity, water, and roads into the land," he told me, "I could probably get thirty thousand" for a single dunum. At other times, people just get lucky. In one story that was related to me, an owner had been desperately trying to sell a 5 dunum plot in the early 2000s, but even for JD 5,000 could find no takers. He gave up trying. In 2013 the land was worth considerably more, and he was still holding on to it. In another case, a cousin of a man I interviewed lived in Jordan, and had tried to sell off 20 dunums of "ruined land [khirab]" before the real estate boom. It seems that he had found a buyer, but the land was family property, and the seller could not get the thirty-five heirs—half in Palestine and half in Jordan—to agree to the sale. It was perhaps a stroke of fortune, as the land's value would increase considerably. But the result was the same: simply holding the land and leaving it idle could earn one far more money than going to the effort of growing anything.

It is not only developers and surveyors, but also village residents, who participate in this process. With the expectation that prices will continue to rise, more and more people are drawn into the market for village lands. Many have sold, but many more still own small plots of land. Some have become active participants, working as brokers, trying their hand at spec-

FIGURE 5. "Land for sale," 2022.

Source: Author.

ulation, and in the case of the Manazel company, even getting involved in development. Indeed, because land prices rose without anyone doing much of anything, just owning land made one a passive participant and potential agent in this process.

Can we say, then, that land has been commodified in the central highlands? A commodity is a good intended for exchange, whose "social form" consists of a use value and an exchange value.[23] The use value of a commodity refers to what it can be used for to fulfill a want or need. The exchange value refers to what the commodity can be exchanged for, which, in capitalist societies, is expressed as a price. For land to be commodified, then, means that both the use and control of land are determined by exchange value (in other words, whoever can pay for land has the right to determine how it is used, and who can use it), and that this has not just happened once or twice but has become general social practice in a given location.

If this is an acceptable definition of this process, then it is reasonable to conclude that land commodification is well underway in the central highlands. While the PA did not privatize common lands or introduce markets, it did help eliminate or bypass "diverse and historically sedimented institutions and social values" that frustrated large-scale purchases and acquisitions by nonresident buyers.[24] The land registration teams that helped institute this subtle transformation did so, in large part, in cooperation with residents, conscripting everyone in the highlands into the real estate market.

INSIDERS AND OUTSIDERS

Those opposed to, or at least dissatisfied with, land commodification offered critiques that referred to violations of village norms. They spoke of how neighbors forgot plot borders, how real estate companies did not offer a fair price, and how new owners had little interest in neighborly relations. In doing so, they articulated a moral boundary between inside and outside, one in which injustice originated from outside the village community.

At first glance, the agricultural land of the highlands does not appear to be divided into plots. There are few fences demarcating individual parcels, or signs warning a passerby of trespassing. But those who work the land know where the borders are. "For those who spent the long hours of daily work within the boundaries of village fields," wrote architect Suad Amiry about her fieldwork in the highlands in the 1980s, "the natural landscape was transformed into a 'cultural landscape' through their own intervention."[25] It was not fences or maps, but terraces, trees, rocks, and other landmarks that denoted boundaries between the land of different families, and seasonal agricultural work that reinforced them.

Today, fewer people remember these boundaries. During land titling, the most difficult plots to survey always belonged to absentee owners, or to those who had never spent much time farming. One man, speaking about his brother who lived abroad, grumbled to the surveyors that "we know every inch of the land and he doesn't even know where Farkha is." Leaving land untended for decades does not only render one's memory a bit hazy. It also results in the transformation of the landscape and the disappearance of landmarks. Fruitless searches and desperate phone calls to a brother or father—usually doomed since any verbal descriptions of the land were meaningless to the hapless owner—resulted in frustrating delays for survey teams. "I don't remember the old names," one man told the surveyors, as we stood overlooking overgrown olive trees and unplowed land.

Those whose connection to the village had been changed or severed with the passing of time had to rely on others to demarcate the borders. During titling, a local guide (*mu'arrif*) often played this role. These guides assisted the land registration teams. They were usually men who had spent their lives in the fields and often knew as much or more about many plots of land than the property owners did. In Qarawa, land registration teams had the help of an elderly resident named Abu Ijbal whose decades as shepherd, watchman, and farmer gave him unparalleled knowledge of the village landscape.[26] When I interviewed Abu Ijbal, he told me that he had also helped smooth over conflicts arising from disagreements that would emerge when people had forgotten where their borders were.[27] On a number of occasions in Farkha, I witnessed a local guide locate landmarks that the owners of the land were ignorant of. At times, he enjoyed rubbing it in. "You don't even know the name of your own uncle," he once told a hapless man who was clearly struggling to remember the names of those who owned the surrounding plots.

Land titling reinforced an important principle of agrarian life: the respect for the land rights of one's neighbor. Indeed, for many of those I spoke with, titling was often seen as aligning with village norms and providing much needed security. A former village council head in Qarawa, who was deeply critical of land titling and of many aspects of the land registration project, put it this way: "even if you stop working your land, or leave the village, or die, the land will be safe" and the borders set for "a thousand years." Land titling was often experienced as a recognition of existing rights and, in the case of encroachments, restoring things to how they had always been.

It was the violation of these property rights that could allow people to locate injustice as originating from outside the village. One illustrative instance happened in Farkha. A man from a nearby town, who had a reputation with the survey team (and, I suspect, with local residents) as a land broker, had purchased a plot of agricultural land adjacent to an area owned by a large real estate company. His claims about the plot's borders raised the suspicions of the survey team, who phoned the neighboring owner. The owner turned out to be an elderly farmer, and he arrived soon after, accompanied by his eldest son. The broker, who had commissioned a private survey of the area and had his own map, pointed out the land that he believed he had purchased. The farmer disagreed.

Both plots were located on a steep slope and separated by a steep rocky outcropping (*arak*) that supported a terrace retaining wall. According to local practice, which the survey team had been following, one measured "from the wall and above" to determine ownership of the outcropping, which in this case meant that it should go to the resident farmer. Gesturing with his walking stick, the farmer explained that he knew where the border was because his family had divided the land, and he had been coming here for decades to cultivate it. The broker demanded that the government survey team include the lower area into his plot, pointing to his map and finally, in a show of frustration, hurling rocks at the points where he thought the retaining wall indicated a border. The farmer, now more confident in his position, took pleasure in pointing out the encroacher's misunderstanding of the landscape ("that's not even a terrace wall you're pointing to!"). The farmer's son, who had become visibly angry, threatened to rent a backhoe to carve away the side of the mountain and make it clear once and for all whose land was whose. At this point, the broker appeared to surrender. But as we were leaving, he reappeared with an elderly man in tow. (We were quite far from the village, so where this man came from is still a mystery to me.) "Go and ask this man about the outcropping, since you don't believe me!" he exclaimed to the lead surveyor.

This conflict illustrates two things. First, it shows another way that agrarian custom was respected, reinforcing the experience that titling constituted a recognition of preexisting norms. Second, it was the attempt to skirt this custom that marked this man not only as engaging in unjust action, but as bringing injustice from the outside into the village. Such an experience fit into a more widely held sentiment. One farmer I met during land titling in Farkha referred to 2007 as the year when "the thieves came." The "thieves," in his telling, were not only the real estate companies, but also the brokers, the lawyers, and the speculators who, he said, were "exploiting the character and naïveté of the peasants [*fallahin*]." Claims like these invoked inequalities that characterized peasant life in the past, with today's speculators and developers the latest outsiders trying to take advantage of the people who lived in the village.[28]

The issue of this land broker brings up a second issue: land sales. When I asked about land sales, people might say it was shameful (*'ayb*) to sell land, that "peasants [*fallahin*] never sell," or that "land is honor [*al-ard 'ard*]."[29]

One man told me that he knew a woman who valued the land so much that he had seen her wipe the dirt off a surface, wrap it in the fold of her dress, and scatter it below her trees. Once, when I was lost outside of Farkha, I drove into a dead end in the groves of a bemused father and son who were harvesting olives. They were curious about what I was doing, and when I told them I was following one of the survey teams working in the village, one of them immediately brought up the real estate company UCI. "They came to us and offered us three times what they paid for the land," he said as he gestured with his hand toward the UCI area. "We told them to weigh a dunum and give us its weight in gold, and they said they couldn't, so we refused to sell."

At issue here is not that one should never sell, but that the price should be fair. After all, villagers had been selling land to one another for quite some time, and many people did sell their land to developers and brokers. According to another man in Qarawa, developers and brokers "took advantage of the situation of the peasants [*fallahin*] and bought land very cheaply, and sold it for more." When I began to investigate the land market, the village council head in Farkha told me that I would have a hard time finding people to talk to about land sales. They'd be embarrassed, he explained, after it came out that they had parted with their land for pennies. While I did find plenty of people to talk with about land sales, it was true that narratives often were tinged with shame or resignation. Buyers acquired land in the late 2000s, and village councils, sellers, and officials at the land registry estimated that a dunum could go for JD 2,000–3,000. Compared to the rising values of land, people spoke about those early buying prices as practically nothing, "a few hundred lira" (in reference to old bank notes that were associated with devaluation in the 1960s and 1970s and eventually replaced by the shekel in 1980 and the new shekel in 1985) or "a cup of coffee."

While many people sold, it was particularly galling to many how outsiders took advantage of those in desperate situations. This included those who desperately needed cash to get by as well as refugees or absentees. Some had fled or were abroad during the 1967 war and had since lived in refugee camps in Jordan; others, also in Jordan, were expelled from Kuwait in the 1990s; and others had migrated to the United States or Europe. According to interviews with current and past village council members, while those in the United States or Europe were generally better off financially, many of those in Jordan, with little chance of returning and in more dire financial straits, were some of the first to sell their shares.[30]

Land sales raise a final issue, that of new owners of land. While clear title increased land values, it also allowed, as one man put it, "a group of investors from outside the village" to control village land. For others, it was the potential of new residents to introduce urban customs. One former village council leader in Qarawa explained to me that a stranger's (*gharib*) actions might clash with local manners. The example he gave me was a bit extreme—imagine a guy, he told me, walking around the village streets with five young women—but the point seemed to be that the more liberal social mores of the city might not be acceptable in the village. And for others, it was less that new owners would make problems for existing social life, than that they would remain strangers. During one drive from Qarawa to the neighboring village of Mazari' al-Nubani, several older farmers pointed out new buildings. One particularly palatial complex belonged to someone from Hebron. They spoke of a nearby village, where after the land settlement was finished, they said, it turned out that half of the land was owned by outsiders. "You don't even know your neighbor anymore," said one as we drove by.

Such behavior stands in opposition to how villagers are supposed to relate to one another. The paradigmatic example here was the conduct of past generations, who embodied hard work and generosity. Abu Ashraf, from Qarawa, recalled how his family members helped one another in the fields, from picking olives to harvesting wheat. "I remember my father had a lot of wheat to harvest, so my uncles and other family members all came to help," he told me. "If you had grapes, it was a grape house," he went on, and you would give the extra to friends and relatives. Today, he concluded, everything except the olive tree has "basically faded and finished [*shibih indathar wa intaha*]," with generosity and cooperation disappearing along with the figs, grapes, almonds, and wheat.

These conflicts reveal what it means to lose village control over land. These critiques are not about the rights of citizens or owners, but about the obligations of families and neighbors. The demands for respect, fairness, and generosity are also firmly attached to specific people, plots, terraces, and trees. They are a bit more specific than laments about a lost past, since they also articulate how those who control village land today should treat one another. And by establishing a moral boundary between the village and the outside, they made clear the ways that they thought land commodification was putting village control further out of reach.

VILLAGE INJUSTICE

Entrenched inequalities and hierarchies are also part of village life. The idyllic village is a common motif in literary and artistic representations of the countryside, and one that has been subject to a great deal of criticism. But both individual experience and collective memory of village life, however, are more complex. Invocations of better days that, at certain times and to certain audiences, might smooth over, as James Scott once put it, "less favorable features of the old order," but they always exist alongside narratives of exploitative landlords, poverty, and oppressive family relationships.[31] This history shaped the social conflicts that land commodification created, and the injustices that these conflicts revealed.

For women, injustice often originated from the most intimate familial relationships. Indeed, the most overt resistance to titling often came not from efforts to resist individual property ownership, but from efforts to preserve patriarchal control over land. While Palestinian women have inheritance rights under both civil and Islamic law, brothers might deny a sister her share of the inheritance, often for the purpose of keeping property under the control of male heirs and within the paternal extended family. In an extensive study published in 2014, the Women's Centre for Legal Aid and Counselling found that women often were pressured to abandon inherited property to brothers, and that those who pursued claims in court faced social stigma and a legal process that could last years.[32] During the land settlement, partition could become contentious when it touched on the question of female inheritance. According to surveyors I spoke to in the PLA, attempts to preserve patriarchal control over land led to overt resistance to land titling and partition.[33] At the end of my fieldwork, when I was examining the published schedules of rights for Farkha, I found several plots that remained undivided. The head of the village council told me that many of these plots were likely the result of family conflicts, including concerns about "losing" land through the marriage of women.

Land titling created a space in which such conflicts could make their way into the open. One such instance occurred during land registration in Qarawa and drew the attention of residents and development experts alike.[34] The stakes were high, since making a legal claim for denied inheritance poses the danger of damaging relations with brothers and, potentially, other family members whom one might need to call on for support later.[35] One former head of the village council explained how contentious it was at the time, and several years later people brought it up when I asked about land titling (a few called it the "woman problem"). After the settlement of title was complete in the village, I was told, a number of these claims remained unresolved.[36]

But such public incidents, at least during my fieldwork, were rare. Instead, conflicts could be far less overt, and pressure far more subtle. Once, for example, I was with a survey team as they registered the land of an elderly woman outside of Farkha. She was accompanied by her son. It was a small plot with a few olive trees and the remains of grapevines hanging onto a terrace in need of repair. The woman noticed that her neighbor had encroached on her property. This was "shameful," she said, indicating where the borders should be, and telling the team that she had papers to prove it. Her son asked who the neighbor was, and when the head of the survey team told him, he shook his head. "Forget it," he told his mother. "We don't want to start a fight." She did not push the issue, but as we walked, she continued to bring it up, and insisted that she had the papers. When one of the surveyors suggested they register a conflict, her son insisted that it was not worth it. The issue was dropped, the plot was mapped, and we moved on. One of the surveyors felt guilty, and continued to bring it up as the day went on. "I won't be able to sleep tonight," she said. "The woman lost her grapevines [*diwali*]," she continued and, holding up a rock, concluded, "If she had wanted us to register this rock in her name, we should have done it."

Private meetings to provide legal advice and public events also illustrated the ways that women experienced injustice as coming from within, rather than outside. These meetings seemed to do little to shore up faith in legal solutions; lawyers and social workers tasked with helping women navigate the claims-making process tried to impress upon them that, given the understaffed courts and difficulties involved in enforcing rulings, formal legal procedures should be a last resort. During one public meeting in Salfit, for instance, several Palestinian lawyers explained to an audience of women how to navigate the claims-making process. Many of the follow-up questions pointed to where the law fell short. What sort of protections do you have if you make a claim against your brothers, and your husband dies? What about familial pressure? Won't fathers who wish to disinherit their daughters simply "sell" their land to their sons? There were no clear solutions. While the legal remedies promised by formal property ownership often fell short, land titling did succeed in revealing, and perhaps exacerbating, very intimate forms of injustice.

People I spoke with also felt that the rising prices of land were affecting relationships between neighbors and kin. They spoke of heirs becoming inflexible and greedy, relatives living abroad who had never shown much interest in land in Palestine suddenly demanding control of property, and siblings sacrificing family peace for small bits of land. Sometimes these conflicts played out during land registration, which revealed minor encroachments that people called "eating" (*akal*) the land, or, if you were really trying to underline your point, "shameful eating" (*akal haram*). This idiom appears in other agrarian societies as well, linking land to subsistence, and viewing its theft as unjust consumption.[37] Many a fight would include claims that one "ate" land that did not belong to them. Such "fights over centimeters," as one man called them, appeared to be more frequent; in the past, people might have just let them go, or not found it worth fighting over in the first place.[38]

The rising prices of land created other sorts of rifts within families. One such instance of family strife created by the sale of family land was related to me by a man I'll call Abu Sayf, whom I met in Bruqin. When I asked Abu Sayf about how agrarian life had changed, he recounted to me how his father, then an old man, had once owned land on one of the large hills outside the village. In the 1970s and 1980s, his parents cultivated this area with wheat, figs, melons, and vegetables. They would never have thought of selling it then, he said, and while everyone else was going to work in Israel, his parents stayed. But as they got older, the work became harder. Their children grew up and found jobs elsewhere. The land fell out of use. Before the real estate boom really got going, a broker from Qarawa inquired about the land, and even though the price the broker offered to Abu Sayf's father was low, he agreed.

His decision led to a serious disagreement among the extended family. Some of the children were furious with their father for agreeing to the sale. Some would later agree to sell their own plots, holding out for a better price. Some refused. His father's land ended up with UCI. But why would you blame the company? he asked me. They "created a market where one didn't exist" and acted "rationally," just as one would expect. "We are the ones behaving like fools," he said, "running around complaining, begging, and crying." Perhaps, he mused, the company had a plan all along. Was it really so surprising that a broker "came and found an old man who doesn't have any support from his sons and bought the land for ten lira?"

While both land broker and company play a role in the loss of land, this story complicates the idea that injustice only comes from outside the village. For Abu Sayf, the broker might have taken advantage of his parents, and the developer might have offered an unfair price. But responsibility was more diffused; he blamed himself, and his siblings, for leaving his parents alone to take care of the land in the first place. This abandonment was not malicious; in fact, it was likely unavoidable. But in the telling of this story, it registered as a failure to support one's family, a failure that could not be blamed solely on a private company that, after all, was just doing what private companies do.

The sense of personal responsibility for the loss of land could also shape how people imagined the future. Abu Amjad, for example, had come out ahead in the land boom. A father of four children, he lives in Qarawa and works in Ramallah for a well-established Palestinian NGO. His brothers are in the United States, and he was entrusted with maintaining the family holdings in the West Bank, which include some 80 dunums in Qarawa as well as property in Ramallah. In 2009 and 2010 the family bought additional agricultural land adjacent to the property they already owned, expecting prices to rise. When I asked him how he was able to purchase land when so many other people were selling, he shrugged: we're lucky, he said, and didn't have a reason to sell land at that time.

Abu Amjad thought of his land as investment for his children. Instead of making money and putting it in the bank for them, "we'll leave them real estate [*aqarat aradi*] that tomorrow will be worth a lot more." Their generation, he explained to me, sees "land as a business." His brothers' children, for instance, grew up in the United States. One day "they will come, sell [the land], and go home." He expected his children would do the same. "I have a daughter," he told me, "who, after graduating at the top of her class in computer science and spending a year and a half searching, could only find a minimum-wage job in Ramallah." His son was doing worse. "When I was growing up in the 1970s and 1980s, I would work in the fields, pick olives, plow. My son, who is finishing university, hasn't had the chance to make a shekel in his life."

Men like Abu Amjad felt personally culpable for the fact that the next generation might have no choice but to sell the land. "My father wanted me to immigrate to the United States with my brothers," Abu Amjad recalled. "I refused. I loved what we had here. But now I feel like I have made a mistake, like I have done wrong not just to myself, but to my children, by staying here." And while people recognized that others might have good reasons to sell their land, or perhaps no other choice, they still worried about the future consequences. Another man from Qarawa put it this way: "The children of our children tomorrow are going to be forced to buy the land we or their grandparents sold for JD 1,000 or 2,000, for 100,000, 150,000 for a half-dunum." More likely, they would never own land in the village again. This prospect weighed on those for whom land ownership was a way to maintain some sort of connection to their village, and to Palestine. While Abu Amjad and others were well aware that land titling and private capital were driving the loss of land, they also felt that it was their fault, too, that they could not provide for their children.

In these narratives, one's own neighbors and kin were to blame for the loss of land, not outsiders. Instead, commodification brought longstanding conflicts out into the open, and frayed relationships that people may have assumed they could rely on. This experience, too, indexed a loss of local control, but one that came from within the heart of the village community, and was felt to be the fault of those who lived there.

JUSTICE WITHOUT RESISTANCE

Spatial scales like global/local or above/below not only help us describe the world, they help make it. Material and discursive practices produce the idea that the state is hovering above us, or capital that is global, and critical investigation of such scalar imaginaries reveals how they are made, and what their evocation can hide.[39] For activists and social movements, this framing of above/outside is a way to talk about corporate land grabbing and dispossession, and to rally support for the resistance that comes from "below." Doing so creates the possibility for a kind of progressive internationalism that links various local communities fighting against predatory corporate and state encroachment. At its most extreme, it grounds a political-theoretical discourse that divides the planet into two camps: as scholar and environmental activist Vandana Shiva puts it, those who view "the planet as private property" and "movements [that] are defending, on a local and global level, the planet as a commons."[40]

Critiques of commodification in the highlands also rely on a kind of spatial thinking. People used boundaries between the village community and its outside to assign responsibility for injustice and suggest how people might act otherwise. But these are difficult boundaries to sustain. Indeed, because land commodification itself spreads seemingly of its own accord, responsibility for the strain and fracture of intimate relationships is difficult to pin on malicious external actors; rather, blame diffuses to the farmers who left, the family members who abandoned one another, and everyone for whom the land became cheap. These conflicts and complaints point to a desire for local control over village land, and a sense of what just conduct would look like. They also illuminate that recourse to the village community cannot provide a stable foundation for land justice.

When we privilege a certain kind of resistance, we risk plowing over the roughness of daily struggles, and the compromises that people make, knowingly or not, to stay on their land. The analytical shortcomings and political dangers of narratives that pit bad corporations against good local communities are well rehearsed at this point.[41] Activists, whether or not they agree with these critiques, may have little immediate use for them. After all, building a local campaign or an international movement requires clear lines between friend and enemy. It is the job of scholars to examine the places that are not easily incorporated into this script, and the people who do not resist as we might expect. In doing so, we can expand our understanding of what land justice might be and gain a clearer understanding of the obstacles that stand in the way of its realization.

Four

BUILDING

LAND FOR THOSE WHO WORK IT

HEALTHY OLIVE TREES. SOLID TERRACE WALLS. PLOWED EARTH, free of weeds. These are a few characteristics of a well-tended plot, or what people call "clean" land. Early on in my fieldwork I enjoyed the good fortune of touring the hills of Farkha with one of the village's best known farmers. Riding in a cart pulled by a donkey, he patiently answered my questions about the landscape and drew my attention to the work that goes into keeping land in such a condition. Over the years I had similar conversations with others, many of whom were proud to tell me about the land that they had spent so much time and effort on. Their labor, and the labor of those who came before them, made this landscape and produced a double sense of belonging: the land belongs to those who work it, just as they themselves belong to the land.

The work of cultivation is also an essential part of land defense. Near the end of my fieldwork, Israeli settlers began to encroach on land outside of Farkha. The Israeli government had declared the area to be state property, granting its legal blessing to the settlers' occupation, while the Israeli military offered armed protection. In response, activists organized different land defense efforts. One involved young people who, in photographs published by the village news service on Facebook, were seen digging holes on a rocky hilltop to plant olive saplings. This act was part of a long tradition of rural anticolonialism, one in which peasant labor was repurposed for the defense of village land and national territory.

On other hills, olive trees were irrelevant for the private developers who now owned the land. Once, during my time with land registration teams in Farkha, we were joined by the lawyer of a large real estate company. He had brought maps of the land that the company owned, and we followed the metal stakes and spray-painted rocks that indicated the extent of the holdings. Much of the land was rocky and uncultivated, but some plots were planted with olive trees. The lawyer told the local guide that they were planning on removing these trees, and wondered if he knew anyone who might want to use them as firewood.

Peasant labor produces different claims to land. Peasant labor practices, and the wider set of cultural values and social norms that give them meaning, have been around for a long time. Even with the decline of agricultural livelihoods, they endure as a means by which Palestinians can establish socially recognized possession, and sometimes legal ownership, of land. Activists, development economists, and agronomists adapted aspects of peasant labor into a broader land defense strategy that combined rural development and ownership claims. Some of the men who cultivated the land in the highlands are also beginning to rethink the meaning of their hard work, using these experiences to critique commodification *and* to demand inclusion in the new real estate economy. These different claims to land are all informed by a principle at the heart of the peasant labor process: land is for those who work it.

PEASANT LABOR

Rather than conceptualizing the peasant as an ideal type, anthropologist Michel-Rolph Trouillot suggested that we instead concentrate on the peasant labor process. What made that process specific, he argued, was that it was the household that carried out agricultural work and controlled the instruments to do so. Relying on the capacities of those who shared a household meant that maintaining family relations was far more important than it might be to, say, a highly mechanized industrial farm.[1] For peasant farmers, land is what you work with, where you work, and where you live.

This labor process determines how people relate to land, and to each other. Peasant farmers often measure land in terms of labor—for instance, how long it takes to plow a given plot—rather than by a dematerialized calculation of surface area.[2] The seasonal cycles of plowing, planting, and harvesting reproduce collective values of solidarity and cooperation, as well as more individualistic values of personal hard work and private ownership. Finally, work is constitutive of rights, both to general membership in the village community and to use, access, and ownership of specific plots of land. Labor distributes responsibilities and creates boundaries, grounding the moral, and often legal, claim that land should be for those who work it.

The defense of peasant rights, especially the idea that land belongs to those who work it, was part of the impetus for anticolonial struggles and postcolonial land reforms. Enclosure and expropriation were catalysts for rural revolt, and demands that the land be given to those who worked it were part of postcolonial "land to the tiller" reforms.[3] Today, peasants and landless people still turn to this principle, and sometimes to the legal legacy of land reform itself, to pressure the state to make good on its promises.[4] At the same time, these struggles often fell short of extending land rights to women, and some internalized colonial tropes about Indigenous land use that justified ongoing dispossession and displacement.[5] Today, "land for those who work it" is an enduring demand that has the potential for both agrarian justice and violent exclusion.

Peasant labor can also justify the spread of capitalist social relations and ideologies. Geographer Sharad Chari, for instance, showed how Indian worker-peasants who become factory owners "renovate" agrarian culture into an ideology based on the hard work of self-made men who transformed "subaltern knowledge [into] capitalist advantage."[6] Anthropologist Tania Li, in her research on the commodification of land in the Indonesian highlands, found that "indigenous concepts emphasizing the value of an individual's hard work combine with market opportunities that are enticing but volatile, and a land regime that enables private enclosure."[7] Sometimes the idea that land should be for those who work it facilitates, rather than thwarts, the commodification of land.

Peasant labor produces rural landscapes that are a palimpsest of these different histories. "Rural politics," argues political ecologist Donald Moore, play out "on the shifting ground of these complex, layered sedimentations and their mutual imbrication."[8] Through their work, rural people make the landscape and imbue it with meaning, while subsequent political conflicts and economic transformations create the opportunities to put the practices and values of cultivation in the service of making new claims to land.

BUILDING THE LAND

In the highlands of Palestine, peasant labor is best understood as a process of building. When speaking to older farmers—I mostly heard this from men, but not exclusively—about their life on the land, they often used the verb "to build" (*'amr*) to describe both their work and its results. While this term is specific to the rural dialect of Palestinian Arabic, it is the Standard Arabic definition of the word, which means "to build," "to make prosper," "to be inhabited or civilized," and "to restore," that illuminates the links between cultivation, wealth, and place.[9] Building the land is long-term, transformative labor, which includes the removal of stones from the soil, the construction of terrace walls and shelters (*qusur,* sing. *qasr*), the seasonal work of upkeep and harvesting, and most crucially, the planting of trees.[10] It is also the creation of collective and personal identities. Cultivation, after all, is not only a "work of improvement exercised upon the agrarian landscape" but also "a labor on the nature of the self" that draws from a deep well of agrarian thought and practice about what constitutes virtue and the good life.[11] This idiom of "building the land" captures the multifaceted, transformative nature of labor, and the sedimented quality of the landscapes it produces.[12]

In precolonial Palestine, the peasant labor process structured village life. In early Ottoman Palestine, "the peopling and cultivation and settledness" of a region were one and the same, and the new Ottoman rulers sought to ensure the regular collection of taxes, working with village leaders to "ensure the regular cultivation and settlement of their villages."[13] The idea that "continuous cultivation" produced rights to land had been part of legal tradition and debate since at least the sixteenth century.[14] The 1858 Ottoman Land Code built on this tradition, recognizing rights created through cultivation and extending the possibility of acquiring unused land through "improvement."[15] Peasants measured land by how long it took to plow, or by the number of trees planted in a given location.[16] Access to land in Palestinian villages was inseparable from the ability to work it. Shares to common land (*masha‘*) in some villages, for instance, depended on the amount of labor, calculated by able-bodied men, that a family could mobilize.[17] Whether or not land was held in common—one historian, for instance, has argued that in the highlands the predominance of tree crops meant that individual land tenure was more common—the spatial distribution of land to the various village families and the need to coordinate various cycles of planting and harvesting, as well as the pasturing of animals, meant that the peasant labor process required a great deal of coordination and detailed knowledge of local conditions.[18]

Palestine's different agricultural environments each gave rise to different kinds of peasant labor. In the highlands, for example, the work of terracing and tree planting is a multigenerational effort. Take the olive tree: When a tree becomes less productive (or "weak"), farmers graft new branches to the tree to replace the older, less productive ones. The most common tree in olive-producing regions is the Nabali cultivar, known colloquially as *rumi* (Roman) or *baladi* (local). It can live for hundreds of years. Given that the lifespan of olive trees is far longer than that of any one of the people that care for them, generations contribute to the life (and renewal) of any single tree. Or take the terraces: "Terracing structures," writes anthropologist Andrew Mathews, "are a testimony to centuries of collective geomorphological work by peasant farmers."[19] Called "chains" (*sinasil*, sing. *sinsila*) in Arabic, terrace walls are built by removing rocks from the soil and stacking them so that they fit together with no adhesive or cement. As with the olive tree, generations of cultivators have worked to terrace the hillsides, repairing older walls after winter rains and extending them to bring more land under cultivation. Indeed, there is practically nothing about this rural landscape that is not the product of generations of human labor.

The work of cultivation provided the means to obtain customary and legal rights to land. The property-making power of labor is nowhere clearer than in co-planting (*mugharasa*) agreements. In co-planting, one party provides the means of production in the form of land, animals, and/or saplings, while the other provides labor over an agreed-upon period of time corresponding to the years it takes for a given tree to bear fruit.[20] After the completion of the agreement, the planter—called *ghares* (planter) or *mu’amarji* ("builder," from the Arabic word ʿamr, "build," with Turkish suffix -ji)—earns rights to a portion of the trees, to land, and sometimes to both. Co-planting agreements may cover different kinds of trees, and in the central highlands of Palestine, the olive tree's economic importance and biophysical characteristics have made it especially appropriate for co-planting.[21] Over the life of the co-planting agreement—as long as fifteen years for olive trees—the cultivator might also have the right to plant seasonal subsistence crops while waiting for the trees to mature.[22] These agreements were an important part of rural life during the late Ottoman and Mandate periods and, according the historian Sarah Graham-Brown, were key to the increase in the number of smallholders in the highlands.[23]

Prior to the Israeli occupation of the West Bank in 1967, many of the practices and values that characterized the peasant labor process were disappearing or changing. The British assault on peasant land tenure had resulted in the drastic decline of common lands (mashaʿ).[24] Co-planting agreements still existed in the highlands but were fewer in number by the end of the 1960s.[25] According to one of the few ethnographic studies during this period, while land ownership still brought a measure of prestige, in the central highlands farming was considered by some to be a degrading occupation that offered little in terms of stability or social advancement.[26]

Under Israeli rule, Palestinians adapted the peasant labor process to their new economic situation. In the 1970s and 1980s, villagers greatly expanded the amount of land under olive tree cultivation. One of the reasons they did so was to cope with migratory wage labor. Peasants replaced seasonal field crops, like wheat and barley, as well as other fruit trees with shorter lifespans, with olive trees. An increase in olive tree–producing nurseries and advances in agronomy helped considerably.[27] Work in construction allowed men to take time off during the harvest. One farmer from Qarawa, recalling how his father would come back from his work in a factory for the harvest, recalled, "You couldn't find one single person in town; everyone was out in the fields." Most families also hired labor from Gaza and Hebron to help pick and sort the olives. These men and women would sleep in the homes of the landowners for the month, and were paid in oil, based on the task they performed within the gendered division of labor.[28] In these years, building the land was part of how peasants adapted to the changes in the political economy, one in which olives became more important in order to adapt to the new regime of migrant labor in Israel.

Since the 1990s, there has been a general growth in olive cultivation and decline in other agricultural pursuits.[29] Grapes, wheat, figs, and various stone fruits have diminished or disappeared altogether. The Israeli confiscation of pasture lands had a devastating effect on animal husbandry across the West Bank in the 1970s, and the expansion of settlements, checkpoints, and fences has only entrenched these enclosures. The highlands have lost much of the complexity that once characterized the agricultural environment, and the peasant labor process has changed accordingly.

Despite these changes, peasant labor remains an important way cultivators can establish a socially recognized presence on the land. In the highlands, a well-cared-for plot is what people call "clean" land. Keeping land clean requires regular maintenance work of plowing, removing stones, and weeding, in addition to occasionally pruning the dead branches off olive trees, or repairing terraces damaged by winter rains. Following anthropologist Katherine Verdery, these various agricultural practices create a "visible economy" that others can understand and evaluate. Clean land demonstrates a "mastery" that demands respect, while the overgrown trees and wild bushes of ruined land are evidence of neglect and abandonment.[30]

This labor also created plot boundaries that reflected the ways that peasants measured and valued land. I learned about these borders on one particularly hot day in Farkha, when I followed the survey team as they mapped the land of an older farmer whom I'll call Abu Hadid. Later, hiding from the sun under a large olive tree, I asked to see the sketch of the plot. It was nowhere near a perfect square: the borders moved across more than eighty points, jagged lines zigzagging up and down the hills, cutting back and forth across terraces, and wrapping around trees and walls. "Until recently," Abu Hadid explained to me, people valued their land according to the olive crop. The borders reflected this history, one in which the people bought land, divided it up among their children, or bestowed it as a dowry, according to the quality of the soil and the trees.

The PA settlement of title attempted to straighten out these borders, but it was easier said than done. The survey teams I spent time with could not force the issue, so they did their best to convince rural landowners to do

it themselves. From meetings in the village councils and mosques to interactions in the field, they extolled the virtues of the straight line. But many
people wanted to keep the existing lines. During my fieldwork, it was older
landowners whom I saw most often insisting on keeping to the traditional
boundaries, often against the advice of the surveyors. I remember one owner
in Farkha who led surveyors along a terrace, followed a stair-like pattern
down a hill, and then looped along a rock. He indicated point after point
where he believed that one surveyor should record a point in the GPS device.
A frustrated team leader tried to explain that so many coordinates so close
together would be lost at the scale of the official map. But this explanation
missed the point. "I don't want to encroach on anyone's land, or anyone on
mine," the man insisted, "so no one can say anything about me." In the final
maps issued by land settlement, one can see the distinction between the
straight lines of the hills given over to real estate, and the crooked lines defining the borders of the plots that are still farmed.

During my time with the land survey teams I realized that some people
continued to own trees without owning ground or, more commonly, to own
very small bits of land within a larger plot owned by someone else. While
I never encountered estimates, it was not an insignificant phenomenon.
During the days I spent with surveyors, I counted at least a dozen: one day,
a small plot with only a single tree; another day three plots, one with four
trees, a second with two, and a third with two; another day, three plots, each
with a single tree; and so on. Farmers tended to respect these sorts of arrangements. In Farkha, I encountered one larger plot of land containing four
trees (belonging to two different people), and the landowner was keen to
emphasize that while he could not claim the trees, the ground around them
belonged to him. Even if a tree appeared to be abandoned, people might re-
frain from claiming it. Several times, men instructed the teams to record
points around an olive tree that had been on their land so long that they were
not even sure who it belonged to.

Even those who greatly resented the presence of trees felt unable to get
rid of them. One farmer pointed out a tree on his land surrounded by a tiny
patch of land that he did not own. He guessed that, long ago, someone sold
the land but insisted on keeping this single tree. "Damn them all [the older
generation]," he lamented, "they loved the trees more than their families

FIGURE 6. Plot boundaries in Farkha. The straight lines and square plots on the left are more typical of real estate development, while agricultural use has resulted in the curving boundary lines on the right.

Image by Wenfei Xu based on data from the Palestinian Land and Water Settlement Commission.

and their children." Another man I met in Farkha was particularly incensed when a tiny bit of land was marked out of his plot to preserve a tree. Not only was he forced into the role of de facto caretaker for a tree that did not belong to him, he told us, but it also prevented him from using the land as he wished. He had been trying to buy out the owner for years, so far without success. "I'm going to dig a well right there," he fumed, "so I'm going to tear up the tree, and dig a well on my land, and put down concrete and all that. I can do that, right? It's my land, no?" He turned to the survey team, perhaps expecting some support. "Just burn it," one of the surveyors suggested.

Suggesting arson was a joke, but the predicament that the olive tree created for the PLA was not. Land titling, informed as it was by the ideal of absolute private property ownership, was supposed to consolidate tree and ground ownership and eliminate small plots. A provision in the law allows for compulsory sale, in effect combining micro-plots or trees with a neighboring plot, but the PLA seemed wary of using it.[31] Instead, different strategies appeared over the course of different land titling projects. PLA employees told me that during land titling in Salfit (which began in 2010 and was largely completed by the time I started my fieldwork), the director registered a small portion of land—roughly equivalent to the shadow cast by the tree—to the tree's owner. By the time the Farkha project started, surveyors were recording free-floating trees in a note on the title, while micro-plots were surveyed without comment. In 2016, some in the PLA were worried that any kind of compulsory sale would result in resistance and undermine support for the project. One surveyor, who would later become the director of the Salfit office, noted with exasperation how difficult it was to convince people to exchange or sell trees or small bits of land. She said, "It is like you've killed one of their sons." When I finished fieldwork in Farkha at the beginning of 2017, it did not seem like a satisfying solution was in sight. In the summer of 2022, I returned to Palestine after pandemic restrictions were lifted and learned that land ownership had been consolidated through compulsory sales. When I asked the mayor about it, he shrugged: people did not always like it, but what could they do?

Building the land is based on precolonial practices and values that have endured the slow annihilation of agrarian Palestine. They have not endured unchanged. Instead, they are part of an agrarian landscape that has been whittled down and thinned out, one in which violations of agrarian custom no longer incite collective resistance. But clean land, crooked borders, errant trees, and small plots all underline the lingering respect that building the land commands among those who still work the land, and grounds an agrarian ethics that is not easily metabolized by new economic relations overtaking the highlands.[32]

DEFENDING THE LAND

Cultivation, or the assumed lack thereof, is key to the Israeli colonization of the West Bank. The seizure of so-called "uncultivated" lands from Palestinians, the transformation of this land into property of the state, and the subsequent use of state lands for settlement expansion provided one important legal tool that facilitated and justified dispossession. Starting in the 1970s, and armed with a legal definition of cultivation that would ensure maximum losses for Palestinians, Israeli experts surveyed the West Bank, reviewed aerial photographs and land registries, and carried out field visits with the goal of declaring as much land as possible to be property of the state.[33] As dispossession and settlement accelerated in the highlands in the 1980s, the question of cultivation became of paramount political importance for those who lived there.

To combat the ideological and legal claims of empty land, Palestinians began planting the land with olive trees. Villagers planted trees in response to state land confiscation orders, foresting projects, and settlement construction.[34] They also engaged in preemptive actions, planting areas they believed would be targeted in the future. Some of these efforts, as one observer noted, were a "spontaneous reaction" to Israeli colonization, and others, as we will see, were organized.[35] As the 1980s progressed, tree plantings were sometimes carried out in tandem with protest marches or sit-ins. Reclaiming land, terracing it, and planting it with trees was a longstanding practice for peasants. So too was the idea that mixing their labor with the land was proof of possession, if not property. Now, however, the *absence* of this labor was being used against them, imbuing cultivation with a new urgency and political meaning.

Beginning in the late 1970s, an ensemble of activists and intellectuals began to explore how to help peasants stay on their land. It was a diverse group of people and included rural activists and village committees, as well as agronomists, surveyors, lawyers, and development economists. Their ideas circulated in the Arabic press; in books, reports, and pamphlets published by the Arab Studies Society and the Arab Thought Forum; and in the pages of the PLO journal *Samed al-Iqtisadi*. They often drew inspiration from peasant agriculture, just as they explored ways to transform it. A group of agronomists and development economists—Abdulrahman Abu 'Arafeh, Yusuf al-Azzeh, and Dawood Istanbuli—wrote that agriculture would need to become a "process of struggle that aims for self-defense [*difa' 'an nafs*]" to enable the "continued existence [*tawajud*] of the people [*sha'ab*] on their land [*fawq ardihi*]."[36] In the struggle against settler colonialism, the labor of building the land became not only the means to defend land in specific villages, but a resource that nourished a much larger project of national land defense.

On the ground, the most visible expression of this project was large-scale tree planting. One early example is from the 1970s, when the Mennonite Central Committee's (MCC) agricultural development arm took up the "mass distribution of saplings," buying trees in bulk from a Nablus-area nursery and then transporting the saplings to threatened villages.[37] In the 1980s, the Palestinian Agricultural Relief Committees (PARC) and the Union of Agricultural Work Committees (UAWC)—both of which were set up by agronomists who, on a voluntary basis, provided extension services to small farmers—became involved with sapling distribution and planting.[38] In the central highlands, voluntary work activists played a role in the fight against the settlement of Ariel. In those days, one older activist told me, the "settlements didn't have fences" and Palestinians, who at the time far outnumbered settlers, planted olive trees as close as possible to the new settlement. According to a contemporary news report, in 1980 "volunteers planted 1,650 olive trees, 600 grapevines and leveled 220 dunums of land [and collected funds] to cover half the cost of the groves" in Farkha, Salfit, and Dier Jarir.[39] To protect land from colonial settlement, a burgeoning network of plant nurseries, activist groups, and village committees distributed and planted trees in threatened areas across the West Bank.

Sapling distribution introduced a new type of olive tree into the Palestinian landscape. The native Nabali cultivar grows slowly; it can take several years to produce olives, and ten to twelve before maturing completely. In the 1970s, growers at the Qasem Abdulhadi Nursery came across a new variety that grew much faster and produced fruit after only six months; they marketed it as "Improved Nabali" (Nabali Muhassan). During the 1980s, the agronomist Said Assaf estimated that a million of these so-called improved saplings were distributed in the West Bank.[40] Palestinians planted this variety widely, especially in the Hebron and Bethlehem districts where olive trees were not widespread and land confiscation was increasing.[41] Economist Ibrahim Matar, who served as the MMC's agricultural development expert, would later argue that the sapling distribution was crucial in transforming Hebron from a "dry zone" to a "green zone."[42]

The career of Matar also helps us see how planting was wrapped up with the protection of private property. Because of his connections in the West Bank countryside, the MCC tasked Matar with assisting Quaker Legal Services in locating rural landowners who would be willing to take their cases to the Israeli courts; he recruited petitioners for three significant cases.[43] Agronomists and surveyors also were tasked with helping provide proof of prior cultivation. Jamal Talab, a prominent activist from the south and now director of the Land Research Center, explained that "agricultural reports"—detailed information about crops, soil, climate, and topography— accompanied the surveyors' maps that served as evidence of property ownership.[44] Land reclamation projects served this purpose as well. In his study of the possibilities for land reclamation in the West Bank, for instance, researcher Khalil al-ʿAlul wrote that in "every Palestinian village," there was still a great deal of "unused private land"; to "protect it" required "the use of every inch."[45]

The protection of ownership was only one part of a larger project of agricultural development. Palestinian development thinking in the 1970s emerged out of an insurgent approach to economic development pioneered in the wake of postwar decolonization, and sought to combine economic and social development with the needs of the liberation struggle.[46] This anticolonial orientation framed economic dependency as a political problem and tried to imagine how, without the sovereign power of a state, development could serve as a means to resist subordination.[47] In the West Bank, one of the problems was mitigating agricultural decline and rural migration.

There was not a consensus around peasant farming, and often Palestinian thinkers argued that modernization was necessary for the development of the agricultural sector and the defense of land. Indeed, as geographer Omar Tesdell points out, many working in the agricultural sector did not understand, or appreciate, rain-fed farming.[48] Abu ʾArafeh, al-Azzeh, and Istanbuli, for instance, argued that irrigation could both break a reliance on rainfall (the unreliability of which, they thought, discouraged risk-taking) and increase productivity.[49] Hisham Awartani represented a different position. He believed that irrigation was important, but he also valued aspects of peasant farming. "Quasi-peasant farming," he thought, could mobilize "large inputs of land and family labour at acceptable levels of efficiency" and as such was "probably more able to survive the strong competition with Israeli produce than most patterns of capital-intensive and market-oriented agricultural production."[50] Awartani argued that successful agricultural development should be evaluated not according to "conventional economic theories" but according to its contribution to "national viability" that included reversing labor migration and land desertion.

Land reclamation was an important part of this approach to agricultural development. Awartani, for example, noted that the neglect of terrace walls led to soil erosion and undermined Palestinian control over land.[51] Both Awartani and al-'Alul argued against Israeli categorizations of land that, they thought, downplayed the feasibility of reclamation. Against an Israeli survey that saw some land as impossible to cultivate, al-'Alul advocated for the construction of agricultural roads and the use of "simple reclamation (non-mechanized)"—based on "traditional" practices using simple tools, animals, and terracing—to encourage farmers to "begin to invest their money and time in land reclamation and use" in hostile market and political conditions.[52] Land reclamation, these experts thought, could confront colonial dispossession through increasing extensive land use and labor-intensive farming, and as such should be supported regardless of cost.[53]

Land defense efforts brought together these different currents. In *al-Zaitun taht al-Ihtilal* (The Olive under Occupation), Jamal Talab and Nuri al-'Uqbi recounted how Israeli troops occupied the village of al-Midya and uprooted more than 3,000 olive trees in the summer of 1986.[54] They detailed how villagers clashed with soldiers and blocked bulldozers, and also brought their demands to the streets of Jerusalem and Tel Aviv. In front of the Premier's Office in Jerusalem, and the Ministry of Agriculture in Tel Aviv, farmers displayed dead tree trunks, left over after the uprooting, which were hung with messages that read: "I am more than sixty years old." Talab and al-'Uqbi's booklet also includes Mandate- and Jordanian-era tax receipts, wills from 1984, and Israeli building permits that serve as evidence of legal ownership. An agricultural report documents the value and age of the damaged trees, names each owner, and calculates losses. In the English section of the book, but not in the Arabic, the authors explicitly note that an "agricultural economist with a PhD" produced the figures. Both an account of one village's struggle and a part of it, this text helps us see the various elements of an agrarian formation of land defense, one in which labor, livelihood, and ownership grounded rights to land and demands for justice.

This approach to land defense informed the recurring battles over land in the 1990s and 2000s. One activist-farmer I interviewed, whom I'll call Abu ʿAmar, illustrates this dynamic perfectly. He lives in a highland village, but a bit farther north than the villages that are the focus of this book. In 1981 he was elected to the local land defense committee of his village, and in 1988 moved to district-level coordination. During these years, he helped plan demonstrations and, according to his count, was involved in planting some 20,000 olive saplings and reclamation work on 1,000 dunums of land.

Abu ʿAmar's own land was caught up in a large state land declaration. He knew the state would ultimately evaluate the extent of cultivation for each plot separately, and did everything he could to ensure that his land would be recognized as cultivated. Doing so came at great expense. He sold his sheep and goats, as well as his wife's gold, to raise the money to employ a contractor to remove hundreds of truckloads of stones from the land. Several years after the declaration and the objections, a government official named Plia Albeck arrived in the village to inspect the land several times. Abu ʿAmar's account of the inspection is worth quoting in full:

> Plia Albeck visited us on the land to determine if it was cultivated or not. Prior to her visit, my land had been set on fire, and everything had been burned. I had older saplings that had been planted, but nothing had remained after the fire. When I told her that the land had been cultivated, there was no proof. I pointed to a spot and moved the ash and ground with my foot, and below there was a buried trunk of a tree. Growing out of it were 15 new branches, trying to push up out of the burned ground. Albeck reached down and touched the soil, digging around the trunk. She was silent. Also, with her was another official, an Iraqi Jew. Everyone was silent as she touched the ground and felt the burned tree. She rested her head in her hands and sighed [he demonstrates this]. Nearby, there was another trace. I had been spraying the trees to protect them against ʿayn tawoos ["eye of the peacock," a condition that results from bugs eating small holes in olive tree leaves]. I had started spraying the night before the fire and left the hose on the ground with the intention of returning in the morning. The hose was gone, but when they burn it left abnormal marks on the ground. Albeck studied and touched these as well, and again was silent. Finally, she said: "I believe you that this was cultivated land.' " Later, it was excluded from the state lands order.

This exclusion provided only temporary respite. In 2002, when Israel began building the Separation Barrier through the village's agricultural area, Abu 'Amar once again began to help coordinate land defense activities, including the weekly Friday marches that would become a fixture of anti-Wall protests in the years to come. In 2004, he received notice that the Israeli authorities again were trying to claim land that he owned as property of the state. The map was wrong, he told me. Still, he had no choice but to return to court.

Farmers like Abu 'Amar did not face the state alone. In the 1990s, agricultural organizations like PARC and UAWC built up their institutional capacity and resources. In the 2000s, PARC began building thousands of kilometers of agricultural roads. Planting projects have also multiplied, and in addition to local land defense and development initiatives, are now part of everything from international campaigns to solidarity tourism experiences.

These projects did not always succeed in strengthening the position of Palestinian farmers. One of the worst mistakes involved Improved Nabali olive trees. As Said Assaf pointed out, this cultivar was neither improved nor Nabali. Although the tree produced olives very quickly, yields dropped dramatically as the tree reached maturity, and the cultivar turned out to be highly vulnerable to pests. Worse still, it was not suitable for rain-fed farming. Assaf noted that even though his research center had publicized these findings in the mid-1980s, not until "older experienced Palestinian farmers raised their voices and called its introduction a 'treason,' did commercial nurseries start switching to producing the Souri (Nabali Baladi) cultivar."[55] In 2010, according to the head of the Palestinian Olive Oil Council, Fayyad Fayyad, the Council carried out a study on the feasibility of moving around a million trees from the drier regions of the south and replanting them farther north, in areas that had more rainfall. It concluded, perhaps unsurprisingly, that this would be far too costly.

Reclamation and planting efforts are ongoing in the central highlands. In the summer of 2022, I visited one project taking place in an area that had long been the site of skirmishes between Palestinian villagers and nearby settlers. The land was still littered with the spent cartridges of tear gas. I walked with a young agronomist who accompanied the farmers, measuring the length of the retaining walls they had built, and nervously watching the road for signs of settlers or military vehicles. High on the mountain, Palestinians had set up a tent and sitting area, another small attempt to hold the high ground and provide opportunities, however minimal, to spend time in the area.

Nearby in Farkha, reclamation had been ongoing on a smaller scale. In the summer of 2019, the Israeli Civil Administration posted notices on the land of Hassan Hajjaj, informing him that his land was state property, and shortly thereafter destroying the improvements he had made to his farm. Hajjaj told the Land Research Center that he had cultivated the land with wheat in the 1980s and 1990s, and then in 2017 had "rehabilitated 4 dunums" and planted almonds, grapes, and olives.[56] Several hills on the outskirts of the village, 1,250 dunums of land in Area C, are under threat of confiscation. The reasons were expected: the land, according to the Israeli authorities, had been left uncultivated.

Following the demolition of Hajjaj's plot, people rebuilt. European activists (who happened to be visiting the village) and residents restored the retaining walls and replanted trees. That same year, the municipality completed agricultural roads, allowing slightly easier access to the area under threat. In 2022, village youth launched a campaign called "The Land Is Ours," planting 800 olive trees in the threatened area, and fencing off 20 dunums. The young men planting the hilltops likely do not see themselves as peasants, nor do they have hopes to work in agriculture. But, as they plant the land, they are enacting a tradition built on peasant labor, one that their parents and grandparents likely did as well, to defend it.

Understanding land defense through building the land helps to center peasant labor in the story of anticolonialism in the West Bank. Scholars have examined in detail the ways that the Israeli state uproots olive trees and plants pines to dispossess Palestinians, and Palestinians replant olive trees to assert counter-claims. Whether this "rivalry between the olive and the pine" is framed as "competing methods for asserting dominion" or as green colonialism against Palestinian environmentalism, most accounts pass over the ways that peasant labor lies at the heart of these planting projects.[57] When we situate tree planting within the deeper history of building the land, we can see how the demand that land should be for those who work it became part of the larger struggle for national liberation that transformed the highland landscape.

INVESTING IN THE LAND

The real estate boom in the highlands in the 2000s made agrarian relations to land far more difficult to maintain. The possibility of selling land discourages long-term investment in agriculture, and the new metric of determining prices asks owners to value their land according to measurements of surface area, proximity to infrastructure, and scenic views, rather than the quality of soil or trees. But in these conditions, villagers did not forget the decades they had spent building the land. Instead, this past offered ways to make claims about who was deserving of the new wealth created by rising land prices, and who was not.

The biography of Abu Iskandar can illuminate the lifelong work involved in acquiring land. I met Abu Iskandar in 2013 and conducted several interviews with him that summer in Bruqin. His story began with his father, who was an officer in the British army. His father sold his land to "go off and drink coffee in Jaffa." Forced to return to the village after 1948, he had to work as a tenant farmer. Abu Iskandar was born shortly thereafter. When he was seventeen, he began to work the land of a large landowner and, after fifteen or sixteen years of "work, work, work [ta'ab, ta'ab, ta'ab]," he acquired the rights to half the land that he cultivated. This achievement stands as an implicit restoration of family standing that, in this telling, seemed to have been tarnished by his father's actions.

For Abu Iskandar, farming coexisted with his life as a laborer. Indeed, much of his working life, and the stories he shared with me, revolved around his life in the construction trade in Israel, first as an unskilled worker, and later, for many years, in refurbishing walls and building interiors. With other young men, he rented an apartment in Jaffa, coming back to the village on the weekends. He learned Hebrew, and shared stories about his relationship with his employer, the recognition he received for his skills, and discrimination he faced for being Palestinian. It was during this time that he acquired more land: a plot in 1988 and another in the early 2000s. Likely, as many other workers did at the time, he was able to invest his earnings in land in the village.[58]

The way that Abu Iskandar talked to me about building the land highlighted the ways that his individual hard work translated into preferential rights. Transforming the land from an unused hillside to an orchard was a lifetime of work. There was the initial effort: clearing rocks with rope, pick, and donkey; building walls to keep out animals; constructing terraces to level out the land. There was also the seasonal work of plowing twice a year, and grafting olive trees. Abu Iskandar recounted how an Israeli guard confronted him when he was grafting one of his trees, presumably near the settlement. When he explained what he was doing, the guard offered to hire him and get him a permit to do similar work on Israeli farms. Abu Iskandar mentioned that he has two brothers who, while they have rights to the land, do not use it. Sometimes, he said, if the harvest is good, I can share with them. But, he stressed, he was the one who put his time and energy into the land.

Another illustrative example is that of Abu Ijbal, whom I met in 2016. I had already heard a lot about him. He was the land expert whose knowledge of the landscape had been so useful to the PA surveyors titling land in Qarawa, and many people I spoke to mentioned him as an example of a committed farmer. Like Abu Iskandar, Abu Ijbal began his conversation with me by talking about his own father. His family was poor and, growing up in the 1950s, he began work early in life. He seemed to have had preternatural entrepreneurial instincts. "There weren't any chickens in the village," he said, and so when he was a boy he rode to nearby villages, bought chickens, and brought them back to Qarawa to sell. When he was a bit older, he bought and sold livestock in Jerusalem, Hebron, Beersheva, and Gaza, while also cultivating various seasonal crops in the village: beans, wheat, barley, and other fodder crops with the help of his family. "My father didn't have more than a quarter of a donkey," he told me, but "by the end of his life ended up with thirteen head of cattle, as a result of my efforts."

In the decades that followed, Abu Ijbal worked in different trades, acquiring land plot by plot. When people began migrating to America, Kuwait, and Europe, Abu Ijbal almost left as well, staying behind because he did not win the visa lottery for Germany. He continued to acquire livestock, including camels; at some point, he remarked, he could have fed the whole village. He worked in Israel for less than a year. He then purchased agricultural and construction machinery and became involved in contracting. He also opened a small shop with a partner. And he invested earnings in land. He purchased 20 dunums in 1965, then another 24 (which, he said, he acquired in exchange for ten ewes), then half a dozen more plots ranging from a few dunums to as many as 30 in Qarawa and the neighboring villages over the following years. This land was often cheap and required work. Speaking of one large plot of 60 dunums, he explained: "I built it up myself, and now it's totally covered with olive trees." Today, the land that he owns has become quite valuable: one plot that he bought in 1966 for JD 100, he said, was worth 35,000 today, and he owned several others located near various real estate projects. He spoke proudly of being able to pass on land to his sons, all located in areas that, due to development or speculation, had appreciated drastically. Money comes and goes, he said, but land is a "treasure" and a "pillar" that remains.

The stories that Abu Ijbal and Abu Iskandar told me can help us understand the ways that men evaluated the rising number of land sales that were occurring because of land commodification. First, men I spoke with excused the sale of land when the seller had "no other choice." Those who fell into this category included refugees in Jordan and poor families living in the village who needed the cash to get by. Second, the sale of land was acceptable when the proceeds of the sale were used to cover an essential family cost—usually to pay for a marriage, build a house for a son, or cover university tuition—or were invested into a "project": the purchase of workshop, a taxi, or a truck that could generate income for the family. Most men I spoke to found ways to justify selling when doing so contributed to supporting a family and conformed to the virtues of responsibility and hard work.

Condemnation fell not on those who sold, but on those who wasted. Sometimes, wasted proceeds were the result of selling too early. At other times, men criticized sales when the proceeds were used to purchase certain kinds of consumer goods that they saw as frivolous. Televisions and new cars were oft-cited examples in accounts of people who "eat" their money and have nothing lasting to show for it. In the conversations I had with fathers and grandfathers, the younger generation received an outsized share of the blame for eschewing productive investment for temporary pleasure. Older men often commented on how younger people spent too much time staring at screens, and not enough time on the land. "They don't know the land or what it's worth," one man told me. "Instead, they rush to sell as soon as they can." These are the ones, he continued, showing off by "driving through the village in a 2016 Jeep, wearing sunglasses and smoking a cigarette." In the same way that sales could be justified to support a family, selling too early in one's life was betraying the family that one did not yet have. "What you should be doing," he concluded, "was preserving your land and enlarging it, so your children and their children have something to live on."

The criticism of seeking fast money was directed not only at young people, but at the developers and brokers who had bought land in the central highlands. The source of anger at the developers, as I have already pointed out, stemmed from their purchases of cheap land, only to resell the same land (often without any visible improvement) for a much higher price. A former head of the village council in Qarawa, for example, called what the developers were doing "confiscation [*musadara*]" of land from those in need. UCI was not engaged in "investment [*isthithmar*]" at all, but "buying in order to sell [*tajara*]." If it was "really about investment," he concluded rhetorically, "why was it being done on A and B land, at the expense of the *falla-hin* [peasants]?" The same criticism was directed at land brokers, and the harshest words fell on local brokers. Abu Amjad, introduced in the previous chapter, explained that before the land settlement, these men "had nothing" and then—he snapped his fingers—they went from "beggars to millionaires overnight." Another man called them beggars, who quickly got rich while others sold their land for "the price of lunch." The criticism of both developers and brokers was that not only did they not know the value of the land, but they had not engaged in any kind of productive labor to improve it.

Abu Mazra' was in his fifties when I met him, and lives with his family in Qarawa. He is one of eight children, of whom one lives in the United States. The others live in the West Bank where they work as teachers, a bus driver, and laborers. Abu Mazra' recalled that his father farmed and tended sheep until the 1970s, when he found a job at the Pilgrim's Palace Hotel (today it is called Golden Walls) in Jerusalem. He worked there for thirty-five years. Abu Mazra' left in the 1980s to work for a construction company in Baghdad. He returned to Palestine in 1984 when the Iran-Iraq war broke out and then went to Saudi Arabia where he worked for a construction company that was building a school. Returning to Palestine in 1987, he found work with an Israeli company. After closure policies made it too difficult to cross the Green Line, he took a job as a driver for an international NGO in the West Bank.

His family did not own a particularly large amount of land, and Abu

Mazra' inherited only 5 or 6 dunums from his father. With his savings, in 2007 or 2008, he and a partner purchased 6 more dunums for JD 30,000. Around 2011, he bought several more. While Abu Mazra' cultivates the land he purchased, its value comes from its location. Just off the main road, it is quite close to several large real estate projects. Pointing to the top of the hill, where Manazel was building the villas for the al-Dira project, he noted that the land sold for JD 100,000, and today is worth far more. "With title [*tabu*] it is stable," he said, and the land is "in my name and no one in the world can encroach on it."

In the highlands, some men are adapting a peasant ethic of hard work to make sense of the new choices and opportunities created by the land market. Their lives provide a glimpse into the way that building the land—the toil of the cultivator, just rewards for hard work, and the imperative of supporting the family—can become available as a moral critique of the new land market. And while a far cry from an explicit defense of the emerging new economy, building the land can be adapted to demanding a share of the new wealth that real estate may bring.

LAND FOR THOSE WHO WORK IT

"Building the land" is animated by the idea that land should belong to those who work it. Whether farming the hills, fighting colonial encroachment, or investing in real estate, Palestinians I spoke with often returned to this basic idea to make moral, legal, and political claims to land. And when they did so, they were adapting "building the land" to the changing political and economic conditions of the highlands.

The idea that land should belong to those who work it has an uncomfortable resemblance to the colonial idea of improvement. When settler farmers mixed their labor with the soil, the argument went, their improvement of the land granted them exclusive property rights over it. Improvement, as legal scholar Brenna Bhandar has argued, is an ideology that fuses the imperatives of agrarian capitalism with an ideology of racial difference that privileges "European forms of cultivation as proof of ownership" and "relegated indigenous people to the margins of civility and deprived them of the status required to be owners of their land."[59]

Philosopher John Locke did not invent the concept of improvement, but he did distill it into a political theory that would prove to be foundational for liberal philosophy and an important justification for colonial domination.[60] According to Locke, God gave man the right to "subdue the earth," and as much land as one "tills, plants, improves, cultivates and can use the product of, so much is his property." Infamously, Locke concluded that "the Indian[s]" failed to cultivate the land and establish private property, their failure to improve the "wild woods and uncultivated wast[e] of America left to nature" providing evidence of a lack of political society.[61] From the forests of the Americas to the deserts of North Africa and beyond, improvement justified European conquest and directly shaped colonial property law, facilitating the ongoing dispossession of native peoples. This ideology survived the demise of formal colonial rule and continues to inform theories of progress and development projects across the postcolonial world, often with disastrous results.[62]

Improvement also justified the conquest and colonization of Palestine. According to the Zionist narrative, Palestine was a wasteland because Palestinians were too backward to cultivate it.[63] For Zionist thinkers, working the land would enable not only the return of the Jewish people to Palestine, but also exclusive Jewish dominion over it. After the establishment of the state of Israel, the ideology of improvement effectively became law. As a result, a great deal of political and scholarly energy has been expended critiquing the claim that settler labor "made the desert bloom," and revealing how the ideological and legal structures underpinning this narrative facilitate the dispossession of Palestinians to this day.[64]

The difference between improving the land and building that land is that while the former is an act of expropriation, the latter is an act of appropriation. This distinction, points out John Bellamy Foster, is at the heart of Marx's economic and ecological critique of capitalism.[65] For Marx, appropriation from nature was at the basis of any human labor process, and a wide variety of property systems. Expropriation, in contrast, was "appropriation without an equivalent (in Marx's terms, also without exchange and without reciprocity)" that characterized the capitalist mode of production.[66] Building the land is an appropriation of nature that produces reciprocal social relationships and requires the upkeep, rather than the exhaustion, of the land. This labor process, and the values it gives rise to, is not free of exploitation of either people or nature. But it is also not driven by the creation of exclusive property rights or the conquest of territory. Instead, it transforms the landscape into something that is at once "mine" and "ours."

Building the land is the basis of land claims that include and exceed legal rights. Many of the legal regimes that Palestinian peasants lived under recognized how working the land could establish rights to own and access it. The Israeli legal system has made Palestinian property rights contingent on a settler-defined definition of cultivation, and private property the only defensible form of legal ownership. But, as we have seen, building the land creates expectations of social conduct that are not protected by law, and calls forth the collective labor of planting to protect village land. It is in these moments, as fragile and fleeting as they may be, that agrarian rights and collective responsibilities that exceed the law come into view.

The transformation of agricultural land into real estate may result in the articulation of peasant labor with a far more financialized, and decidedly nonagrarian, relationship to land. Personal experiences of working the land and the veneration of individual hard work can just as easily provide justifications for arbitrary distributions of generational wealth, while the commodification of land creates material incentives for men to claim that it is their labor alone that has the power to create private ownership.[67] It is not difficult to see how these aspects of building the land could be mobilized in support of an ideology of possessive individualism that justifies the dominion of men over property.[68]

Building the land belongs within a larger tradition of agrarian justice. From Ireland to India to China and beyond, the idea that the land should belong to those who work it has animated liberation struggles and postcolonial land reforms. The demand for "land to the tiller" saw the redistribution of land to small farmers and peasants, just as the different forms of property that these reforms sought to implement—from state communes to private ownership—represented divergent visions for the future of agrarian societies.[69] And while this egalitarian moment, as historian Donald Low called it, may have ended, the demand for land to the tiller lives on in today's rural social movements. The Palestinian highlands are part of this struggle, and the people who live there reveal the possibilities and limits of a demand for justice built on the idea that land belongs to those who work it.

Five

RETURNING

AGRARIAN EXPERIMENTS IN THE HIGHLANDS

PEASANTS, WE ARE TOLD, ARE ROOTED IN THE LAND. FOR REFORM-
ers and governments of all stripes, peasant rootedness was a problem that
needed to overcome.[1] For revolutionaries and anticolonial thinkers, the
peasant was often seen in a more positive light, representing the "soul of
the nation."[2] "The peasant who stays put is a staunch defender of tradition,"
Frantz Fanon wrote in his influential work, *The Wretched of the Earth*, and
"had constantly clung to a virtually anticolonial way of life. From time im-
memorial the peasants had more or less safeguarded their subjectivity from
colonial imposition thanks to stratagems and balancing acts worthy of a ma-
gician."[3] It is this quality of being rooted that, whether they are being condemned or celebrated, makes peasants visible as significant historical actors.

The Palestinian peasant, too, has been the subject of different narratives emphasizing rootedness. In their search for traces of biblical customs,
nineteenth-century European missionaries and scholars put the peasant
(*fallah*) at the center of historical-racial theory to explain, in the words of
one early Orientalist, how "the fellaheen of Palestine [were] the modern
representatives of those old tribes which the Israelites found settled in the
country."[4] Early Zionist settlers appropriated elements of Palestinian peas-

ant culture while also slotting the peasant into a narrative of backwardness that justified Jewish settlement and sovereignty. Later, Palestinian artists and intellectuals fashioned the peasant into a symbol of Palestinian nationalism and steadfastness (*sumud*). There has been a series of critiques of the ways that this nationalist discourse has romanticized the peasant community, erasing the antagonisms of agrarian society in favor of a homogeneous, unchanging peasant village.[5] But even these critiques do not suggest that rootedness might not exhaust the peasant's qualities.

To understand land struggle in the highlands, we need to emphasize a different quality of peasant life: transformation. In the village of Farkha, residents organize voluntary work projects, sell organic olive through a farmer's cooperative, care for an impressive number of home gardens, and operate an experimental farm. These are all rooted in peasant farming practices, but practices that farmers, activists, and intellectuals have transformed and put toward new political and social ends. Importantly, these projects are all shaped by the movement of people and ideas in and out of Farkha, turning the village into a site for figuring out new ways of making a living, providing food, rebuilding social solidarity, and farming. Palestine is often talked about as a colonial laboratory, one where Israel tests military hardware, counterinsurgency tactics, and surveillance technology before exporting them to the rest of the world.[6] Farkha gives us a different model, an anticolonial laboratory to experiment with new ways of relating to the land.

Animating all these different efforts is the hope of return. These various experiments provide a way of repairing displacement and disconnection caused by land dispossession, labor migration, or never having the opportunity to farm in the first place. My goal here is to expand our thinking of "return" to include the Palestinians in the West Bank who, while never being displaced from their homes, were still forced off the land. In doing so, we can reconceptualize "return" as a set of practices that, while not foregoing legal rights entirely, is far more invested in the renovation of agrarian ethics, knowledge, and labor to create claims to the land, and to defend a collective Palestinian presence upon it.

DISPOSSESSION AND RETURN

For those who have been dispossessed and expelled, return often has a crucial agrarian element. For Indigenous movements, struggles for the restoration of political and legal rights over a territory are often accompanied by the regeneration of traditional agricultural practices, and the re-creation of ecological and social relations severed by colonial genocide.[7] Black agrarianism is also animated by the idea of return, both to farming and sometimes to the American South itself, and the creation of an autonomous land base.[8] And by occupying abandoned plantations and unused estates, organizations of landless peasants do the same.[9] All of these projects confront different histories of displacement and dispossession, and are united by the demand that returning is a step toward addressing longstanding injustices.

From these disparate experiences, we can distill several important points about the politics of return. First, return is a transformative process, both for the potential returnees and the place to which they hope to return. It must be. Displacement is a violent, and often prolonged, separation between people and land that weakens land-based knowledge and degrades the landscapes that such knowledge was embedded in. Projects of return are always engaged in agricultural education, ecological restoration, and land reclamation. But we should not assume that it is possible, or even desirable, to restore either people or land to a preexisting, pristine condition. Instead, going back is always an act of bringing something new into existence.

Second, return takes a long time. It is a process of trial and error, a path strewn with projects that have broken down and movements that have been beaten back or defeated. As such, projects of return are always preoccupied with epistemological questions, and often devise innovative means of preserving and transmitting to young people memories about a place, practical knowledge of farming, and histories of struggle. Return unfolds over multiple generations, and those at the forefront are always faced with the task of adapting what has been passed on to them to the specific opportunities and limits of the conjuncture they inhabit.

Finally, the goal of return is the creation of an enduring presence on the land. A range of actors and alliances share in the broader struggles for return, but they have different, and sometimes incompatible, visions of what life back on the land should look like. For everyone involved, return is essential to addressing dispossession and displacement. But it is in the messy and often conflictual process of establishing collective presence, what we might call the *practices of return*, that returnees work out what land justice means.

DISPLACEMENT IN PLACE

Israel's occupation of the West Bank led to a drastic economic transformation that, as political economist Leila Farsakh has shown, amounted to the "transformation of the Palestinian economy from an agrarian to a service-oriented economy directed towards Israel."[10] From the 1970s to the early 1990s, between 28 percent and 33 percent of the West Bank labor force was employed in Israel, most of whom hailed from villages or refugee camps. Palestinians left to work in Israel not only because Israeli employers could offer higher wages, but because settler colonial rule resulted in "de-development," preventing capital investment and destroying the institutions that could support a robust Palestinian economy.[11] De-development was particularly pronounced in Palestinian agriculture, driving the decline of agriculture's share of GDP, employment, and the amount of land under cultivation.[12] The result, concludes Farsakh, was the creation of a structural dependency on Israel that, in the West Bank and Gaza Strip, "saw the improvement of its inhabitants' individual welfare at the same time as the deterioration of its national productive capacity to grow independently from Israel and to absorb its growing labour force."[13]

The incorporation of Palestinians as workers in Israel transformed everyday life in the rural West Bank. Men of working age increasingly only spent weekends and holidays in the village. During the week, construction workers often lived at their job sites, while those working service jobs in Israeli cities might share a small room with other migrant workers. Consumption patterns also changed. With more disposable income, peasant families could afford to eat meat on a weekly basis, buy clothing more regularly, and purchase appliances like television sets.[14] And, as detailed in chapter 1, the landscape itself also began to reflect the ways that agriculture had become less central for household livelihoods.

Such changes had myriad effects. For children, now growing up with fewer of the seasonal events and rituals of peasant farming, agriculture was becoming less important to their socialization.[15] Women took on more of the

agricultural work, just as wage labor increased their reliance on their hus-
bands and decreased their dependency on their natal households.[16] For older
generations, new consumer pleasures and freedoms caused anxiety about
alienation and moral corruption.[17] "The attachment of the new generations to
the land is of a more remote nature than that of their parents," wrote several
researchers about one highland village in the early 1980s, "despite a strong
effort on the part of the family to instil [sic] a sense of identification with the
land and the homeland in their children."[18] In one report in the Palestinian
publication *Al-Fajr Weekly*, a twenty-five-year-old named Sami, working as a
waiter in a Jerusalem hotel, tells a reporter that the olive harvest is akin to
"an annual punishment" and describes the land as "no more than a personal
belonging of our elders."[19] If we define place as a space that "an individual or
group imbues with special meaning, value, and intention," then what these
various experiences attest to is the diminishing capacity of agrarian relationships to produce a sense of place and the divergence of political and literary "land rhetoric" from experiences of those who lived in the highlands.[20]

For those who had no land to begin with, there might be little to stay
behind for. Higher incomes allowed villagers to pay off debts and buy farmland and, at times, urban real estate.[21] Access to wages undermined the
power of large landlords over their tenants, with some landlords appealing
to the Israeli government to intervene to close the border to migrants.[22]
Sahar Khalifeh's 1976 novel *Wild Thorns* is a poignant exploration of these
new class antagonisms. In one scene, a young revolutionary from a once
powerful Nablus family returns to Palestine to find the family's land abandoned, tended only by an elderly caretaker. After enduring the young man's
questions, the old farmer finally rebukes him:

> Why are you so angry with me? I'm just a hired hand. I've been here all
> my life. I don't own any land. I don't own anything. My son Shahada was
> a hired hand too. And he still is. The land isn't mine or Shahada's, so
> why should we care about it? Why should we die for it? Don't give me
> that! Nobody ever came and asked about us when we were nearly dying
> of starvation. But now, now you've come! Why?[23]

For the poor and the landless, money earned in hotels and factories undermined existing forms of rural power and privilege. Indeed, rural hierarchies

created the social inequalities and exclusions that made many people eager to leave village life behind.

Scholars have mostly thought about the incorporation of Palestinian peasants and refugees into the Israeli economy in terms of labor migration. They have demonstrated the ways that push and pull factors are intertwined, with the dispossession of land fueling labor migration, which in turn enabled the dispossession of more land.[24] They have shown how the management of Palestinian labor is an important aspect of Israeli state power, enabling the recruitment of collaborators, the exercise of collective punishment, and the control of entire populations.[25] And they have explored how specific kinds of Palestinian politics, and demands for justice, emerge around labor in Israel.[26]

But this scholarship is a focus on those who leave, rather than on the places they leave from. When we turn our gaze to the village, a fuller picture of displacement comes into view. When scholars speak of displacement, they often mean forced migration, or the process by which people are violently dispossessed and expelled from their homes; in the Middle East, the Palestinian Nakba of 1948 is the paradigmatic example.[27] But we can also think of "displacement in place." "Instead of referring solely to the movement of people from their places of belonging," argues literary scholar Rob Nixon, this understanding of displacement "refers rather to the loss of the land and resources beneath them, a loss that leaves communities stranded in a place stripped of the very characteristics that made it inhabitable."[28] In the highlands of the West Bank, displacement was not the outcome of an extraordinary rupture. Instead, what was happening there looked like what was, and is, happening to rural places across the world: disinvestment, outmigration, and agricultural decline. What was different was that these changes provided openings for Israel to seize land and expand settlements, making return both a local and a national imperative.

Framing the adverse incorporation of Palestinian peasants into the Israeli economy in terms of displacement can help us understand the relationship between expulsion, dispossession, and exploitation. Often, we think of return in relation to exile. The right of return, after all, is the defining demand of Palestinian refugees, one that galvanized the Palestinian revolution and, whether in terms of legal campaigns, cultural production, commemoration, or individual and collective attempts to return, has been at the center of refugee politics ever since.²⁹ Displacement in the West Bank had very different political, legal, and cultural coordinates, in which departure might take years, and losses were not immediately visible. These were the problems that agronomists, young radicals, and farmers confronted when they began to think of what it would take for people to return to the land or, better yet, to not have to leave in the first place.

BACK TO THE LAND

In the 1970s and 1980s, the problem of land loss and labor migration began to preoccupy Palestinian activists and agricultural experts. In her expansive 1974 study of Palestinian olive farming, botanist Sumaya Farhat-Naser argued that Israeli policy was resulting in land abandonment, soil degradation, and agricultural decline.³⁰ In the introduction to her study, Bakir Abu Kishk, an expert on colonial land policy and Palestinian agriculture inside Israel, raised the alarm that the weakening of agriculture facilitated Israeli land confiscation and settlement.³¹ In 1981, these concerns appeared in the papers and discussions of the Development for Steadfastness Conference in the West Bank. "Leaving the land and leaving it waste [*bur*]" was a grave threat, argued one of the conference participants, and efforts must be organized "to return to the planting of the land."³² Other participants dramatically called the transformation of peasants into wage workers "the suicide of agriculture on the altar of city life."³³ It was in this political context that voluntary work youth groups and agricultural aid organizations each developed ways of supporting land defense and agricultural livelihoods. When Palestinian workers lost their jobs in Israel and returned to peasant farming during the First Intifada, these groups helped make going back to the land a revolutionary practice.

In 1972, a small group of young people began to meet in Ramallah. What began as a reading group eventually became a movement that set itself the task of creating a nationalist spirit among youth through the provision of services to the community. Their main practice would be what they called "voluntary work."³⁴ These activists drew on peasant tradition, cosmopolitan leftism, and Palestinian struggles in Israel, combining them into a form of collective labor that, they hoped, would be the basis for a radical political transformation.

First, peasant tradition. Voluntary work activists drew on the principle of 'awna (alternatively transliterated oneh), which refers to the collective labor that went into peasant agriculture and home construction. It is similar to the tradition of the "work party" that is common in many other agrarian contexts.[35] 'Awna was embedded in the horizontal structures of cooperation as well as vertical structures of patriarchal authority that constituted peasant farming. Plowing, planting, and harvesting are all time-sensitive tasks that require collective discipline and labor, and peasants expected kin and neighbor to pitch in if they had finished in their own fields.[36] It was also expected that if a man were too ill to carry out a task, then someone in the clan would come to his aid.[37] Home construction in the villages also relied on collective labor, its completion celebrated by a feast and an exchange of gifts after which "the owner and his family would thank everyone for their help and promise to be present at the next village 'oneh."[38] As part of the common good, agrarian cooperation was not so much an individual choice as a duty that made one a member of the village community.[39]

Second, cosmopolitan leftism. Muharram Barghouti, who was one of the founders of the movement, told me that "we were affected by the global left [al-yasar fil 'alam], and especially the Communists." At the time, the main factions of the Palestinian liberation movement were all part of this global left, constituted by transnational networks of fighters, activists, artists, filmmakers, and writers. In the West Bank, only the Communist Party was not explicitly proscribed by Israel and thus able to organize more openly. For voluntary work, Barghouti recalled that the inspiration of the All-Union Leninist Young Communist League, or Komsomol, was especially important, both for its organizational focus on youth and labor and for the ways in which it sought to instill discipline and abolish social hierarchies that prevented national unity. The ideas that nourished these young activists were not limited to Marxism, but were part of an eclectic, and international, cultural milieu.[40] One activist from Ramallah whom I spoke to, a young woman at the time, recalled a vibrant cultural moment: the socialist realism of Maxim Gorky as well as Hemingway; the songs of Marcel Khalifeh and Sheikh Imam, and slogans that linked Korea, Vietnam, and Palestine into an international anti-imperial axis.

Third, Palestinian struggles in Israel—in particular local politics in the city of Nazareth. Nazareth, celebrated in the Christian tradition as the hometown of Jesus, was a small town before 1948. Due to its importance for Western Christians, the town was left standing and spared the fate of most other Palestinian population centers during the Nakba. It grew dramatically as a result, absorbing thousands of displaced Palestinians who would end up constituting a third of the population.[41] After 1948, Nazareth became the largest Palestinian city left in what was now Israel, and in the years that followed was at the center of Palestinian cultural and political life.

Communist politics were an important part of that life. The city had a strong Communist Party that, after several decades of repression, succeeded in winning the 1975 municipal election. The party put the charismatic poet Tawfiq Zayyad into the mayor's seat. The Israeli government sought to undermine Zayyad's administration by withdrawing state funding, and the new mayor put out a public call to the residents of Nazareth to volunteer to help keep the city running.[42] In response, residents formed neighborhood committees to repair streets, maintain public spaces, paint schools, and otherwise lower government expenditures. At the same time, political forces in Nazareth were organizing against the Israel government's plan to confiscate Palestinian land.[43] In the spring of 1976, the closure of private land in three villages resulted in a massive strike and protest on March 30, now commemorated annually as Land Day.

It was during these battles that Nazareth hosted the first voluntary work camp. Held in the summer of 1976, the four-day event combined labor with cultural activities and lectures. The next year, Zayyad would describe the purpose as follows: "We will come out from this camp more united and organized, not only in the battle for development and construction but also for knowledge and culture. Let our camp be a festival of work and dignity in the morning and a festival of culture in the evening."[44] In the years that followed, the voluntary work camp would bring thousands of Palestinians from Israel and the occupied territories to Nazareth. Bakr Hammad, from Farkha, was a young man working in Israel at the time and was one of the early participants in the Nazareth festival. Many more would join him. From the occupied territories, the Higher Committee for Voluntary Work sent 1,200 volunteers to a voluntary work camp in Nazareth in 1981, and 3,000 in 1982.[45] At its height in 1985, some 4,000 volunteers converged on the city. For many people I spoke to, time spent in Nazareth was the defining moment of their early political lives.

Voluntary work activists brought these ideas and experiences together to support farmers. Beginning in 1976, voluntary work groups assisted in distributing trees, clearing brush and stones, and planting areas that owners worried might face confiscation. They also helped pave roads and clean up village schools. Barghouthi estimated in 1981 that the movement had mobilized 4,500 volunteers to engage in land reclamation and cultivation on Land Day, in March. Just a month later, in April, Israel arrested 200 people who had gathered for voluntary work to defend 1,000 dunums of "common land" belonging to the residents of Nahalin, a village outside of Bethlehem.[46] Farkha was one of the first villages in the area to form a voluntary work committee, with young men joining efforts across the West Bank. There were many such efforts in the central highlands themselves, often in response to threats of dispossession: in April 1983 volunteers reclaimed land to protect it from confiscation in Jibya, Nabi Saleh, and Um Safa; in September 1984 a two-day work camp was organized in Kobar, where 2,000 dunums were under threat of confiscation, to prepare land for planting.[47] These are only a few examples of voluntary work activities that, as the 1980s progressed, were taking place across the West Bank and Gaza Strip.

In Farkha, the voluntary work committee found ways to sustain their activities. Hammad recounted how activists rented land, harvested the olives with voluntary workers, sold the oil, and put the proceeds into voluntary work. They set up bazaars in the village (at the time, there were not many shops, and people would have to travel to Nablus for shopping) and asked the merchants to donate a percentage of the profits. They brought tanks to olive presses to collect donations of oil from farmers during the olive harvest. Their communist leanings did not prevent them from selling prayer calendars during Ramadan to raise funds. These various activities functioned not only to sustain the organization and land defense, but also to instill in the members a sense of self-sufficiency and belonging. The ultimate point was to concretize the nationalist slogan "land is identity" through forms of cooperative work that could produce new political subjects, or "building the Palestinian person [*bina' al-insan al-Filastini*]," as Barghouti put it, that would contribute to the task of liberation.[48]

In the 1980s, Palestinian agronomists would form their own groups to help keep Palestinians on the land. Volunteers established the Palestinian Agricultural Relief Committees (PARC) and the Union of Agricultural Work Committees (UAWC) to provide extension services focusing on "small peasant farmers."[49] PARC, which was loosely affiliated at the time with the Communist Party, had set up its base in the Salfit, making it especially important in the region. Throughout the 1980s, PARC would support farmers with technical advice and various kinds of material assistance.

Agronomists and voluntary work activists cooperated with one another to assist farmers. PARC worked with the voluntary work committees to set up "agricultural work camps."[50] Ismail Daiq, one of the founders of PARC, reported that the organization had advised the voluntary work movement on the distribution and planting of olive saplings, and the reclamation of 27,000 dunums of land.[51] In 1982, near the end of his short tenure as the head of the Rural Research Center at al-Najah University, Hisham Awartani produced an agricultural strategy for the occupied territories that cited these successes and suggested ways of scaling them up within a broader strategy of agricultural development.[52]

The highlands were also important sites of agrarian experimentation. In the late 1970s and into the 1980s, the Jordan Cooperative Organization (JCO) received some $30 million in development funds. But these were directed toward traditional elites and large landowners, who controlled the large cooperatives.[53] In 1986, the activist Ghassan Jarrar described "experiments [tajarub]," held in Birzeit, Kobar, Kufr Nameh, ʿAyn al-Diwak, Dhahriya, and Bethlehem, in anticapitalist modes of agricultural production.[54] In Birzeit, for example, he detailed how a landowner gave young activists 9 dunums for a period of five years. With the assistance of local farmers, volunteers planted wheat and onions, which they sold in the village. For Jarrar, the Birzeit experience demonstrated an alternative to the moribund cooperative system and, he hoped, a fleeting vision of what could be a "revolutionary alternative [to the] domination of the capitalist market."[55]

After the outbreak of the First Intifada in 1987, peasant farming become more important economically and politically. Closures and strikes forced thousands of Palestinian workers back into their villages. Many returned to agriculture or found themselves trying their hand at it for the first time. Subsistence farming was celebrated as part of the national struggle, with Unified National Leadership of the Uprising calling for a "return to our soil," citing the example of the Vietnamese who "defeated US tyranny not only by the gun but also by the wise use of their land."[56] Marxist intellectual Adel Samara's theory of popular protection posited that Palestinians would need to rely on popular power and labor-intensive, family farming as part of a broader effort to delink from the Israeli economy, reclaim "ruined land [*khirab*]," and "retrain the peasant [*i'ada ta'hil al-falah*]," especially younger people, whose separation from the land had taken a toll on their ability to farm.[57] He imagined an expansive project, one beginning with family gardens and a few animals, that would gradually grow, leading to the collectivization of agrarian relations of production and property.[58] While people often had little choice but to go back to farming, the uprising created the social and political conditions for new ways of thinking about the radical potential of peasant agriculture.

During the Intifada, both the voluntary work groups and agricultural aid organizations were involved in supporting efforts toward building self-sufficiency and self-determination. Voluntary work cadres helped organize boycotts, mutual aid, and underground education efforts.[59] They also helped farm. "Voluntary work committees have been active everywhere to work all available agricultural land so that maximum self-sufficiency in food production can be obtained with minimum reliance on Israeli or imported produce," a PARC bulletin from 1988 reported.[60] Agricultural development groups distributed vegetable seedlings and encouraged small-scale animal husbandry to support the expansion of home gardens, a longstanding peasant institution that helped provision rural households.[61] They helped villages to organize household economic projects, often run by new women's committees. And they also carried out land reclamation. In an interview, one of the founders of UAWC told me that the organization engaged in a "reclamation operation" in the middle of the uprising, opening agricultural roads between villages and into agricultural lands. The overall result, according to a PARC interim report in 1988, was a "return to the land [...] in camps, villages and towns throughout the West Bank, committees were formed to sow every inch of available land."[62]

One of the most successful projects took place in the central highlands. At the beginning of the Intifada, Palestinians from Salfit working in the nearby settlement of Ariel were fired. Forced back into agriculture, they built greenhouses, revived areas that had fallen into disuse, and reclaimed marginal lands. "The combination of available workers, agricultural expertise, and high levels of enthusiasm for the back-to-the-land movement," argues political scientist Glen Robinson, who carried out fieldwork in the area during this time, "produced a virtual green revolution in Salfit during the Intifada."[63]

What happened in the highlands did not lead to a lasting transformation of agrarian production or social relations. Instead, as the years dragged on, daily hardships and brutal counterinsurgency undermined the revolutionary potential of the uprising. The Oslo Accords, the first of which was signed in 1993 by the Palestinian leadership in exile, marked the end of the First Intifada and the gradual demobilization of its mass movements.[64] In the years that followed, those in charge of building a Palestinian state in the occupied territories evinced little interest in the collective voluntary work or localizing food production. But the practical experiences, organizational forms, and political theories of these rural struggles did not disappear. Instead, village activists would rethink them as they fought for return in a post–Oslo world.

AGRARIAN EXPERIMENTS IN THE HIGHLANDS

The political and economic forces arrayed against peasant farming are, to put it bluntly, overwhelming. Even though there has been nominal Palestinian self-government since the 1990s, settler colonial power has only become more entrenched. Dispossessed by Israel and neglected by the PA, the declining number of peasant farmers find themselves cobbling together support from the various NGOs that effectively direct agricultural development in the West Bank. In Farkha, activists have worked within these constraints, creating a series of agrarian experiments that adapt the radical traditions of the 1980s to keep people on the land, or to encourage them to come back.

First, activists managed to keep the practice, and spirit, of voluntary work alive. At the center of this effort is the voluntary work festival. At the height of the summer, young participants converge on Farkha to celebrate and carry out voluntary work. As of 2022, it has been held annually for twenty-seven years, except for 2020 and 2021, when the festival was canceled on account of the coronavirus pandemic.

I had the opportunity to attend the festival twice, in 2013 and in 2022. The festival itself is a blend of youth summer camp, political education, and community service. In 2022, for example, organizers divided the volunteers into groups and set them to different tasks: painting the walls of classrooms and other public spaces, building a new wall at the village school, and building terraces in the village's experimental farm. Lectures focused on political issues in Palestine and abroad, while in conversations during the day and storytelling over dinner, older volunteers recounted the history of the movement and the festival. During the penultimate day of the festival, organizers unveiled a statue in the center of the village dedicated to Tawfiq Zayyad. They also planted a tree in a garden nearby in honor of Mohammed Nafa', a communist activist who had died several years earlier.

The festival is also a place for creating solidarity. Participants come from across the West Bank (due to Israel's closure of the Gaza Strip, Gazans have not been able to attend since 2005), and delegations from Nazareth visit as well. They are joined by international volunteers. During one day of the camp in 2022, festival participants boarded a bus to the village of Beit Dajjan, outside of Nablus. Volunteers cleaned out a municipal park that had been overtaken with weeds, and then joined the weekly march protesting the land confiscation. At the base of the hill, they were blocked by soldiers and dispersed with rubber bullets and tear gas. Against the disempowering paternalism of humanitarian aid, the festival offers an alternative politics based on land defense and anti-imperialist internationalism.

Voluntary work does not only happen during the summer festival. Throughout the year, voluntary work groups help clean and maintain public spaces like roads and schools. They are also an important resource during emergencies. Throughout the pandemic lockdowns, crews distributed food and medical supplies. The municipality also encouraged people to help farmers in other villages, arranging purchases of vegetables from Deir Ballut and melons from the Jordan Valley. In 2022, when Israeli forces sealed off the checkpoint connecting the central and northern West Bank, the village council offered to provide a place for stranded commuters. These efforts are part of a project to make the collective ethos of voluntary work part of daily life.

Voluntary work crews have also tried to transform threatened land into a place that people could access. In 2019, as I discussed in the first chapter, the Israeli authorities bulldozed a Palestinian farm in an area known as al-Batin, on the legal pretext that it was located within a 1,250 dunum area that had been declared state lands back in 1982. In 2021 the Israeli authorities announced their intention to expand the Ariel settlement into al-Batin. In addition to planting the area with olive trees, youth groups also came up with plans to build a 3 dunum public park in the area, accessible by trails and a bike path, and began work on this project in 2022. In the summer of 2023, however, settlers tore down the fencing that had been erected around the perimeter of the planned park. Threats from armed settlers, under the guard of Israeli soldiers, led to the suspension of reclamation efforts. At the end of October 2023, settlers uprooted trees and broke ground on a new road connecting the hill of al-Batin to Ariel. Shortly after the road was paved in October 2024, settlers established a new outpost.

Voluntary work is a practice of return in two interrelated ways. First, it represents the regeneration of an ethic of collective labor that has its roots in the peasant labor process, and that activists have transformed through various community events and projects. Second, sometimes these projects are part of a larger effort to return to areas that are at risk of being lost. While paramilitaries, soldiers, and settlement infrastructure may have blocked, at least for now, the recovery of al-Batin, the collective energies that voluntary work can summon will remain a vital aspect of future struggles to get the land back.

Some of the same activists who keep up the tradition of voluntary work also helped establish a cooperative. Since the 1990s, the emergence of new olive oil sectors in the Middle East and Europe, coupled with Israeli restrictions at home, undermined the competitiveness of Palestinian olive oil.[65] By the early 2000s, the closure of checkpoints and the long lockdowns of the Second Intifada totally cut farmers off from markets.[66] In the central highlands, a glut of oil pushed prices down below production costs. Around 2005 in Farkha, 1 kilo of oil was selling for 7–9 New Israeli Shekels (NIS) (about $2.00). It was at this point that farmers began to explore ways of selling oil in new markets that, they hoped, would enable them to make some semblance of a living.[67]

The first experiment began in Mazari' al-Nubani, a village next to Farkha and now a member of the Bani Zaid al-Sharqiyya cooperative. PARC helped farmers in both villages obtain organic certification through a certifying body in Egypt (at the time, the only other option was in Israel) in 2005, and fair trade certification later. Producers sell their oil to al-Reef, a private fair trade company owned by PARC, at an agreed-upon price, and al-Reef then sells the oil in European and North American markets. In 2022, the cooperative had eighteen members (of an estimated two hundred farmers in the village) producing organic olive oil on 400 dunums of the 3,500 dunums planted with olive trees. Early on, members of the cooperative told me that organic certification allowed them to sell oil for NIS 14 per kilo. Today, production costs are higher (NIS 14–15), but even in the worst years, they said, oil does not sell for less than NIS 26.5. Like small producers elsewhere, farmers can obtain a higher price through organic and fair trade certification, relying on solidarity markets and affluent consumers in the Global North.[68]

Palestinian olive producers did not use chemical fertilizers and insecticides heavily, meaning that organic certification did not require drastic changes to farming practices.[69] 'Ali, a member of the Farkha cooperative, showed me how farmers integrated many longstanding practices into organic farming. He was seventy years old when we met in 2022. At the age of fourteen he began helping in the fields, but it was not until age thirty, in 1982, when he returned from work in Kuwait, that farming became an occupation. He described how spraying a mixture of hot pepper, garlic, lemon, and water on leaves can help deal with pests; showed me how farmers stack cut branches in a small pile below olive trees to draw flies away; and pointed out how animal manure was laid in circles around trees to fertilize them in the summer. For 'Ali, these kinds of practices had the potential to keep costs down and ensure that farmers did not become dependent on Israeli pesticides and fertilizers.

It is the processing of olive oil that has changed. To keep acidity at the level required by international standards, farmers must press olives the same day they are picked (if olives are left to sit in bags, they heat up, and higher temperature increases the acidity level) and must store oil in stainless steel containers.[70] Thus, farmers participating in organic certification have modified the tradition of collective work, or 'awna. While cooperative members would help each other when they could, people generally did not harvest at the same time, and the creation of a cooperative did not precipitate a return to collective harvesting. Instead, as one farmer explained to me, "collective work [*amal al-jamai'*]" is expressed by "collective pressing [*asr al-jamai'*]." During the harvest, those who pick their olives on a given day mix them together in the late afternoon, weigh their share, and press the olives together. This form of cooperation is new and took some convincing to implement. In Farkha, for instance, different areas produce olives that yield varying amounts of oil, depending on soil, sunlight, and humidity, as well as the type and age of the tree. Collective pressing requires that individual farmers surrender whatever benefit they may think their land provides, and accept a share based on weight, rather than on the quality of their olives. This new requirement demands a subtle reworking of agrarian tradition to make Palestinian oil appropriate for a new market.

These efforts have necessitated new relationships with producers across the central highlands. The Farkha cooperative works closely with two other cooperatives, Bani Zaid al-Gharbiyya and Bani Zaid al-Sharqiyya, each of which contain several villages from the western and eastern parts of the Bani Zaid, respectively. Access to affordable fertilizer is an issue for farmers, and members of cooperatives have worked together to produce fertilizer that meets organic standards. In the past, each home would have access to a *mizwi*, or pit, where they would dry manure for use as fertilizer. This practice disappeared, however, with the precipitous decline of animal husbandry in the village. In 2012, Farkha and Bani Zaid al-Sharqiyya cooperatives began a compost project, supported by several NGOs that operate in the area.[71] It is located in the village of Khirbet Qeis, on land belonging to a member of the cooperative, where there is machinery for sifting, sorting, and packaging fertilizer created from a combination of straw (*qish*), cuttings from olive trees, olive pomace (*jift*), and cow manure purchased from a farm outside of Salfit. When I visited the site, piles of fertilizer had finished drying under the sun, ready to be bagged and distributed.

Perhaps the most important endeavor was the acquisition of a new, Italian-made olive press. To obtain a loan, the three cooperatives created a private company called Our Agricultural Land (Arduna al-Zaraiyya). A loan for the press—$300,000, and an additional $60,000 in interest payments—

was obtained through al-Reef in 2015. Payments are made with profits from olive oil. While the cooperatives had hoped to finish payments after five years, they were forced to extend the loan to seven. They hoped that, following the 2022 harvest, they would be able to finish payments in 2023. The new press is far faster and more efficient than older presses in the area, while ownership allows the cooperatives to be in control of the production process. Over the past several years, they have also integrated a machine to compress leftover pomace into bricks, which can be used as fuel for household and commercial heating.

Olive trees are not the only sort of agricultural activity in the central highlands. Farkha, for instance, is full of gardens. In 2022, according to the head of the village council, there were 230 home gardens in the village. Gardens are planted with all sorts of things: fruit trees that include figs, almonds, stone-fruits, citrus, guava, pomegranates; greens like *mulukhiyya* (jute mallow) and arugula; vegetables like onions, garlic, peppers, corn, and potatoes; and herbs like mint and *za'atar* (thyme); and flowers that attract bees and other beneficial insects. Grapevines provide fruit and shade. Some people keep pigeons, chickens, and rabbits as well. In addition to food, gardens provide places to gather and entertain, and sources of small gifts for friends, family, and visitors.

Voluntary work groups have helped support home gardens. During the pandemic lockdowns, people in Farkha spent far more time in their gardens, when the need to save money and the inability to travel made producing one's own food more important. Because the annual Voluntary Work Festival was canceled, the organizers formed the Farkha International Festival Volunteers League, collecting donations from international participants to support various initiatives in the village. The League, in cooperation with the village council, worked on a campaign to buy produce from local families and distribute it to those in need, and provided seeds and saplings for people to expand their gardens. In the spring of 2020, the village council held a competition, sending judges to visit homes to find the village's top ten gardens. It also had its more serious side, with the village council head telling me that the gardens were part of a "home resistance economy" (*al-iqtisad al-manzali al-muqawim*), his language evoking the radical hopes for self-sufficiency that emerged in the First Intifada.

Farming and gardening can also be practices of return. By shoring up household incomes and provisioning families and neighbors, cooperatives and home gardens make it possible for people to stay connected to one another, and to land-based practices. Their effects become most visible during times of crisis, when having access to a market or fresh vegetables cannot be taken for granted. But they also matter when they fade into the background, shaping cooperation at the olive press, providing spaces to spend time with friends and neighbors, and creating the opportunity for mundane acts of reciprocity. These practices are part of what makes it possible for some people to stay on the land, and also what makes the village into a place that others desire to come back to.

Finally, in 2015, an experimental farm in Farkha began operating. The farm was a collaboration between Saad Dagher, who today is probably the best known figure in Palestine's agroecology movement, and activist farmers in Farkha. Dagher told me that he began experimenting with agroecological principles in the early 2000s at his farm in Mazari' al-Nubani, a village that neighbors Farkha. In 2009, he began to work with the Arab Agronomists Association. In 2013, he also became acquainted with Tamera, an eco-village network. Through the Association, he worked with farmers in Farkha, in particular Hammad (whom Dagher knew through his work at PARC), to design Qamar al-Balad as an agroecological farm. The experimental farm is the result of networks that cross the central highlands, as well as Farkha's reputation for farming and voluntary work.

Voluntary work was important for transforming the site into a place suitable for farming. It is located on 14.5 dunums of land, rented from the Islamic Waqf on a twenty-year contract. In 2013, when I first began research in Farkha, I recorded in my field notes that the site was a prime example of ruined land. Voluntary labor helped build Qamar al-Balad, with young people helping to clear brush, move rocks, and terrace the hillside. In 2022, volunteers reclaimed an area of the hill. Working with several older men who had experience in building retaining walls—built by gathering stones from the ground and stacking them to support terraces—lines of volunteers filled buckets with small stones to fill in the cracks and passed large stones to serve as the base. Others worked with picks to break apart larger stones into manageable sizes. A backhoe helped remove larger rocks, enlarge the terrace by removing part of the hillside, and spread the excess dirt to flatten the ground. After a week of work, a new addition to the farm had appeared.

The experimental farm is also a site for regenerating agriculture. Currently, five families oversee Qamar al-Balad, selling produce across the West Bank. There are olive, lemon, and almond trees, and a variety of herbs. A small cistern feeds into a drip irrigation system, which, in the summer of 2022, was used to irrigate hot peppers that belonged to the Farkha's Women's Association. There are new grapevines, growing on metal trellises set up along the terraces, and protected by a fence.[72] Since my final visit, farmers have set up a plastic greenhouse, and there are plans to raise chickens, pigeons, and other poultry.

The farm is also a place to learn about agriculture. According to Hammad, many volunteers and experts have visited since its opening, making Qamar al-Balad a hub for curious agronomists, farmers, and environmental activists. In the center of the farm is a shaded sitting area. The educational visit that I happened to find myself at was a group of high school students from Nazareth. They came during the 2022 festival, helping to move and stack rocks for the retaining wall. Afterward, they sat with Hammad as he explained the importance of growing healthy food, why they refrained from using chemicals, and how they created compost. The group's chaperone would occasionally interrupt, asking him to define a word or explain a process. These sorts of meetings are an opportunity to learn a bit more about farming by experiencing what it looks, feels, and smells like to spend time on the land.

Qamar al-Balad is part of the project to make Farkha into an eco-village.[73] Some of these efforts, like eco-tourism, have yet to bear fruit. Others, like the introduction of solar panels, have reduced village dependence on the Israeli grid. We should see sustainable farming and sustainable energy as based in an insurgent tradition of rural development, one in which not having to buy Israeli products or electricity is a step in the direction of agrarian self-determination.

The activities at the experimental farm are also practices of return. The labor and ethics of voluntary work, olive farming, and home gardening are part of the building and upkeep of the farm. They have created a place where people can come and learn, even for a day, about the pleasures and hardships of agrarian life. Here, those who have farmed all their life can meet those who do not know the first thing about it, creating opportunities to experiment with what going back to the land might mean.

Considered together, these different agrarian experiments show us how return is also about the transformation of village life. Many of the activist farmers I interviewed are themselves returnees who had at various points left the village and worked in the Gulf, in Israel, and later in factories in nearby settlements. They wanted to make farming possible, both for those who cultivate land now, and those who might come after them. I asked many farmers about the future, but it was 'Ali's response that stuck with me. He told me that he hopes that his children will take care of the land the way that he does now. "Every year," he said, "I go out with them and tell them about the land, tell them where it came from. I hope that they will develop it. Not that they will do it like their grandfathers, but that they will develop it further."

THE WORK OF RETURN

Of all the farming techniques I learned about during my research, grafting is the one I have always found most fascinating. Walking through olive groves, one might catch sight of young, white scions fastened by a cloth to the gnarled bark of old trees. 'Ali explained to me how trees are combinations of different rootstocks and branches, and how one must periodically graft new shoots onto the tree, to ensure that it continues to produce. When one looks at an olive tree, it can appear to a single, unchanging organism. But for farmers, it is a slow work in progress. And since a tree lives far longer than any single farmer, generations share in the work of making any single tree.

We might extend grafting as a metaphor for the agrarian experiments underway in the central highlands. Roots matter, of course, and activists draw on peasant traditions for many of their efforts. But they also branch out. Each new project is a branch, creating different relationships between farmers, development professionals, international activists, and renegade agronomists, and bringing the village into contact with new movements, markets, and networks. As people rebuild the land and renew agricultural traditions, they are not just returning to their roots; they are also grafting and waiting to see what grows.

What might grow are new ways of being a peasant. Today, "peasant" is a collective political identity for farming communities and social movements across the globe.[74] They are not demanding, as sociologist and food sovereignty activist Annette Desmarais puts it in her history of La Via Campesina, a "romanticized return to an archaic past," but instead "reaffirming the lessons from *their* histories and reshaping the rural landscape to benefit those who work the land."[75] By making voluntary work a part of village life, supporting agricultural livelihoods, and creating opportunities to learn about the land, these experiments in the central highlands make it possible for people to (re)establish agrarian relationships to land informed by peasant ethics and practices. What they become will not resemble the peasantries of old; they may not even call themselves peasants. Instead, what matters is the possibility that these agrarian relationships will become a meaningful part of social life and political identity, and worth sacrificing something to defend.

Transformation is important precisely because settler colonialism consigns the colonized to an unchanging past. This operation of power works through a discourse that represents "the native" as backward and traditional, and a distribution of material resources that deprives colonized peoples of the resources required to transform their societies. This form of domination produces what Fanon called "an organized petrification of the peasantry."[76] "They will not allow us to develop our village so that it shares features with the city, or to move with our city into a contemporary space," wrote the poet Mourid Barghouti in his memoir about visiting—he refuses to call it return—his home in the central highlands after three decades of exile. "The Occupation forced us to remain with the old," he continued. "That is its crime. It did not deprive us of the clay ovens of yesterday, but of the mystery of what we would invent tomorrow."[77] The agrarian experiments in the highlands are a rejection of the colonial idea that village life is nothing more than, as Barghouti put it, a "bouquet of 'symbols.'" Instead, they are dynamic practices of self-determination.

Return is open-ended, and people cannot do it alone. Like the peasant labor process that so often inspires its practices, returning demands collective energy and cooperation. For those organizing voluntary work crews, running cooperatives, and building experimental farms, land justice is enacted through the hard work of reclaiming the places and relationships that make agrarian life possible. Return, then, is more than just going back; it is a commitment to the liberatory possibilities of making something new.

Conclusion

MANY LAND JUSTICES

THE PROLIFERATION OF CONFLICTS OVER OWNERSHIP, TERRITORY, and sovereignty has made the question of land one of the most important political questions of the present moment.[1] Peasants, Indigenous peoples, and other communities are often on the frontlines, with longstanding local and national struggles for land now taking on a sense of planetary significance. From land occupations by "an urban proletariat with peasant characteristics" to the "translation" of food sovereignty, they are changing how we understand land politics and challenging us to rethink frameworks that divided the world into urban and rural, North and South, or modern and traditional.[2] Most important, they are showing us new ways to think about and fight for land justice.

The agrarian resurgence in Palestine is part of this global upheaval. Seed banks are preserving local (*baladi*) seeds by distributing them to farmers.[3] Home gardens, agroecological farms, and cooperatives are appearing in villages, cities, and refugee camps.[4] Renewed interest in traditional farming and food has seen the creation of new projects that are confronting the fragmentation and isolation of rural places. Internationally, from cookbooks to fair trade olive oil, it is increasingly likely that people encounter Palestinians through food and agriculture, while movements for climate justice, food sovereignty, and Indigenous rights are increasingly making common cause with

Palestinian farmers. In other words, the regeneration of land-based practices and identities in Palestine has created new ways for people to understand the Palestinian struggle, and new relationships of solidarity and support.

This resurgence offers a critique that is anticolonial and predominantly anticapitalist. For many Palestinian intellectuals, today's agricultural cooperatives carry on the tradition of the resistance economy, and offer the basis for food sovereignty.[5] For critics of Palestinian neoliberalism, "experiments in permaculture, rooftop gardening, and promoting local biodiversity in crops" point toward the possibility of escaping the trap of "economic peace" and moving toward the possibility of "economic resistance."[6] "Whether it is in Haiti, Honduras, India, or Palestine," argue Vivien Sansour and Alaa Tartir, "small-scale family farming represents the last frontier of resistance to a worldwide capital-driven political system that dilutes people's identities and strips them of their food sovereignty in order to ensure elite political and economic dominance of both human and natural resources."[7] The political critique that is emerging from this resurgence asks us to understand the Israeli occupation, the PA's economic policies, and the agendas of donors and NGOs as a complex formation of power that maintains Palestinian subjugation to Israeli and Western interests. It draws on Palestinian anticolonial traditions, reworking them in the hope of breaking the relations of domination that emerged after the peace process of the 1990s and continue to forestall liberation.

But this resurgence is also enmeshed within capitalist economies and liberal political structures. Fair trade and organic markets may offer "fair wages, healthy and safe working conditions, [and] environmental stewardship."[8] But they also institute new forms of market discipline on farms, and conscript Indigenous identity as a marketing device.[9] Local markets may create new forms of dependency on urban middle-class tastes (and incomes), and produce a romantic agrarian imaginary that is divorced from the realities of rural life in Palestine.[10] Nor is it really feasible to escape from philanthropic organizations or NGOs, which many activists and organizations still rely on for grants, salaries, and other forms of support. These agrarian projects do not offer a clean break from settler colonialism or capitalism. Instead, they work through, and sometimes against, the markets, class relations, and institutions of these dominant orders.

The different struggles for land that I have recounted in *Plots and Deeds* are a microcosm of what is happening in Palestine, and indeed across the globe. The people who live in these villages face colonial powers that dispossess them, economic forces that price them out, political schemes that ignore them, and ideologies that both celebrate or condemn them as atavistic and unchanging. They are not only fighting against settlers and soldiers, but also fighting to convince their families and neighbors that peasant agriculture and agrarian values are worth defending. They show us that the forces that drive agrarian annihilation also shape the practices and subjectivities of those who decide to resist. And as they fight for the return of the land, and to return to it, they teach us what land justice means in Palestine.

THE MOSAIC OF LAND JUSTICE

Peasant farming gives rise to a specific formation of land justice. Through recourse to the practices and values embedded in peasant farming, people in the highlands position themselves as the rightful owners and occupiers of the land, as possessors of knowledge about the landscape, and as having the right to determine what rural places should be like. But while peasant farming grounds a powerful set of claims and practices, it is also not the only way that Palestinians relate to land, or think about land justice.

Commercial agriculture in the West Bank gives rise to a different set of issues. While smallholder agriculture is prevalent in the highlands, there are large commercial farms in the West Bank, too. The Jordan Valley is a prime example. There, the fertile soil and unique climate enable the year-round cultivation of a wide variety of fruits and vegetables. After the Nakba, refugees became sharecroppers and agricultural workers, their labor fueling the introduction of capitalist agriculture to the Valley, encouraging land purchases and bringing nearly all arable land under cultivation.[11] Israel established agricultural settlements in the Jordan Valley in the 1970s; today, 87.5 percent of the Valley is classified as Area C, which has both dispossessed Palestinian farmers and enabled settler farms to expand. Dispossessed Palestinians—men, women, and children—provide cheap labor; in 2017, for instance, 60 percent of the workforce in the Valley worked on Israeli settlement farms.[12] New arrangements of Palestinian agribusiness create further ecological and social problems. The expansion of Palestinian date plantations over the past few decades, for example, has undermined longstanding arrangements of water usage and land access, inadvertently displacing sharecroppers.[13] And like real estate in the highlands, these date plantations have also provided a way for Palestinian capital to merge business with land defense.[14] The issues surrounding agricultural labor, resource access, and sharecropping make for a set of struggles quite different from those faced by peasant farmers in the highlands, and a formation of land justice that will emerge from the specific social, political, and ecological changes wrought by colonization and agribusiness in the Valley.

Pastoralists have different relationships to land and have faced different sorts of injustice. Pastoralism is often associated with Palestinian Bedouin, but villagers in both the highlands and the lowlands also had significant holdings of animals, and need for pastures. We might take the Jahalin Bedouin as an example. Israel expelled many Bedouin from their homes in the Naqab (today part of southern Israel), forcing them to rebuild their lives in the West Bank. In the early 1950s, the Jahalin eventually settled in the hills outside of Jerusalem. They planted limited crops for animal feed, traveled as far north as Jenin and as far east as Jordan for pasture, sold dairy products and meat in Jerusalem markets, worked in construction, and worked in agriculture through sharecropping agreements with local landowners.[15] The occupation of the West Bank devasted the pastoral economy. The closure of most open grazing areas meant that the number of sheep dropped by 36 percent in the first five years of occupation and continued to decline, albeit not as sharply, as the years wore on.[16] Those who entered these areas—now classified as state lands, military zones, or natural parks—risked having their animals confiscated by the Israeli authorities.[17] The Jahalin and others like them have been forced into the peripheries of the West Bank, and today are subject not only to military bulldozers, but also to paramilitary gangs that have begun to force them from their homes. The result is the destruction of a pastoral mode of life, one in which enclosures and forced displacements compound the dispossession and exile of the Nakba.

Palestinians in exile offer another vantage point for considering land justice. During the 1967 war, 250,000 people fled the West Bank, and only 17,000 were allowed to return.[18] Since then, many more have left to work and live abroad: in the United States, Europe, and the Gulf. As I have mentioned in this book, villagers noted that it was refugees who, having lived in Jordan since 1967 with no prospects of return, sold land to developers and brokers. But it is also through buying land that the descendants of Palestinian refugees and migrants can establish claims and connections to Palestine again. One man, who along with a group of friends from Europe and the United States had bought land in the hills of Farkha, told me that it might not be Jaffa (where his father had been expelled from in 1948), but it was still land in Palestine.[19] For those with the right passports and enough money, the spread of private property and transformation of agricultural land into real estate is a way to imagine return.

Even for those who have no hope of immediate return, property ownership is a way to express solidarity with other Palestinians. In 2022, for example, refugees in Gaza organized the Kushan Baladi (My Country's Deed) initiative in response to the settler takeover of homes in the Jerusalem neighborhood of Sheikh Jarrah. These refugees were not from Jerusalem; instead, they were responding to the broader implications of the Israeli claim that Palestinians in the neighborhood were not the legal owners because they did not possess the proper legal documents. In one video report about Kushan Baladi, we see people meeting in a home the Jabalia refugee camp who have gathered Ottoman and British deeds to prove that they had once owned land and houses in the what is now Israel, and to remind their children of their right to return.[20] Today Jabalia, like much of northern Gaza, has been laid waste. It is likely that both these people and their deeds are buried in the rubble.

While we do not often think about Gaza in agrarian terms, land justice is just as important there as it is in the West Bank. In the aftermath of the Nakba, this tiny sliver of southern Palestine was inundated with 200,000 refugees, joining the 85,000 residents of Gaza City and surrounding villages left standing. Land ownership was concentrated in the hands of a few powerful families, and after the Nakba they hired these refugees, many of whom had once been peasants, to work in the citrus plantations of Gaza.[21] After 1967, Israel turned these peasant-refugees into a reserve of cheap labor.[22] Those who still farmed, whether they owned the land or worked as tenants, have been gradually squeezed between the expanding cities and refugee camps that ate into farmland from one side, and a militarized zone of Israeli control on the other.[23] Over the past several decades, "environmental warfare" has turned the agricultural landscape into a means of war, not only destroying crops, degrading soils, and killing farmers, but also transforming what people grow, and how they do it.[24] Agrarian annihilation is both the origin and condition of Gaza, and a place where multiple struggles for land justice converge.

The fight for land in the central highlands that I have focused on in *Plots and Deeds* is but one piece of a larger mosaic of land justice in Palestine. Even a cursory look at this mosaic shows us the ways that settler colonialism has torn apart the agrarian fabric of historic Palestine. Repairing it requires a political solution, and no amount of tinkering can take the place of self-determination and sovereignty. Yet the diverse array of Palestinian relationships to land, and the different struggles over who should control it, mean that even if the occupation ended tomorrow, many important social, legal, and environmental questions would remain unresolved. Whatever forms land justice takes cannot be confined to the achievement of state sovereignty or enforcement of international law, but must incorporate the diverse claims, needs, and aspirations of those who work and live on the land.

LAND JUSTICE AFTER OCTOBER 7

October 7, 2023, completely transformed the political landscape. That morning, Hamas and other Palestinian resistance groups launched a coordinated assault on the military forces enforcing the siege of the Gaza Strip. The speed at which they broke through, and the subsequent battles inside Israeli population centers, the massacres of civilians, and the taking of hostages back to Gaza, shattered the Israeli military's aura of invincibility, and the Israeli government's policy of managing (and never resolving) the Palestinian question. Almost immediately, Israel unleased the full force of its arsenal on the entire population of the Gaza Strip, where the level of death and destruction quickly crossed the line into genocide.[25] The extent of the devastation has been assiduously documented, yet the scale and scope of the loss are still unimaginable.

As I put the final touches on this manuscript in February 2025, there is a fragile ceasefire in place. How long it will hold remains unclear. But as increasingly powerful Israeli ethnonationalists clamor for the recolonization of Gaza, and a newly elected US president floats the idea of expelling the entire Palestinian population and turning the Strip into a luxury real estate development, it is clear that this ceasefire marks only an interruption, rather than an end, to genocide.

Over the past sixteen months we have witnessed a new phase of agrarian annihilation. According to analyses of satellite imagery, 64–70 percent of tree crops and 58 percent of greenhouses have been damaged or destroyed, and 90 percent of Gaza's livestock killed.[26] Despite Israel's decades-long closure of the Gaza Strip and the limited amount of arable land available, Gazan farmers had managed to meet many of the food needs of the population. Today, that food system is shattered. Gazans now rely on humanitarian aid, with malnutrition and hunger threatening the lives of those who have been able to avoid being killed by bullets and bombs.[27]

This aerial view, while vital for making sense of the horrifying scope of the war, tells us little about the specific places that Israel has wiped out. Take al-Mawasi. According to a report from Joan Mandell, who spoke to farmers who grew vegetables in this coastal area in the 1980s:

> The *muwasi* are level areas of sand near the sea. The farmer digs until he reaches sand of a certain density, indicating sweet water. In the summer, when the water table is lower, he bulldozes away the top layer of sand to form a barrier for the field. In the winter, he pushes the sand back on top of the field so that it does not turn into a swamp. At the time of the Mandate, only a small portion of *muwasi* land had been cultivated. As untended sandy land, it was considered state domain. *Muwasi* cultivation expanded under the Egyptian administration. The owners of registered land began farming plots next to their own, in a checkerboard fashion. According to one *muwasi* farmer, this coastal area, including that now confiscated by Katif, was slated for distribution to Palestinian peasants under an Egyptian land distribution scheme interrupted by the 1967 war.[28]

It was also once home to a variety of wildlife. According to journalist Fred Peace, Gazan ecologist Abdel Fattah Abd Rabou "has recorded 135 bird species there, including many Palestine sunbirds, as well as 14 species of mammals and 20 of reptiles."[29] In 2024, Israel designed al-Mawasi a so-called humanitarian safe zone, forcing thousands of displaced Palestinians to take shelter there. Today, al-Mawasi is known not for its unique agricultural practices or ecological diversity, but as the site of a massacre of ninety Palestinians, killed by Israeli airstrikes. Different bombings leveled the Islamic University of Gaza, where Abu Rabou once did his research. When contacted by Pearce to discuss the effect of the war on Gaza's environment, he responded, "Now I am not able to communicate at all [. . .] because five of my children were lost during the Israeli war on Gaza and my house was completely destroyed."[30]

Nor can statistics or satellite images tell us much about the people that Israel has killed. One such person was the young farmer and agricultural engineer Youssef Abu Rabie, whose story I learned about from the writer Luke Carneal. Abu Rabie came from a farming family, and led a project that brought around one hundred farmers together to cultivate more than 300 dunums in Beit Lahiya.[31] The Israeli invasion destroyed his family's farmland and greenhouse, but even amid war, they managed to return and replant. In a short video from *Al-Jazeera* in August 2024, we see him standing in front of small strips of cultivated land in front of the ruins of a bombed building.[32] According to an interview from September 2024, he reported that they been able to harvest enough jute mallow (*mulukhiya*) and zucchini to distribute to their neighbors and to shelters, and establish a nursery to provide growers with peppers, eggplant, and other vegetables.[33] Even during the worst bombardments of northern Gaza in October 2024, he had managed to plant an array of vegetables and leafy greens. He was killed on October 21, 2024.[34]

There is also a war, albeit one of a far different scale and intensity, happening in the West Bank. The Israeli military had been attacking West Bank refugee camps, often strongholds of Palestinian armed resistance, before the war on Gaza began. It has escalated since, with airstrikes and invasions in Jenin, Tulkarm, and Nablus. Settler assaults on Palestinians and their property were on the rise before October 2023. Since then, the Israeli government has encouraged them, arming and inciting settlers who, under the guard of the Israeli military, have carried out pogroms and terrorized smaller communities in the peripheries of the West Bank.

Land grabbing is the object of the war in the West Bank. The seizure and colonization of land in Farkha, with the subsequent expulsion of several Bedouin families and vandalism of Palestinian homes and farms, is part of a much larger story. Across the West Bank, settlers are establishing outposts and sealing off entire areas, while government authorities have initiated another cycle of state land claims.[35] Communities that have faced decades of periodic home demolitions find themselves displaced at gunpoint by soldiers and paramilitaries.[36] In yet another sign of the demise of the Oslo era, the state has seized land in Area B, while settlers discuss ways to contain Palestinians in built-up population centers.[37] From Farkha, to Bethlehem, to the Jordan Valley, to the hills of southern Hebron, land dispossession is increasingly accompanied by population transfer. To paraphrase what a former colleague from Stop the Wall told me while explaining its work on the most recent expulsions: apartheid at least had the pretense of legality; whatever is coming next will be far worse.

Even as legal avenues close, Palestinians will still be forced to turn to property ownership to defend land. Indeed, law's failures often incite more, not less, psychic and material investment in legal promises and direct collective energies toward imbuing such claims with the "the air of legality."[38] The more the Israeli state ignores the law, the more Palestinians will find themselves compelled to register, title, and make legal claims. The need to do something, even if it might not work, justifies going to the Israeli courts where Palestinian rights will be ignored, just as it justifies making thousands of title deeds that the Israeli authorities will not honor. As a result, we have the paradox in which a proliferation of legal claims, discourses, and frameworks accompanies a growing disillusion that the law—from property to human rights to international treaties—can offer protection, much less justice.

Within the Palestinian enclaves, the pressures of land commodification are likely to increase. Real estate development is no longer the subject of exuberant development conferences or hopeful newspaper headlines. But property in the Palestinian hinterlands will remain an attractive site of investment, and sometimes the only investment, for families and corporations alike. The shrinking amount of land that Palestinians can access will only push prices upward. Colonial violence will accelerate the commodification of land, and the concomitant destruction of peasant farming, in the shrinking space that Palestinians can still farm.

This means that those on the rural periphery are on the frontlines of land defense, even as their ability to stay on that land faces growing threats from all sides. Today land justice seems ever more impossible to realize, and ever more vital to fight for. It was in the hope of understanding one path that this struggle has taken, and offering something to those who carry it forward, that I wrote this book.

Notes

Introduction

1. Mazin B. Qumsiyeh, *Popular Resistance in Palestine: A History of Hope and Empowerment* (London: Pluto Press, 2011). On the figure of the peasant, see Ted Swedenburg, "The Palestinian Peasant As National Signifier," *Anthropological Quarterly* 63, no. 1 (1990): 18–30; Salim Tamari, "Soul of the Nation: The Fallah in the Eyes of the Urban Intelligentsia," *Review of Middle East Studies* 5, no. 5 (1992): 74–83.

2. The term "neoliberal Palestine" comes from Ali Abunimah, *The Battle for Justice in Palestine* (Chicago: Haymarket Books, 2014). The writing on neoliberalism in the West Bank is extensive, and the foundational texts include Toufic Haddad, *Palestine Ltd.: Neoliberalism and Nationalism in the Occupied Territory* (London: IB Tauris, 2016); Adam Hanieh, "The Internationalisation of Gulf Capital and Palestinian Class Formation," *Capital & Class* 35, no. 1 (2011): 81–106; Adam Hanieh, *Lineages of Revolt: Issues of Contemporary Capitalism in the Middle East* (Chicago: Haymarket Books, 2013); Christopher Harker, *Spacing Debt: Obligations, Violence, and Endurance in Ramallah, Palestine* (Durham, NC: Duke University Press, 2020); Raja Khalidi and Sobhi Samour, "Neoliberalism As Liberation: The Statehood Program and the Remaking of the Palestinian National Movement," *Journal of Palestine Studies* 40, no. 2 (2011): 6–25; Kareem Rabie, *Palestine Is Throwing a Party and the Whole World Is Invited: Capital and State Building in the West Bank* (Durham, NC: Duke University Press, 2021). This boom built on an earlier phase of liberalization, a result of the Oslo peace process and consolidation of the PA in the city in the 1990s. See Kareem Rabie, "Remaking Ramallah," *New Left Review* 111 (2018): 43–60; Lisa Taraki, "Urban Moder-

nity on the Periphery: A New Middle Class Reinvents the Palestinian City," *Social Text* 26, no. 95 (2008): 61–81.

3. Kareem Rabie, "Ramallah's Bubbles," *Jadaliyya* (blog), January 18, 2013, http://www.jadaliyya.com/Details/27839/Ramallah%E2%80%99s-Bubbles.

4. So much so that Human Rights Watch used what has been happening in Bruqin and the surrounding area for the past twenty years or so as evidence that Israel was guilty of the crime of apartheid. See Human Rights Watch, "A Threshold Crossed: Israeli Authorities and the Crimes of Apartheid and Persecution" (Human Rights Watch, 2021).

5. This is not to say that the legal rights are respected or protected; we only need to look to Gaza, where detailed knowledge of Israeli war crimes has done little to slow the genocide.

6. On the history that got us to this point in Palestine, see Lori Allen, *The Rise and Fall of Human Rights: Cynicism and Politics in Occupied Palestine* (Stanford: Stanford University Press, 2013); Noura Erakat, *Justice for Some: Law and the Question of Palestine* (Stanford: Stanford University Press, 2019); Lisa Hajjar, "Human Rights in Israel/Palestine: The History and Politics of a Movement," *Journal of Palestine Studies* 30, no. 4 (2001): 21–38. It also means that in Palestine, everyone from Islamic resistance movements to neoliberal technocrats turns to this legal discourse as well. On the use of liberal discourse by Hamas, see Tareq Baconi, *Hamas Contained: The Rise and Pacification of Palestinian Resistance* (Stanford: Stanford University Press, 2018).

7. For a critical discussion of this turn, see Kareem Rabie, "What Do We Talk About When We Talk About Political Economy?" *Jadaliyya* (blog), September 29, 2015, https://www.jadaliyya.com/Details/32527/What-Do-We-Talk-About-When -We-Talk-About-Political-Economy. For a discussion of the lacunae in Palestinian studies surrounding property ownership, see Beshara Doumani and Paul Kohlbry, "Introduction: Claiming Property, Claiming Palestine," *Comparative Studies of South Asia, Africa and the Middle East* 43, no. 3 (2023): 245–48. The few studies that have directly addressed some of these questions include Andy Clarno, *Neoliberal Apartheid: Palestine/Israel and South Africa after 1994* (Chicago: University of Chicago Press, 2017); Samir Harb, "Imaginary and Autonomy: Urbanisation, Construction, and Cement Production in Palestine," PhD diss., University of Manchester, 2020; Fadia Panosetti and Laurence Roudart, "Evolving Regimes of Land Use and Property in the West Bank," *Jerusalem Quarterly* 89 (2022): 10–31; Rabie, *Palestine Is Throwing a Party and the Whole World Is Invited*.

8. Michel-Rolph Trouillot defines peasant labor as "an institutionalized process through which a household performs agricultural labor on a unit over which it

exerts a form of control that excludes similar groups, with instruments of work which it also controls in an exclusive manner and which generally represent less of an input than the labor itself." Michel-Rolph Trouillot, *Peasants and Capital: Dominica in the World Economy* (Baltimore: Johns Hopkins University Press, 1988), 4. For similar definitions of "peasant," see Marc Edelman, "What Is a Peasant? What Are Peasantries? A Briefing Paper on Issues of Definition," paper presented at First Session of the Intergovernmental Working Group on a United Nations Declaration on the Rights of Peasants and Other People Working in Rural Areas, Geneva, July 2013, 15–19; Teodor Shanin, *Peasants and Peasant Societies* (Harmondsworth, UK: Penguin, 1971); Deborah Bryceson, "Peasant Theories and Smallholder Policies: Past and Present," in *Disappearing Peasantries? Rural Labour in Africa, Asia and Latin America*, ed. Deborah Bryceson, Cristóbal Kay, and Jos Mooij (London: Intermediate Technology Publications, 2000), 1–36.

9. Trouillot, *Peasants and Capital*, 9. The potential for some sort of autonomy is what makes peasants so important for various anticapitalist theorizations. For a recent example, see Jan Douwe Van der Ploeg, *The New Peasantries: Struggles for Autonomy and Sustainability in an Era of Empire and Globalization* (London: Routledge, 2009). There is a large literature exploring whether the noncommodified aspects of peasant labor can support noncapitalist economic relationships (and resistance) while also providing a subsidy to capital. For a helpful discussion, see Ann Laura Stoler, "Plantation Politics and Protest on Sumatra's East Coast," *The Journal of Peasant Studies* 13, no. 2 (1986): 124–43.

10. A. Haroon Akram-Lodhi, "The Ties That Bind? Agroecology and the Agrarian Question in the Twenty-First Century," *The Journal of Peasant Studies* 48, no. 4 (2021): 687–714; Miguel A. Altieri, "Applying Agroecology to Enhance the Productivity of Peasant Farming Systems in Latin America," *Environment, Development and Sustainability* 1, no. 3–4 (1999): 197–217; Stephen R. Gliessman, *Agroecology: The Ecology of Sustainable Food Systems*, 3rd ed. (Boca Raton: CRC Press, 2014; Robert McC. Netting, *Smallholders, Householders: Farm Families and the Ecology of Intensive, Sustainable Agriculture* (Stanford: Stanford University Press, 1993).

11. La Via Campesina, "About La Via Campesina," https://viacampesina.org/en/international-peasants-voice/.

12. Reflecting on the relative absence in the anthropology of the Middle East of (agrarian) political economy at the end of the 1980s, Lila Abu Lughod asked rhetorically, "Are there household economies only in Africa? Is there peasant resistance only in Asia? Is there capitalist transformation of rural areas only in Latin America?" Lila Abu-Lughod, "Zones of Theory in the Anthropology of the Arab World," *Annual Review of Anthropology* 18 (1989): 267–306, at 299. Max Ajl's recent assessment of the

literature is as follows: "The Arab region is not part of broader discussions on the agrarian question (AQ), while the AQ is essentially absent in studies of the region." Max Ajl, "Does the Arab Region Have an Agrarian Question?" *The Journal of Peasant Studies* 48, no. 5 (2021): 955–83. And as Caroline Abu-Sada pointed out, the agricultural sector in Palestine receives "little media and public attention." See Caroline Abu-Sada, "Cultivating Dependence: Palestinian Agriculture under the Israeli Occupation," in *The Power of Inclusive Exclusion: Anatomy of Israeli Rule in the Occupied Palestinian Territories*, ed. Sari Hanafi, Adi Ophir, and Michal Givoni (New York: Zone Books, 2009), 413–29, at 426.

13. Elia T. Zureik, "Transformation of Class Structure among the Arabs in Israel: From Peasantry to Proletariat," *Journal of Palestine Studies* 6, no. 1 (1976): 39–66; Henry Rosenfeld, "From Peasantry to Wage Labor and Residual Peasantry: The Transformation of an Arab Village," in *Process and Pattern in Culture*, ed. Robert Manners (Chicago: Aldine Publishing, 1964), 211–34; Najwa Hanna Makhoul, "The Proletarianization of Palestinians in Israel: A Study of Development and Class Formation," PhD diss., MIT, 1978. For a critique of some of this work, see Talal Asad, "Anthropological Texts and Ideological Problems: An Analysis of Cohen on Arab Villages in Israel," *Economy and Society* 4, no. 3 (1975): 251–82. On the history of the relationship between Israeli scholars, military intelligence, and the conquest and governance of Palestinian villages, see Gil Eyal, *The Disenchantment of the Orient: Expertise in Arab Affairs and the Israeli State* (Stanford: Stanford University Press, 2006).

14. For some of the main scholarly works, see Hisham Awartani, "Agricultural Development in the West Bank: An Economic and Political Study of the Development of Rain-Fed Farming in the West Bank," PhD diss., University of Bradford, 1982; Rema Hammami, "Between Heaven and Earth: Transformations in Religiosity and Labor among Southern Palestinian Peasant and Refugee Women, 1920–1993," PhD diss., Temple University, 1994; Alex Pollock, "Realist Methodology and the Articulation of Modes of Production: An Analysis of Palestinian Peasant Household Production in the North Jordan Valley of the Occupied West Bank/the Central Highlands of Palestine," PhD diss., University of Strathclyde, 1987; Kathy Glavanis and Pandeli Glavanis, eds., *The Rural Middle East: Peasant Lives and Modes of Production* (London: Zed Books/Birzeit University, 1989); Salim Tamari, "The Dislocation and Re-Constitution of a Peasantry: The Social Economy of Agrarian Palestine in the Central Highlands and the Jordan Valley, 1960—1980," PhD diss., University of Manchester, 1983.

15. "I was fully aware of how the place was saturated with academic and other researchers who help to form what some have called 'the Palestine industry,' " wrote

John Collins about his 1996 fieldwork, noting that "many Palestinians with whom I spoke had already been interviewed multiple times by journalists, human rights workers, and scholars." See John Collins, *Occupied by Memory: The Intifada Generation and the Palestinian State of Emergency* (New York: NYU Press, 2004), 3. If Abu Lughod could say in the 1980s that anthropologists tended to avoid "the political minefield of the conflict over Palestine" in favor of safer "prestige zones," by the 1990s Palestine was becoming, if not a prestige zone, than at least a place that was extensively researched. On the proliferation of anthropological work on the Palestinians (which also illustrates the absence of engagement of agrarian studies and rural fieldwork), see Khaled Furani and Dan Rabinowitz, "The Ethnographic Arriving of Palestine," *Annual Review of Anthropology* 40 (2011): 475–91; Sa'ed Atshan, "The Anthropological Rise of Palestine," *Journal of Palestine Studies* 50, no. 4 (2021): 3–31.

16. Rochelle Davis, *Palestinian Village Histories: Geographies of the Displaced* (Stanford: Stanford University Press, 2011); Susan Slyomovics, *The Object of Memory: Arab and Jew Narrate the Palestinian Village* (Philadelphia: University of Pennsylvania Press, 1998); Ted Swedenburg, *Memories of Revolt: The 1936–1939 Rebellion and the Palestinian National Past* (Fayetteville: University of Arkansas Press, 2003).

17. Courtney Fullilove, "'Famine Foods' and the Values of Biodiversity Preservation in Israel-Palestine," *Isis* 113, no. 3 (September 1, 2022): 625–36; Jumana Manna, "Where Nature Ends and Settlements Begin," *E-Flux Journal* 113 (November 2020), https://www.e-flux.com/journal/113/360006/where-nature-ends-and-settlements -begin/; Anne Meneley, "Blood, Sweat and Tears in a Bottle of Palestinian Extra-Virgin Olive Oil," *Food, Culture & Society* 14, no. 2 (2011): 275–92; Anne Meneley, "Discourses of Distinction in Contemporary Palestinian Extra-Virgin Olive Oil Production," *Food and Foodways* 22, no. 1–2 (2014): 48–64.

18. Imad Sayrafi, "Political Ecology and the Social Solidarity Economies within the Power Matrix in Rural Palestine" (Birzeit: Center for Development Studies, Birzeit University, 2022); Omar Loren Tesdell, "Shadow Spaces: Territory, Sovereignty, and the Question of Palestinian Cultivation," PhD diss., University of Minnesota, 2013; Omar Tesdell, Yusra Othman, and Saher Alkhoury, "Rainfed Agroecosystem Resilience in the Palestinian West Bank, 1918–2017," *Agroecology and Sustainable Food Systems* 43, no. 1 (2019): 21–39.

19. Abunimah, *The Battle for Justice in Palestine,* 120. Also see Vivien Sansour and Alaa Tartir, "Palestinian Farmers: A Last Stronghold of Resistance," *Al-Shabaka* (blog), 2014, https://al-shabaka.org/briefs/palestinian-farmers-a-last-stronghold-of -resistance/.

20. This formulation comes from Henry Bernstein, *Class Dynamics of Agrarian Change* (Sterling, VA: Kumarian Press, 2010), 4. There is an emerging body of schol-

arship working across these two fields, one that I hope *Plots and Deeds* helps advance. It includes Natalia Gutkowski, *Struggling for Time: Environmental Governance and Agrarian Resistance in Israel/Palestine* (Stanford: Stanford University Press, 2024); Gabi Kirk, "Commodifying Indigeneity? Settler Colonialism and Racial Capitalism in Fair Trade Farming in Palestine," *Historical Materialism* 31, no. 2 (2023): 236–68; Fadia Panosetti and Laurence Roudart, "Land Struggle and Palestinian Farmers' Livelihoods in the West Bank: Between De-agrarianization and Anticolonial Resistance," *The Journal of Peasant Studies* (November 10, 2023): 1–23.

21. On peasant farming in the highlands and the surviving sense of local identification, see Beshara Doumani, *Rediscovering Palestine: Merchants and Peasants in Jabal Nablus, 1700–1900* (Berkeley: University of California Press, 1995). For examples of rain-fed farming practices, see Ismail Daiq, *The Local Knowledge System for Plant Protection and Soil Conservation in Rain-Fed Agriculture in the West Bank, Palestine* (Berlin: Margraf, 2005); Tesdell, Othman, and Alkhoury, "Rainfed Agroecosystem Resilience in the Palestinian West Bank, 1918–2017."

22. The amount of agricultural land in each village is derived from Applied Research Institute—Jerusalem (ARIJ) village profiles. The entire surface area of the West Bank, according to PA agricultural census data, is 5.66 million dunums, of which 1.04 million are under cultivation in the West Bank today.

23. Around 9.5 percent of farms above 20 dunums account for 61 percent of the total land. Larger commercial farms are more concentrated in Jenin and the Jordan Valley, while farms in the highlands tend to be smaller and more oriented toward subsistence farming. See Jacques Marzin, Ahmad Uwaidat, and Jean-Michel Sourisseau, "Study on Small-Scale Agriculture in the Palestinian Territories" (Rome: FAO, 2019).

24. These statistics come from the 2021 census, published in 2023. According to the census, 81.5 percent of holders were forty years old and up, 92 percent were men; 81 percent of agricultural holdings belong to individuals (around 13 percent belong to households), and they account for 72 percent of the total agricultural land (12 percent belong to households). Of these holdings 91 percent are considered "owned or owned like possession," and they account for 76 percent of the total agricultural land. Palestinian Authority Ministry of Agriculture and Palestinian Central Bureau of Statistics, "Agriculture Census: 2021" (Ramallah: Palestinian Central Bureau of Statistics/Ministry of Agriculture, 2023).

25. Throughout the 1980s, the number of "owner-operators" increased to 91 percent of West Bank farmers. Most of the work was done by unpaid family members, primarily women, children, and the elderly. In 2011, according to Palestinian statistics, "the 292,000 workers employed in agriculture, about 94 per cent are unpaid

family members." UNCTAD, "The Besieged Palestinian Agricultural Sector" (New York: United Nations, 2015). For current conditions, see Marzin, Uwaidat, and Sourisseau, "Study on Small-Scale Agriculture in the Palestinian Territories," 8–12.

26. Farkha, Qarawa, and Bruqin have populations of 1,650 people, 3,415 people, and 4,047 people, respectively, according to the most recent census. Most farms in the West Bank are classified as small farms, most farmers in the West Bank and Gaza Strip qualify as "small-scale family farming," and most of them produce primarily for subsistence. Today, 81 percent of all land is rain-fed, most of it concentrated in the highlands. Marzin, Uwaidat, and Sourisseau, "Study on Small-Scale Agriculture in the Palestinian Territories." In the 1990s, according to the agricultural economist Hisham Awartani, 95 percent of the cultivated area of the West Bank was rain-fed. Hisham Masoud Awartani, *The Agricultural Sector of the West Bank and the Gaza Strip* (Geneva: UNCTAD, 1993).

27. Marzin, Uwaidat, and Sourisseau, "Study on Small-Scale Agriculture in the Palestinian Territories," 8.

28. Henry Bernstein, "Agrarian Questions from Transition to Globalization," in *Peasants and Globalization*, ed. A. Haroon Akram-Lodhi and Cristóbal Kay (London: Routledge, 2012), 251–73. For an earlier critique of the term "peasant" that hits some of the same notes, see Anthony Leeds, "Mythos and Pathos: Some Unpleasantries on Peasantries," in *Peasant Livelihood: Studies in Economic Anthropology and Cultural Ecology,* ed. Rhoda Halperin and James Dow (New York: St. Martin's Press, 1977).

29. Van der Ploeg, *The New Peasantries.* Contemporary peasant organizations have both proudly claimed "peasant" as a collective political identity and radically transformed what peasant farming, culture, and politics mean today. See Annette Aurelie Desmarais, *La Via Campesina: Globalization and the Power of Peasants* (London: Pluto Press, 2007); Marc Edelman, *Peasant Politics of the Twenty-First Century: Transnational Social Movements and Agrarian Change* (Ithaca: Cornell University Press, 2024).

30. Trouillot, *Peasants and Capital*, 12.

31. The use of "autonomy" can sometimes wrongly imply the desire for autarky or total self-sufficiency, and pass over the importance of interdependence, both inside and outside whatever spatial unit counts as local. See Kees Jansen, Mark Vicol, and Lisette Nikol, "Autonomy and Repeasantization: Conceptual, Analytical, and Methodological Problems," *Journal of Agrarian Change* 22, no. 3 (2022): 489–505.

32. Key texts include Awartani, "Agricultural Development in the West Bank"; George Kurzom, *Towards Alternative Self-Reliant Agricultural Development* (Birzeit: Development Studies Program/Birzeit University, 2001); Adel Samara and Shehada Awda, *Al-Himayya al-Sha'biyya* (Popular Protection) (Damascus: Dar Kan'an li-l-

Darasat wa-l-Nashr, 1988); Adel Samara, *Beyond De-Linking: Development by Popular Protection vs. Development by State* (Ramallah: al-Mashriq al-A'amil for Cultural and Development Studies, 2005). On approaches to the resistance economy, see Tariq Dana, "Localising the Economy as a Resistance Response: A Contribution to the 'Resistance Economy' Debate in the Occupied Palestinian Territories," *Journal of Peacebuilding & Development* 15, no. 2 (2020): 192–204; Rayya El Zein, "Developing a Palestinian Resistance Economy through Agricultural Labor," *Journal of Palestine Studies* 46, no. 3 (2017): 7–26; Faiq Mari, "Masha' of the Periphery: Collective Labor and Property in Palestinian Liberation Struggle," PhD diss., ETH Zurich, 2024.

33. For an early, and ambitious, attempt to preserve and scale up traditional knowledge, see Daiq, *The Local Knowledge System for Plant Protection and Soil Conservation in Rain-Fed Agriculture in the West Bank, Palestine.* For examples of new approaches to agriculture, see Luna Alqamar, "Farming As Resistance: Reviving Indigenous Agricultural Practices in Palestine," *Vice*, July 12, 2018, https://www.vice.com/en/article/3kyzej/farming-as-resistance-reviving-indigenous-agricultural-practices-in-palestine; Nadine Fattaleh and Adam Albarghouthi, "Agroecology, from Palestine to the Diaspora," *Science for the People Magazine* (blog), August 1, 2022, https://magazine.scienceforthepeople.org/vol25-1-the-soil-and-worker/agro-ecology-from-palestine-to-the-diaspora/.

34. La Via Campesina, "La Via Campesina Delegation Visited Palestine in December 2024: Notes from Their Daily Diaries (Part 1)," *La Via Campesina—EN* (blog), January 16, 2025, https://viacampesina.org/en/2025/01/la-via-campesina-delegation-visited-palestine-in-december-2024-notes-from-their-daily-diaries-part-1/. La Via Campesina has a long history of support for Palestinians, with several members visiting PLO leader Yasser Arafat during the Israeli siege of his Ramallah compound in 2002. See Desmarais, *La Via Campesina*, 29–30. Despite this history of solidarity, however, the movement lacks a broad base of organizational support in the region, and only one organization, the Union of Agricultural Work Committees (UAWC), is an official member from Palestine.

35. Brenna Bhandar, *Colonial Lives of Property: Law, Land, and Racial Regimes of Ownership* (Durham, NC: Duke University Press, 2018); Gary Fields, *Enclosure: Palestinian Landscapes in a Historical Mirror* (Berkeley: University of California Press, 2017).

36. Clarno, *Neoliberal Apartheid*; Leila Farsakh, *Palestinian Labour Migration to Israel: Labour, Land and Occupation* (London: Routledge, 2005).

37. Abunimah, *The Battle for Justice in Palestine*; Rabie, *Palestine Is Throwing a Party and the Whole World Is Invited*; Linda Tabar and Samia Al-Botmeh, "Real Estate Development through Land Grabs: Predatory Accumulation and Precarity in Palestine," *New Political Economy* 26, no. 5 (2021): 783–96.

38. For a helpful introduction to critical agrarian studies, see China Sajadian,

"Critical Agrarian Studies," in *International Encyclopedia of Human Geography*, ed. Audrey Lynn Kobayashi, 2nd ed. (Amsterdam: Elsevier, 2020), 17–23. This multidisciplinary field emerged around the study of peasants, and has since grown to include the study of various processes of agrarian change. See Henry Bernstein and Terence J. Byres, "From Peasant Studies to Agrarian Change," *Journal of Agrarian Change* 1, no. 1 (2001): 1–56; Harriet Friedmann, "Origins of Peasant Studies," in *Handbook of Critical Agrarian Studies*, ed. A. Haroon Akram-Lodhi et al. (Northampton, MA: Edward Elgar Publishing, 2021), 15–24.

39. For a critical journalistic account that gives a good sense of the scope of the problem, see Fred Pearce, *The Land Grabbers: The New Fight over Who Owns the Earth* (Boston: Beacon Press, 2012). For reviews of this literature that illustrate its extent, see Derek Hall, "Primitive Accumulation, Accumulation by Dispossession and the Global Land Grab," *Third World Quarterly* 34, no. 9 (2013): 1582–1604; Ruth Hall et al., "Resistance, Acquiescence or Incorporation? An Introduction to Land Grabbing and Political Reactions 'from Below,'" *The Journal of Peasant Studies* 42, no. 3–4 (2015): 467–88; Wendy W. Wolford et al., "Global Land Deals: What Has Been Done, What Has Changed, and What's Next?" *The Journal of Peasant Studies* (2024): 1–38; Marc Edelman, Carlos Oya, and Saturnino M Borras, "Global Land Grabs: Historical Processes, Theoretical and Methodological Implications and Current Trajectories," *Third World Quarterly* 34, no. 9 (2013): 1517–31; Ben White et al., "The New Enclosures: Critical Perspectives on Corporate Land Deals," *The Journal of Peasant Studies* 39, no. 3–4 (2012): 619–47; Saturnino M. Borras Jr. et al., "Towards a Better Understanding of Global Land Grabbing: An Editorial Introduction," *The Journal of Peasant Studies* 38, no. 2 (2011): 209–16.

40. Important exceptions that engage with the past and present of colonial dispossession include Liza Grandia, *Enclosed: Conservation, Cattle, and Commerce among the Q'eqchi' Maya Lowlanders* (Seattle: University of Washington Press, 2012); Fouad Makki, "Development by Dispossession: *Terra Nullius* and the Social-Ecology of New Enclosures in Ethiopia," *Rural Sociology* 79, no. 1 (2014): 79–103.

41. Wolford et al., "Global Land Deals, 24."

42. Shiri Pasternak, *Grounded Authority: The Algonquins of Barriere Lake against the State* (Minneapolis: University of Minnesota Press, 2017), 25–26.

43. Baruch Kimmerling, "Sovereignty, Ownership, and 'Presence' in the Jewish-Arab Territorial Conflict: The Case of Bir'im and Ikrit," *Comparative Political Studies* 10, no. 2 (1977): 155–76; Omar Jabary Salamanca et al., "Past Is Present: Settler Colonialism in Palestine," *Settler Colonial Studies* 2, no. 1 (2012): 1–8; Patrick Wolfe, "Settler Colonialism and the Elimination of the Native," *Journal of Genocide Research* 8, no. 4 (2006): 387–409.

44. UNCTAD, "The Besieged Palestinian Agricultural Sector," 7. On the forms of

uncertainty and disorder this military regime creates for farmers, see Irene Calis, "Routine and Rupture: The Everyday Workings of Abyssal (Dis)order in the Palestinian Food Basket," *American Ethnologist* 44, no. 1 (2017): 65–76.

45. Saad Amira, "The Slow Violence of Israeli Settler-Colonialism and the Political Ecology of Ethnic Cleansing in the West Bank," *Settler Colonial Studies* 11, no. 4 (2021): 512–32; Gabi Kirk, "Confronting the Twin Crises of Climate Change and Occupation in Palestine," *Arab Studies Journal* 30, no. 2 (2022): 90–95; D. A. Jaber, "Settler Colonialism and Ecocide: Case Study of Al-Khader, Palestine," *Settler Colonial Studies* 9, no. 1 (2019): 135–54; Mazin B. Qumsiyeh and M. Abusarhan, "An Environmental Nakba: The Palestinian Environment under Israeli Colonization," *Science for the People* 1, no. 21 (2020): 1969–89.

46. Awartani, "Agricultural Development in the West Bank," 93.

47. Farsakh, *Palestinian Labour Migration to Israel,* 96–98.

48. Abu-Sada, "Cultivating Dependence: Palestinian Agriculture under the Israeli Occupation."

49. D. Asher Ghertner and Robert W. Lake, "Introduction: Land Fictions and the Politics of Commodification in City and Country," in *Land Fictions: The Commodification of Land in City and Country*, ed. D. Asher Ghertner and Robert W. Lake (Ithaca: Cornell University Press, 2021), 1–25, at 9. For some examples, see Sai Balakrishnan, "Recombinant Urbanization: Agrarian–Urban Landed Property and Uneven Development in India," *International Journal of Urban and Regional Research* 43, no. 4 (2019): 617–32; Natalia Mamonova and Lee-Ann Sutherland, "Rural Gentrification in Russia: Renegotiating Identity, Alternative Food Production and Social Tensions in the Countryside," *Journal of Rural Studies* 42 (2015): 154–65; Ieva Snikersproge, "Who Are Neorurals? Or, How Capitalist Time Discipline Dilutes Political Projects and Makes It Difficult to Propose an Alternative," *Economic Anthropology* (2023); William Thomson, Cynthia Gharios, and Rami Zurayk, "From Silk to Concrete: Exploring the Socio-Spatial Aspects of the Agrarian Question(s) in Mount Lebanon," *The Journal of Peasant Studies* (2022): 1–23.

50. On this point, but in an urban context, see Hiba Bou Akar, *For the War Yet to Come: Planning Beirut's Frontiers* (Stanford: Stanford University Press, 2018).

51. El Zein, "Developing a Palestinian Resistance Economy through Agricultural Labor," 13.

52. For Justine Williams and Eric Holt-Giménez, "land justice" is the idea that "people and communities that have been historically oppressed have a right to land and territory" and "recognizes the central role of land in culture, in society, and in relations of power, as well as its restorative, protective, and healing potential." It resonates with Jennifer Franco and Saturnino Borras's idea of "land sovereignty,"

which posits that land should belong "to the people who work it, care for it and live on it, and the people belong to a particular land as a people." See Justine M. Williams and Eric Holt-Giménez, eds., *Land Justice: Re-Imagining Land, Food, and the Commons* (Oakland, CA: Food First Books, 2017); Jennifer Franco and Saturnino M. Borras Jr., "A 'Land Sovereignty' Alternative? Towards a Peoples' Counter-Enclosure" (Amsterdam: Transnational Institute, July 2012). Also see Sara Safransky, "Land Justice as a Historical Diagnostic: Thinking with Detroit," in *Social Justice and the City*, ed. Nik Heynen (London: Routledge, 2020), 199–212.

53. Katherine Verdery, *The Vanishing Hectare: Property and Value in Postsocialist Transylvania* (Ithaca: Cornell University Press, 2003), 18–19.

54. Christian Lund, *Nine-Tenths of the Law: Enduring Dispossession in Indonesia* (New Haven: Yale University Press, 2020), 8.

55. John Bellamy Foster, *Marx's Ecology: Materialism and Nature* (New York: Monthly Review Press, 2000), 158.

56. Trouillot, *Peasants and Capital*, 5–6.

57. For examples, see Tania Murray Li, *Land's End: Capitalist Relations on an Indigenous Frontier* (Durham, NC: Duke University Press, 2014); Martha Mundy and Richard Saumarez Smith, *Governing Property, Making the Modern State: Law, Administration and Production in Ottoman Syria* (London: IB Tauris, 2007); Netting, *Smallholders, Householders*.

58. See, in order, Awartani, "Agricultural Development in the West Bank"; and Abdulrahman Abu Arafeh, Yusuf al-Azzeh, and Dawood Istanbuli, "Al-Waqaʿ al-Ziraʿiyya fi al-Minatiq al-Muhtala wa-Dururat al-Tanmiyya" (The Agricultural Situation in the Occupied Areas and the Requirements of Development), and Dawood Istanbuli, "Al-Insan al-Ziraʿi" (The Agricultural Individual), both in *Muʾtamir al-Tanmiyya min Ajl al-Sumud* (Development for Sumud Conference) (Jerusalem: Arab Thought Forum, 1983).

59. Charles Anderson, "Will the Real Palestinian Peasantry Please Sit Down? Towards a New History of British Rule in Palestine, 1917–1936," LSE Middle East Centre Paper, 2015; Rashid Khalidi, *Palestinian Identity: The Construction of Modern National Consciousness* (New York: Columbia University Press, 1997).

60. Stuart Banner, *Possessing the Pacific: Land, Settlers, and Indigenous People from Australia to Alaska* (Cambridge, MA: Harvard University Press, 2009); Charles R. Hale, "Neoliberal Multiculturalism," *PoLAR: Political and Legal Anthropology Review* 28, no. 1 (2005): 10–19; Paul Kohlbry, "Palestinian Counter-Forensics and the Cruel Paradox of Property," *American Ethnologist* 49, no. 3 (2022): 374–86; Paul Nadasdy, " 'Property' and Aboriginal Land Claims in the Canadian Subarctic: Some Theoretical Considerations," *American Anthropologist* 104, no. 1 (2002): 247–61.

61. Edward W. Said, *The Question of Palestine* (New York: Vintage, 1992), 7–8.

62. Said, *The Question of Palestine*, 4.

63. Beshara Doumani, "Palestine versus the Palestinians? The Iron Laws and Ironies of a People Denied," *Journal of Palestine Studies* 36, no. 4 (2007): 49–64, at 60.

64. On the one side lie the forces of imperialism and colonialism that view "the planet as private property"; on the other are "movements defending, on a local and global level, the planet as a commons." Vandana Shiva, *Earth Democracy: Justice, Sustainability, and Peace* (Berkeley, CA: North Atlantic Books, 2015). Other representative accounts include Silvia Federici, *Re-Enchanting the World: Feminism and the Politics of the Commons* (Oakland, CA: PM Press, 2018); Massimo De Angelis, *Omnia Sunt Communia: On the Commons and the Transformation to Postcapitalism* (London: Zed Books, 2017). While the land sovereignty framework is open to different forms of land tenure, it too favors the commons. See Franco and Borras Jr., "A 'Land Sovereignty' Alternative?"

65. Peter Linebaugh, "Palestine & the Commons: Or, Marx & the Musha'a," *CounterPunch*, March 1, 2024, https://www.counterpunch.org/2024/03/01/palestine-the-commons-or-marx-the-mushaa/. Representative accounts include Bhandar, *Colonial Lives of Property*; Khaldun Bshara, "Rural Urbanization: The Commodification of Land in Post-Oslo Palestine," in *Reclaiming Space: The 50 Village Project in Rural Palestine*, ed. Khaldun Bshara and Suad Amiry (Ramallah: Riwaq, 2015), 93–103; Fields, *Enclosure*.

66. For an exception that acknowledges the different uses of property (notably, including *waqf*), see Noura Alkhalili, "Enclosures from Below: The Mushaa' in Contemporary Palestine," *Antipode* 49, no. 5 (2017): 1103–24; Noura Alkhalili, "Protection from Below: On Waqf between Theft and Morality," *Jerusalem Quarterly* 70 (2017): 62. Faiq Mari's dissertation, which was published as I was finishing the final revisions on this manuscript, provides an account of *masha'* that explores questions of property and political economy. See Mari, "Masha' of the Periphery."

67. Between my first visit in 2013 and my final visit in 2022, I did around 160 semi-structured interviews in Arabic or English, depending on the native tongue and preference of those I was talking to. Some were as short as twenty minutes, others lasted an hour or more. Usually, they were somewhere in the middle. Sometimes I recorded the interviews with the permission of the speaker. Often I chose not to, and took notes in shorthand that I would type out the same evening.

68. Doing historical research on Palestine requires assembling an archive. There is no central Palestinian archive, and none of the land registries—controlled by Jordan, Israel, and the PA—is open to researchers. To put together sources, I gathered historical data from government ministries in Amman and in the Israeli State

Archives. In the archives of a few village councils, I found documents covering land registration and agriculture before 1967. In libraries across the West Bank and Israel, I found Palestinian works on law and agronomy, as well as collections of Palestinian and Israeli newspapers. Lawyers, property owners, and former leaders of land defense committees saved records of evidence and decisions, and the court cases and legal documents I draw on come from them.

69. Ghertner and Lake, "Introduction: Land Fictions and the Politics of Commodification in City and Country." This is, for example, part of what was at stake in the debate over the role of "absentee" owners in selling land to Zionists before 1948. See Rashid Khalidi, "A Question of Land," *Journal of Palestine Studies* 17, no. 1 (1987): 146–49.

70. John Collins, *Global Palestine* (London: Hurst, 2011), 16.

71. For a few important works that testify to the centrality of Palestine to the question of global justice, see Abunimah, *The Battle for Justice in Palestine*; Collins, *Global Palestine*; Erakat, *Justice for Some*.

Chapter 1

1. Settler arson is common in the West Bank, and Palestinian researchers have documented several cases of settlers burning olive trees in Bruqin over the years. Incidents documented by the Land Research Center include the following: October 13, 2011 (burning 340 trees); October 9, 2018 (cutting down 42 trees); January 3, 2019 (uprooting 30 saplings and 20 older trees); and June 2020 (uprooting saplings). Some of these incidents are also discussed by Human Rights Watch. See Human Rights Watch, "A Threshold Crossed: Israeli Authorities and the Crimes of Apartheid and Persecution" (Human Rights Watch, 2021), 101–4. Many more likely go unreported, as they often occur in areas that are hard to reach and that owners may have given up on reaching.

2. Land Research Center (LRC), "Ravaging 10 Dunums in Farkha Village/Salfit Governorate," October 7, 2019, http://poica.org/2019/10/ravaging-10-dunums-in-farkha-village-salit-governorate/.

3. "Ruined land" is a "perceptual term" that carries different meanings for different users. In their classic *Land Degradation and Society*, Piers Blaikie and Harold Brookfield note that the use of the term "degradation" to talk about land "implies 'reduction to a lower rank.' The rank is in relation to actual or possible uses and reduction implies a problem for those who use the land." To illustrate how degradation is a "relative measurement" and open to "multiple interpretations," they provide the following example: "To a hunter or a herder the replacement of forest by savanna with a greater capacity to carry ruminants would not be perceived as degradation.

Nor would forest replacement by agricultural land be seen as degradation by a colonizing farmer." Piers Blaikie and Harold Brookfield, *Land Degradation and Society* (London: Methuen, 1987), 4.

4. Following Ann Stoler, the concept of ruination offers a "counterpoint to emergency" and tries to make visible "less perceptible effects of imperial interventions and their settling into the social and material ecologies in which people live and survive." As "an act, a condition, and a cause," ruination helps us understand ruins not as "inert remains," but as a complex process that registers how "imperial formations persist in their material debris, in ruined landscapes and through the social ruination of people's lives." See Ann Laura Stoler, " 'The Rot Remains': From Ruins to Ruination," in *Imperial Debris: On Ruins and Ruination*, ed. Ann Laura Stoler (Durham, NC: Duke University Press, 2013), 1–35, at 3–4 and 10.

5. Michael Perelman, *The Invention of Capitalism: Classical Political Economy and the Secret History of Primitive Accumulation* (Durham, NC: Duke University Press, 2000).

6. This interplay of violence, law, and labor is key in Marx's account, and has been elucidated by later commentators. See Liza Grandia, *Enclosed: Conservation, Cattle, and Commerce among the Q'eqchi' Maya Lowlanders* (Seattle: University of Washington Press, 2012); Karl Marx and Ernest Mandel, *Capital: Volume 1: A Critique of Political Economy*, trans. Ben Fowkes (New York: Penguin Classics, 1992).

7. Massimo De Angelis, "Marx and Primitive Accumulation: The Continuous Character of Capital's Enclosures," *The Commoner* 2, no. 01 (2001): 1–22; David Harvey, *The New Imperialism* (Oxford: Oxford University Press, 2003); Michael Levien, *Dispossession without Development: Land Grabs in Neoliberal India* (Oxford: Oxford University Press, 2018); Ben White et al., "The New Enclosures: Critical Perspectives on Corporate Land Deals," *The Journal of Peasant Studies* 39, no. 3–4 (2012): 619–47. For a helpful summary overview of some of these debates in agrarian studies, see Derek Hall, "Primitive Accumulation, Accumulation by Dispossession and the Global Land Grab," *Third World Quarterly* 34, no. 9 (2013): 1582–1604.

8. Marx and Mandel, *Capital*, 876.

9. Jeanette M. Neeson, *Commoners: Common Right, Enclosure and Social Change in England, 1700–1820* (Cambridge, UK: Cambridge University Press, 1996).

10. Neeson, *Commoners*, 30–34.

11. On the long history of enclosure, see Gary Fields, *Enclosure: Palestinian Landscapes in a Historical Mirror* (Berkeley: University of California Press, 2017); Grandia, *Enclosed*. On the diffusion of European racial ideology and property, especially the ideology of improvement, see Stuart Banner, *Possessing the Pacific: Land, Settlers, and Indigenous People from Australia to Alaska* (Cambridge, MA: Harvard University

Press, 2009); Brenna Bhandar, *Colonial Lives of Property: Law, Land, and Racial Regimes of Ownership* (Durham, NC: Duke University Press, 2018); Roxanne Dunbar-Ortiz, *An Indigenous Peoples' History of the United States* (Boston: Beacon Press, 2014); John C. Weaver, *Great Land Rush and the Making of the Modern World, 1650–1900* (Montreal: McGill-Queen's University Press, 2003).

12. Liz Alden Wily, "Looking Back to See Forward: The Legal Niceties of Land Theft in Land Rushes," *The Journal of Peasant Studies* 39, no. 3–4 (2012): 751–75; White et al., "The New Enclosures."

13. Chris Chen, "The Limit Point of Capitalist Equality," *Endnotes* 3 (2013): 202–23.

14. Ruth Wilson Gilmore, *Golden Gulag: Prisons, Surplus, Crisis, and Opposition in Globalizing California* (Berkeley: University of California Press, 2007), 76, 178.

15. Marx and Mandel, *Capital*, 784.

16. Giovanni Arrighi, "Labour Supplies in Historical Perspective: A Study of the Proletarianization of the African Peasantry in Rhodesia," *The Journal of Development Studies* 6, no. 3 (1970): 197–234; Ann Laura Stoler, "Plantation Politics and Protest on Sumatra's East Coast," *The Journal of Peasant Studies* 13, no. 2 (1986): 124–43.

17. Bernard Magubane and Nzongola Ntalaja, eds., "Imperialism and the Making of the South African Working Class," in *Proletarianization and Class Struggle in Africa* (San Francisco: Synthesis Publications, 1983), 19–56, at 23.

18. Achille Mbembe, "Necropolitics," trans. Libby Meintjes, *Public Culture* 15, no. 1 (2003): 11–40.

19. Jeff Halper, "The 94 Percent Solution," *Middle East Report* 216 (Autumn 2000): 14–19; Jeff Halper, "Warehousing a 'Surplus People,' " *Palestine Chronicle*, September 11, 2008. On technology and enclosure in Gaza, see Helga Tawil-Souri, "Digital Occupation: Gaza's High-Tech Enclosure," *Journal of Palestine Studies* 41, no. 2 (2012): 27–43. Andy Clarno also draws on warehousing and surplus population to frame his discussion of Bethlehem. See Andy Clarno, *Neoliberal Apartheid: Palestine/Israel and South Africa after 1994* (Chicago: University of Chicago Press, 2017).

20. David Lloyd and Patrick Wolfe, "Settler Colonial Logics and the Neoliberal Regime," *Settler Colonial Studies* 6, no. 2 (2016): 109–18, at 112. On the world to come, see, for instance, John Collins, *Global Palestine* (London: Hurst, 2011) ; Silvia Federici, "Palestine Is the World (2002)," *PM Press* (blog), March 14, 2024, https://blog.pm-press.org/2024/03/14/palestine-is-the-world-2002/. The planetary generalization of dispossession and human disposability has made surplus populations a central question for those invested in questions of emancipatory politics. See, for example, Joshua Clover, *Riot. Strike. Riot: The New Era of Uprisings* (New York: Verso Books, 2016). For a discussion of the urban bias of much of this writing, see Michael Levien,

Michael Watts, and Hairong Yan, "Agrarian Marxism," *The Journal of Peasant Studies* 45, no. 5–6 (2018): 853–83.

21. On "agrarian milieux," see Levien, *Dispossession without Development*, 17–20.

22. Scott Atran, "Hamula Organisation and Masha'a Tenure in Palestine," *Man* (1986): 271–95; Beshara Doumani, *Rediscovering Palestine: Merchants and Peasants in Jabal Nablus, 1700–1900* (Berkeley: University of California Press, 1995); Susynne McElrone, "From the Pages of the Defter: A Social History of Rural Property Tenure and the Implementation of Tanzimat Land Reform in Hebron, Palestine (1858–1900)," PhD diss., New York University, 2016.

23. Johann Büssow, *Hamidian Palestine: Politics and Society in the District of Jerusalem 1872–1908* (Boston: Brill, 2011); Doumani, *Rediscovering Palestine*.

24. Michael Sfard, "A Guide to Housing, Land and Property Law in Area C of the West Bank" (Norwegian Refugee Council, 2012), 22.

25. Beshara Doumani, "Endowing Family: Waqf, Property Devolution, and Gender in Greater Syria, 1800 to 1860," *Comparative Studies in Society and History* 40, no. 1 (1998): 3–41.

26. Atran, "Hamula Organisation and Masha'a Tenure in Palestine"; Birgit Schaebler, "Practicing Musha: Common Lands and the Common Good in Southern Syria under the Ottomans and the French," in *New Perspectives on Property and Land in the Middle East*, ed. Roger Owen and Martin Bunton (Cambridge, MA: Harvard University Press, 2000), 241–312. While *masha'* was not recognized by the Land Code, new scholarship has shown that Ottoman administrators tolerated, or at least could often do little about, such arrangements. See McElrone, "From the Pages of the Defter: A Social History of Rural Property Tenure and the Implementation of Tanzimat Land Reform in Hebron, Palestine (1858–1900)"; Amos Nadan, "Reconsidering Peasant Communes in the Levant, c. 1850s–1940s," *The Economic History Review* 74, no. 1 (2021): 34–59.

27. On the prior existence of private property in the highlands, see Doumani, *Rediscovering Palestine*. For an updated discussion, see Amos Nadan, "The Route from Informal Peasant Landownership to Formal Tenancy and Eviction in Palestine, 1800s–1947," *Continuity and Change* 36, no. 2 (2021): 233–56.

28. Rashid Khalidi, *Palestinian Identity: The Construction of Modern National Consciousness* (New York: Columbia University Press, 1997); Nadan, "The Route from Informal Peasant Landownership to Formal Tenancy and Eviction in Palestine, 1800s–1947."

29. Sir Ernest Dowson was the main architect of this transformation in Palestine and, like the consultants who would follow him decades later, advocated and administered land reform in Egypt, Iraq, and Transjordan, as well as farther afield in Zanzibar, Uganda, the Gold Coast, Kenya, and Singapore. Michael R. Fischbach,

State, Society, and Land in Jordan (Boston: Brill, 2000); Bhandar, *Colonial Lives of Property*; Geremy Forman, "Settlement of the Title in the Galilee; Dowson's Colonial Guiding Principles," *Israel Studies* 7, no. 3 (2002): 61–83.

30. As Martin Bunton writes, "*musha'* clearly touched the colonial imagination in a vivid way, mostly since it was seen to reflect an earlier stage in the 'natural' evolution of social and economic institutions. Many officials likened *musha'* to the commons, and the perceived tragedies thereof, in an earlier period of European history." See Martin P. Bunton, *Colonial Land Policies in Palestine 1917–1936* (Oxford: Oxford University Press, 2007), 9.

31. Riyad Mousa, "The Dispossession of the Peasantry: Colonial Policies, Settler Capitalism, and Rural Change in Palestine, 1918–1948," PhD diss., University of Utah, 2006; Rachelle Taqqu, "Peasants into Workmen: Internal Labor Migration and the Arab Village Community under the Mandate," in *Palestinian Society and Politics*, ed. Joel S. Migdal (Princeton: Princeton University Press, 1980), 261–85.

32. For a discussion of the progress made by the British settlement of title, see Dov Gavish, *A Survey of Palestine under the British Mandate, 1920–1948* (New York: Routledge, 2005). On resistance, see Noura Alkhalili, "Enclosures from Below: The Mushaa' in Contemporary Palestine," *Antipode* 49, no. 5 (2017): 1103–24; Charles Anderson, "Will the Real Palestinian Peasantry Please Sit Down? Towards a New History of British Rule in Palestine, 1917–1936," LSE Middle East Centre Paper, 2015.

33. Anderson, "Will the Real Palestinian Peasantry Please Sit Down?" 21–22.

34. Charles W. Anderson, "From Petition to Confrontation: The Palestinian National Movement and the Rise of Mass Politics, 1929–1939," PhD diss., New York University, 2013; Charles Anderson, "When Palestinians Became Human Shields: Counterinsurgency, Racialization, and the Great Revolt (1936–1939)," *Comparative Studies in Society and History* 63, no. 3 (2021): 625–54.

35. Rashid Khalidi, *Palestinian Identity: The Construction of Modern National Consciousness* (New York: Columbia University Press, 1997). On later iterations of peasant identity and land struggle, see Ted Swedenburg, "The Palestinian Peasant As National Signifier," *Anthropological Quarterly* 63, no. 1 (1990): 18–30.

36. Diana Allan, "Introduction: Past Continuous," in *Voices of the Nakba*, ed. Diana Allan (London: Pluto Press, 2021), 1–19; Rashid Khalidi, *The Hundred Years' War on Palestine: A History of Settler Colonialism and Resistance, 1917–2017* (New York: Metropolitan Books, 2020), 60.

37. Meron Benvenisti, *Sacred Landscape: The Buried History of the Holy Land since 1948* (Berkeley: University of California Press, 2000); Shira N. Robinson, *Citizen Strangers: Palestinians and the Birth of Israel's Liberal Settler State* (Stanford: Stanford University Press, 2013).

38. Geremy Forman and Alexandre Kedar, "From Arab Land to 'Israel Lands':
The Legal Dispossession of the Palestinians Displaced by Israel in the Wake of 1948,"
Environment and Planning D: Society and Space 22, no. 6 (2004): 809–30; Sabri Jiryis,
"The Legal Structure for the Expropriation and Absorption of Arab Lands in Israel,"
Journal of Palestine Studies 2, no. 4 (1973): 82–104.

39. On the land settlement, see Geremy Forman, "Israeli Settlement of Title in
Arab Areas: The Special Land Settlement Operation in Northern Israel (1955–1967),"
PhD diss., University of Haifa, 2005. Here is how Meron Benvenisti described the use
of military emergency regulations: "First the land would be declared 'a closed area,'
where Arabs were barred from entering the plots they had under cultivation, making
it impossible for them to tend them. Then the minister of agriculture would, in ac-
cordance with the regulations, send 'warnings' to the Arab farmers, informing them
that if they did not cultivate their landholdings, these would be classified as fallow.
Since the Arabs were prevented by the closure orders from working their land, it was
in due course declared 'fallow,' and the minister would then transfer it to Jewish
farmers." Benvenisti, *Sacred Landscape*, 165.

40. Henry Rosenfeld, "From Peasantry to Wage Labor and Residual Peasantry:
The Transformation of an Arab Village," in *Process and Pattern in Culture*, ed. Robert
Manners (Chicago: Aldine Publishing, 1964), 211–34; Elia T. Zureik, "Transformation
of Class Structure among the Arabs in Israel: From Peasantry to Proletariat," *Journal
of Palestine Studies* 6, no. 1 (1976): 39–66.

41. Jeffrey D. Reger, "Olive Cultivation in the Galilee, 1948–1955: Hegemony and
Resistance," *Journal of Palestine Studies* 46, no. 4 (2017): 28–45.

42. Geremy Forman's dissertation details the legal aspects of this struggle. See
Forman, "Israeli Settlement of Title in Arab Areas," 243–50. For an account from one
of the prominent lawyers involved in land defense at the time, see Hanna Nakkara,
Mudhakkarat Muhami Filastini: Hanna Dib Naqqarah, Muhami al-ʾard Wa-al-Shaʾab
(Memoirs of a Palestinian Laywer: Hanna Deeb Nakkara, Lawyer of the Land and
the People), ed. Atallah Said Copty, 2nd ed. (Beirut: Institute for Palestine Studies,
2011).

43. Reger, "Olive Cultivation in the Galilee, 1948–1955."

44. Natalia Gutkowski, *Struggling for Time: Environmental Governance and
Agrarian Resistance in Israel/Palestine* (Stanford: Stanford University Press, 2024),
24.

45. Gutkowski, *Struggling for Time*.

46. From Ottoman surveys we learn that olives were the main crop in these villages, followed by cereals like wheat and barley, as far back as the 1500s. See Amy
Singer, *Palestinian Peasants and Ottoman Officials: Rural Administration around*

Sixteenth-Century Jerusalem (Cambridge, UK: Cambridge University Press, 1994), 77–78.

47. These activities went well beyond the immediate labor processes of plowing, planting, and harvesting. Walid Rabie's account of the fig harvest, for example, written in the early 1970s, details the experiences of children sent by their parents to check for ripe fruit, the hiring of guards, the construction of temporary shelters for those who would need to stay in the fields, and the preparation of meals in the fields. These activities socialized children into the gendered division of labor. Girls helped to prepare food and were given the responsibility of keeping the shelter clean, helping prepare them to care for a household of their own. Boys helped more directly with harvest, assisting the men as they picked fruit and restored the terraces of the fields. See Walid Rabie, "Mawsem al-Tin fi Biladi" (The Fig Season in My Country), *Heritage and Society* 4 (1975): 3–16.

48. Abdulla M. Lutfiyya, *Baytin: A Jordanian Village* (London: Mouton & Co., 1966), 26 and 30–31.

49. Hisham Awartani, "Agricultural Development in the West Bank: An Economic and Political Study of the Development of Rain-Fed Farming in the West Bank," PhD diss., University of Bradford, 1982, 101–3.

50. Jamil Hilal, "West Bank and Gaza Strip Social Formation under Jordanian and Egyptian Rule (1948–1967)," *Review of Middle East Studies* 5 (1992): 33–73.

51. In the central highlands, "peasant indebtedness to wealthy landlords" remained the main source of differentiation until the end of British rule. See Salim Tamari, "The Dislocation and Re-Constitution of a Peasantry: The Social Economy of Agrarian Palestine in the Central Highlands and the Jordan Valley, 1960–1980," PhD diss., University of Manchester, 1983, 226–27. Yearly reports from the Jordanian Department of Lands and Surveys that I viewed in Amman, for example, continued sounding alarms about rural debt from 1950 all the way until 1967. There is a lack of detailed research on debt during this period. Awartani argues that by 1967, a combination of state institutions and private firms provided short-term credit at reasonable rates to West Bank agriculturalists, while Hilal argues that small producers were by and large left to the whims of moneylenders. Michael Fischbach argues that in 1963, the Temporary Law Amending the Land Tax Law eliminated taxes on rain-fed land and lifted some pressure on the peasants. See Hisham Awartani, "Agricultural Development in the West Bank: An Economic and Political Study of the Development of Rain-Fed Farming in the West Bank," PhD diss., University of Bradford, 1982, 140–43; Michael R. Fischbach, "The Implications of Jordanian Land Policy for the West Bank," *Middle East Journal* 48, no. 3 (1994): 492–509, at 503; Jamil Hilal, *Al-Diffa al-Gharbiyya: Al-Tarkib al-Ijtima'i wa-*

al-Iqtisadi (1948–1974) (West Bank: Economic and Social Structure) (Beirut: PLO Research Center, 1974), 155.

52. According to Jamil Hilal, by the mid-1960s, the West Bank was producing 60 percent of Jordan's fruit, and 80 percent of Jordan's olives. Historian Jeffrey Reger has argued that "planting by Palestinians in the early Jordanian period continued at nearly the same rate as the Mandate period. The significance of this fact is to show that, at least in the olive sector, Palestinian agriculture continued to expand, rather than stagnate, as has been popularly assumed." See Hilal, "West Bank and Gaza Strip Social Formation under Jordanian and Egyptian Rule (1948–1967)"; Jeffrey Drew Reger, "Planting Palestine: The Political Economy of Olive Culture in the 20th Century Galilee and West Bank," PhD diss., Georgetown University, 2018.

53. Petitions from mukhtars of Qarawa and Kafr Ayn (in Arabic), Israel State Archive (hereafter ISA), MGA 38/25, Metan Ha-Levaot l-Ha-Khaklaot (Giving Loans for Agriculture), August 6, 1959.

54. Agriculture Inspection Committee Report 1960–1961 (in Arabic); ISA 38/26, File: "Khaklaot–Keleli (Agriculture–General)," August 25, 1961. In neighboring Kafr Ayn, accusations surfaced that the village mukhtar and some local merchants had manipulated the official beneficiary list in order to siphon off hundreds of kilos of wheat, leading to an extensive police investigation, the interrogation of multiple witnesses, and the involvement of the local governor. See Correspondence and Testimonies Related to Theft of Grain Shares in Kafr Ayn and Its Sale in Surrounding Villages (in Arabic); ISA, MGA 39/1, April 1961.

55. See Correspondence between Sub-Governor of Ramallah, Governor of Jerusalem, Minister of National Economy, and Minister of Agriculture (in Arabic); ISA, MGA 39/19, File: Khaklaot (Agriculture): February 1961–February 1963, especially April 1962.

56. Correspondence between Sub-Governor of Ramallah, Governor of Jerusalem, and Ramallah District Village Councils (in Arabic); ISA, MGA 39/9, File: "Batsoret–Ramallah (Drought–Ramallah) May–October 1963." While these files do not include requests from the villages in question, they do include nearby villages, leading me to suspect that the whole area was likely affected.

57. See Marisa Escribano and Nazmi El-Joubeh, "Migration and Change in a West Bank Village: The Case of Deir Dibwan," *Journal of Palestine Studies* 11, no. 1 (1981): 150–60; Lutfiyya, *Baytin*; Tamari, "The Dislocation and Re-Constitution of a Peasantry: The Social Economy of Agrarian Palestine in the Central Highlands and the Jordan Valley, 1960–1980."

58. Joel S. Migdal, *Palestinian Society and Politics* (Princeton: Princeton University Press, 1980), 63.

59. Adel Samara, "The Political Economy of the West Bank 1967–1987: From Peripheralization to Development," in *Palestine: Profile of an Occupation* (London: Zed Books, 1989), 7–31, at 20.

60. The Israeli Jews who began to colonize the territories enjoyed the rights and privileges of Israeli citizenship. The Palestinian Arabs who lived there were direct subjects of military rule. The military ruled directly until 1981, and then indirectly through a governing apparatus called the Civil Administration.

61. Awartani, "Agricultural Development in the West Bank"; Leila Farsakh, *Palestinian Labour Migration to Israel: Labour, Land and Occupation* (London: Routledge, 2005); Neve Gordon, *Israel's Occupation* (Berkeley: University of California Press, 2008); Reger, "Planting Palestine." According to the Palestinian Agricultural Relief Committees (PARC), "the budget for agricultural research declined from $59,000 in 1972 to $14,600 in 1981" and "the number of extension workers declined from 464 in 1975 to 219 in 1987." Samir Abed-Rabbo and Doris Safie, eds., *The Palestinian Uprising: FACTS Information Committee, Jerusalem* (Belmont: Association of Arab-American University Graduates, 1990), 296–97.

62. In the early years, according to Gordon, "the Palestinians who worked in Israel earned anywhere from 10 to 100 percent more than they would have if they worked in the territories, depending on their occupations. As a result, the average daily wages of all employees from the West Bank rose by 35 percent in the period 1970–74 and by 13 percent during the period 1974–79. In the Gaza Strip, wages rose by 50 and 18.4 percent, respectively." Wage differences, according to Lila Farsakh, gradually decreased. See Farsakh, *Palestinian Labour Migration to Israel*; Gordon, *Israel's Occupation,* 64–65.

63. Yusif Sayigh, "Dispossession and Pauperisation: The Palestinian Economy under Occupation," in *The Palestinian Economy: Studies in Development under Prolonged Occupation*, ed. George T. Abed (London: Routledge, 1988), 260–61.

64. The Land Code classified agricultural lands as *miri*. The sultan held ultimate right of ownership (*rakaba*), and cultivators had extensive use rights (*tassaruf*). Those who cultivated land for a period of ten years could apply for a title deed. *Miri* land that was left uncultivated for three years could become *mahlul,* giving the sultan (in effect, the Ottoman state) the right to transfer it to others. Finally, *mawat,* or "dead" land, referred to land deemed unsuitable for cultivation, and the Ottoman government encouraged its reclamation. The point of the Land Code was to increase tax revenues by encouraging agriculture and creating a private market for land. Israeli legal doctrine was different. It claimed *miri* lands that had not been titled by the Jordan government were state property. It included *mahlul* land not cultivated for three years, *miri* land not cultivated for ten consecutive years, and *mawat* land.

This interpretation amounted to a radical transformation of Ottoman law, one whose intent was not to increase agricultural production, but to transfer as much land as possible from Palestinian cultivators to exclusive Israeli state control for use in settlement expansion. See Yehezkel Lein and Eyal Weizman, "Land Grab: Israel's Settlement Policy in the West Bank" (Jerusalem: B'Tselem, 2002).

65. Ian Lustick, "Israel and the West Bank after Elon Moreh: The Mechanics of de Facto Annexation," *Middle East Journal* 35, no. 4 (1981): 557–77.

66. Raja Shehadeh, "The Land Law of Palestine: An Analysis of the Definition of State Lands," *Journal of Palestine Studies* 11, no. 2 (1982): 82–99; Aziz Shehadeh, "From the Court Records: 1. The Concept of State Land in the Occupied Territories," *The Palestine Yearbook of International Law Online* 2, no. 1 (January 1, 1985): 163–87.

67. Their opportunity came in the 1970s, when an elected government favorable to their project faced an economic crisis that began to make it more difficult to build housing and obtain mortgages in Israel. While it is well established that the Israeli Supreme Court provided the legal basis for colonization on "state lands" in the 1979 Elon Moreh ruling, what is less remarked upon is that, according to geographer Yael Allweil, "in November 1979, as inflation rates reached 80 percent, the Israeli government issued decision no. 145 to expand settlements in Judea and Samaria, Gaza, the Golan, and the Jordan Valley on state land managed by the JA." Yael Allweil, "Neoliberal Settlement As Violent State Project," *ACME: An International Journal for Critical Geographies* 19, no. 1 (2020): 70–105, at 81.

68. See Allweil, "Neoliberal Settlement"; David Newman, "Settlement as Suburbanization: The Banality of Colonization," in *Normalizing Occupation: The Politics of Everyday Life in the West Bank Settlements*, ed. Marco Allegra, Ariel Handel, and Erez Maggor (Bloomington: Indiana University Press, 2017), 34–47.

69. Salim Tamari, "Building Other People's Homes: The Palestinian Peasant's Household and Work in Israel," *Journal of Palestine Studies* 11, no. 1 (1981): 31–66.

70. Tamari, "The Dislocation and Re-Constitution of a Peasantry: The Social Economy of Agrarian Palestine in the Central Highlands and the Jordan Valley, 1960–1980," 236.

71. Awartani worried that agricultural decline might be much worse than suspected, since statistics did not account for "vast areas of deserted tree orchards which, nominally, are still in production." Tamari noted "widespread neglect" of the olive crop in north Ramallah. See Awartani, "Agricultural Development in the West Bank," 110; Tamari, "The Dislocation and Re-Constitution of a Peasantry: The Social Economy of Agrarian Palestine in the Central Highlands and the Jordan Valley, 1960–1980," 225. Also see Sumaya Farhat-Naser, *Zaytun Filastin Wa-Mushkilatuha* (Olives of Palestine and Their Problems) (Birzeit: Birzeit University, 1980); Dawood

Istanbuli, "Al-Insan al-Zira'i" (The Agricultural Individual), in *Mu'tamir al-Tanmiyya min Ajl al-Sumud* (Development for Sumud Conference) (Arab Thought Forum, 1982), 15.

72. The various crops that anchored village life were a yearlong concern, and those who worked the land spent a great deal of time dealing with the requisite tasks. For a survey of these activities in the central highlands during this time, see Munir Naser, "Al-Nashat al-Zira'i l-Falah Bir Zeit 'ala Mudar al-Sina" (The Agricultural Activities of the Birzeit Peasant over the Year), *Heritage and Society* 1 (1974): 70–80.

73. Sayigh, "Dispossession and Pauperisation," 264–68. He uses the term "primitive appropriation."

74. Tamari, "Building Other People's Homes"; Reger, "Planting Palestine." In Deir Ballut, Omar Tesdell and his co-authors found that labor migration not only changed the gendered division of labor, but resulted in increased crop diversity. See Omar Tesdell, Yusra Othman, and Saher Alkhoury, "Rainfed Agroecosystem Resilience in the Palestinian West Bank, 1918–2017," *Agroecology and Sustainable Food Systems* 43, no. 1 (2019): 21–39.

75. Sobhi Samour, "The Palestinian Economy between Settler Colonial Invasion and Neoliberal Management," PhD diss., School of Oriental and African Studies (SOAS), 2016. There has been a great deal written on this issue. See, for example, Yael Berda, *Living Emergency: Israel's Permit Regime in the Occupied West Bank* (Stanford University Press, 2017); Farsakh, *Palestinian Labour Migration to Israel*; Tobias Kelly, *Law, Violence and Sovereignty among West Bank Palestinians* (Cambridge, UK: Cambridge University Press, 2006).

76. Samour, "The Palestinian Economy," 177.

77. Israel denies Palestinians access to 99 percent of Area C. This affects not only construction, but also any kind of urban planning, agricultural development (much of Area C is some of the most prized arable land in the West Bank), and even humanitarian aid. See Leilani Farha, "Area C Is Everything: Planning for the Future of Palestine" (Oslo: Norwegian Refugee Council, 2023); Nir Shalev and Alon Cohen-Lifshitz, "The Prohibited Zone, Israeli Planning Policy in the Palestinian Villages in Area C" (Jerusalem: Bimkom–Planners for Planning Rights, 2008). For an ethnographic study of how this permit regime affects highland farmers, see Irene Calis, "Routine and Rupture: The Everyday Workings of Abyssal (Dis)order in the Palestinian Food Basket," *American Ethnologist* 44, no. 1 (2017): 65–76.

78. For calculations of lost land, which includes land taken for settlement construction, covered by Area C, and projected to be lost behind the Separation Barrier, see Land Research Center (LRC), "Olive Seedlings and Metal Corners Stolen by Set-

tlers in Bruqin Village Land—Salfit Governorate—POICA," June 6, 2020, http://poica.org/2020/06/olive-seedlings-and-metal-corners-stolen-by-settlers-in-bruqin-village-land-salfit-governorate/.

79. Sophia Stamatopoulou-Robbins, *Waste Siege: The Life of Infrastructure in Palestine* (Stanford: Stanford University Press, 2020).

80. As early as 2005 the Land Research Center noted that "the area has been visited by a number of local and foreign Human Rights and juristic delegations," and subsequent years would see more visits and reports by various researchers, human rights organizations, and NGOs, all of which documented the effects on human health, water, and soil. These have included B'Tselem, Land Research Center, Applied Research Institute–Jerusalem, UNICEF, the Palestinian Hydrology Group, and Human Rights Watch. For details, see Saad Amira, "The Slow Violence of Israeli Settler-Colonialism and the Political Ecology of Ethnic Cleansing in the West Bank," *Settler Colonial Studies* 11, no. 4 (2021): 512–32; Eyal Hareuveni, "Foul Play: Neglect of Wastewater Treatment in the West Bank" (Jerusalem: B'Tselem, 2009); Human Rights Watch, "A Threshold Crossed: Israeli Authorities and the Crimes of Apartheid and Persecution."

81. On al-Matwi, Saad Amira writes that the spring was "once a popular tourist destination" and has now "lost its value through a combination of boars and sewage." See Amira, "The Slow Violence of Israeli Settler-Colonialism and the Political Ecology of Ethnic Cleansing in the West Bank," 526.

82. According to a resident of Bruqin interviewed by a human rights organization in 2009, "Nobody eats the produce we grow, especially the vegetables, because my family and neighbors are afraid that the juice in the vegetables is contaminated by the wastewater." Human Rights Watch notes: "it was recounted to us that some farmers graze animals near the wastewater discharges, especially in the summer when the only green grass that can be found is around sewage water. Although scientific analyses have yet to be done, residents and populations in the surrounding area believe that the heavy metals and chemicals have contaminated the milk of local livestock, and as a result, dairy products from the area are reportedly difficult to sell." Penny Johnson encountered this sentiment as well. See Hareuveni, "Foul Play: Neglect of Wastewater Treatment in the West Bank," 32; Human Rights Watch, "A Threshold Crossed: Israeli Authorities and the Crimes of Apartheid and Persecution"; Penny Johnson, *Companions in Conflict: Animals in Occupied Palestine* (New York: Melville House, 2019).

83. As anthropologist Radhika Govindrajan points out, wild boars are a "weed species" because, "like weed plants, they seek out and thrive in contexts that are often characterized as 'human dominated.'" Radhika Govindrajan, *Animal Intima-*

cies: Interspecies Relatedness in India's Central Himalayas (Chicago: University of Chicago Press, 2019). For reporting on this question, which goes back more than a decade, see Nora Lester-Murad, "Do Pigs Fly—Or Is This a Matter of Human Rights?" *The View from My Window in Palestine* (blog), December 14, 2012, https://noralestermurad.com/do-pigs-fly-or-is-this-a-matter-of-human-rights/; Ben Hattem, "The Wild Boar and Feces Epidemic in Palestine," *Vice* (blog), January 3, 2014, https://www.vice.com/en/article/exmnya/the-wild-boar-and-feces-epidemic-in-palestine; Rawan Samamreh, "Wild Boars in Palestine Are Being Weaponized by Israeli Colonialism," *Mondoweiss* (blog), November 13, 2022, https://mondoweiss.net/2022/11/wild-boars-in-palestine-are-being-weaponized-by-israeli-colonialism/. For discussion on responsibility, see Amira, "Slow Violence"; Johnson, *Companions in Conflict*.

84. Amira, "Slow Violence," 524.

85. Caroline Abu-Sada, "Cultivating Dependence: Palestinian Agriculture under the Israeli Occupation," in *The Power of Inclusive Exclusion: Anatomy of Israeli Rule in the Occupied Palestinian Territories*, ed. Sari Hanafi, Adi Ophir, and Michal Givoni (New York: Zone Books, 2009), 413–29, at 426.

86. For extensive documentation, see Abu-Sada, "Cultivating Dependence"; Farsakh, *Palestinian Labour Migration to Israel*; Sara M. Roy, *The Gaza Strip: The Political Economy of de-Development* (Washington, DC: Institute for Palestine Studies, 1995); UNCTAD, "The Besieged Palestinian Agricultural Sector" (New York: United Nations, 2015).

87. Gordon, *Israel's Occupation*, 2.

88. Clarno, *Neoliberal Apartheid*, 112.

89. Abu-Sada, "Cultivating Dependence."

90. Such practices—which anthropologist Robert Netting ascribes to "smallholders," and which others might call "indigenous" or "agroecological"—are often uniquely appropriate to local ecological conditions and provide a knowledge base that rural people draw on and transform. Robert McC. Netting, *Smallholders, Householders: Farm Families and the Ecology of Intensive, Sustainable Agriculture* (Stanford: Stanford University Press, 1993). On the endurance of traditional knowledge in the West Bank, see Ismail Daiq, *The Local Knowledge System for Plant Protection and Soil Conservation in Rain-Fed Agriculture in the West Bank, Palestine* (Berlin: Margraf, 2005); Tesdell, Othman, and Alkhoury, "Rainfed Agroecosystem Resilience in the Palestinian West Bank, 1918–2017."

91. For an account of this organizing from one of the participants, see Palestinian Grassroots Anti-Apartheid Wall Campaign (Stop the Wall) and Addameer, "Repression Allowed, Resistance Denied: Israel's Suppression of the Popular Movement

against the Apartheid Annexation Wall" (Ramallah: Stop the Wall, 2009). For an overview, see Michael J. Carpenter, *Palestinian Popular Struggle: Unarmed and Participatory* (London: Routledge, 2018).

92. After Hamas won the Palestinian elections in 2006, a failed coup (backed by Britain and the United States) resulted in a Palestinian political split. Hamas stayed in power in the Gaza Strip, while Fatah seized control of the West Bank.

93. Raja Khalidi and Sobhi Samour, "Neoliberalism As Liberation: The Statehood Program and the Remaking of the Palestinian National Movement," *Journal of Palestine Studies* 40, no. 2 (2011): 6–25; Kareem Rabie, *Palestine Is Throwing a Party and the Whole World Is Invited: Capital and State Building in the West Bank* (Durham, NC: Duke University Press, 2021).

94. Located 9 km north of Ramallah, it has cost $1.5 billion, and it is supposed to house 40,000 people. On the city, see Rabie, *Palestine Is Throwing a Party,* 8. As of 2024, the city is only a quarter full. See Sarah Treleaven and Jamie Levin, "The Impossible Promise of Building a New Palestinian City," *The Walrus*, April 8, 2024, https://thewalrus.ca/rawabi/.

95. For instance, see Ali Abunimah, *The Battle for Justice in Palestine* (Chicago: Haymarket Books, 2014); Uri Davis, "Rawabi Remains Settler-Colonial Sub-Contractor," *BDS Movement* (blog), March 31, 2011, https://bdsmovement.net/news/rawabi-remains-settler-colonial-sub-contractor; Tina Grandinetti, "The Palestinian Middle Class in Rawabi: Depoliticizing the Occupation," *Alternatives* 40, no. 1 (2015): 63–78.

96. Ruth Wilson Gilmore demonstrates how the crisis of commercial agriculture, and the related collapse of local rural economies, led to the abandonment or idling of thousands of acres of farmland in California. Gilmore, *Golden Gulag*, 64–70.

97. For some examples, see Clarno, *Neoliberal Apartheid*; Samir Harb, "Imaginary and Autonomy: Urbanisation, Construction, and Cement Production in Palestine," PhD diss., University of Manchester, 2020; Maha Nassar et al., "Agricultural Land Use Change and Its Drivers in the Palestinian Landscape under Political Instability, the Case of Tulkarm City," *Journal of Borderlands Studies* 34, no. 3 (2019): 377–94; Fadia Panosetti and Laurence Roudart, "Evolving Regimes of Land Use and Property in the West Bank," *Jerusalem Quarterly* 89 (2022): 10–31; Linda Tabar and Samia Al-Botmeh, "Real Estate Development through Land Grabs: Predatory Accumulation and Precarity in Palestine," *New Political Economy* 26, no. 5 (2021): 783-796.

98. Outside of Bethlehem, Andy Clarno argues that these "neoliberal enclosures" have become spaces of a landscape where restaurants, hotels, and villas of the Pales-

tinian elite stand in stark contrast to the refugee camps and villages of the dispossessed. Clarno, *Neoliberal Apartheid*, 96–97.

99. Farshad A. Araghi, "Global Depeasantization, 1945–1990," *The Sociological Quarterly* 36, no. 2 (1995): 337–68; Mike Davis, *Planet of Slums* (New York: Verso, 2006).

100. Levien, Watts, and Yan, "Agrarian Marxism"; Tania Murray Li, "To Make Live or Let Die? Rural Dispossession and the Protection of Surplus Populations," *Antipode* 41, no. s1 (2010): 66–93; Pauline E. Peters, "Land Appropriation, Surplus People and a Battle over Visions of Agrarian Futures in Africa," *The Journal of Peasant Studies* 40, no. 3 (2013): 537–62.

Chapter 2

1. For discussions of "neoliberal Palestine," see Ali Abunimah, *The Battle for Justice in Palestine* (Chicago: Haymarket Books, 2014); Raja Khalidi and Sobhi Samour, "Neoliberalism As Liberation: The Statehood Program and the Remaking of the Palestinian National Movement," *Journal of Palestine Studies* 40, no. 2 (2011): 6–25; Kareem Rabie, *Palestine Is Throwing a Party and the Whole World Is Invited: Capital and State Building in the West Bank* (Durham, NC: Duke University Press, 2021).

2. Brenna Bhandar, *Colonial Lives of Property: Law, Land, and Racial Regimes of Ownership* (Durham, NC: Duke University Press, 2018); K-Sue Park, "Money, Mortgages, and the Conquest of America," *Law & Social Inquiry* 41, no. 4 (2016): 1006–35; Robert Nichols, *Theft Is Property! Dispossession and Critical Theory* (Durham, NC: Duke University Press, 2020).

3. William Cronon, *Changes in the Land: Indians, Colonists, and the Ecology of New England* (New York: Hill & Wang, 2011), 69.

4. By "sovereignty," I am following Cronon not to mean the specific form of European political authority over a discrete territory, but to distinguish between land tenure within a political community, and the relationship between different political authorities.

5. Cronon, *Changes in the Land*.

6. Patrick Wolfe, "Settler Colonialism and the Elimination of the Native," *Journal of Genocide Research* 8, no. 4 (2006): 387–409, at 400.

7. Allan Greer, *Property and Dispossession: Natives, Empires and Land in Early Modern North America* (Cambridge, UK: Cambridge University Press, 2018), 3.

8. Stuart Banner, *Possessing the Pacific: Land, Settlers, and Indigenous People from Australia to Alaska* (Cambridge, MA: Harvard University Press, 2009); David A. Chang, *The Color of the Land: Race, Nation, and the Politics of Landownership in Oklahoma, 1832–1929* (Chapel Hill: University of North Carolina Press, 2010); Charles R.

Hale, "Neoliberal Multiculturalism," *PoLAR: Political and Legal Anthropology Review* 28, no. 1 (2005): 10–19; Paul Nadasdy, "'Property' and Aboriginal Land Claims in the Canadian Subarctic: Some Theoretical Considerations," *American Anthropologist* 104, no. 1 (2002): 247–61; Joel Wainwright and Joe Bryan, "Cartography, Territory, Property: Postcolonial Reflections on Indigenous Counter-Mapping in Nicaragua and Belize," *Cultural Geographies* 16, no. 2 (2009): 153–78.

9. Kristen Alff, "Changing Capitalist Structures and Settler-Colonial Land Purchases in Northern Palestine, 1897–1922," *International Journal of Middle East Studies* 55, no. 4 (2023): 675–92; Yossi Katz, *The "Business" of Settlement: Private Entrepreneurship in the Jewish Settlement of Palestine, 1900–1914* (Jerusalem: Hebrew University Magnes Press, 1994); Gershon Shafir, *Land, Labor and the Origins of the Israeli-Palestinian Conflict, 1882–1914* (Berkeley: University of California Press, 1996).

10. While this is not his explicit argument, historian Kenneth Stein documents all of this in detail. See Kenneth Stein, *The Land Question in Palestine, 1917–1939* (Chapel Hill: University of North Carolina Press, 1984).

11. Again, Kenneth Stein provides extensive evidence for these practices: Stein, *The Land Question in Palestine, 1917–1939*. Also see Raya Adler, "The Tenants of Wadi Hawarith: Another View of the Land Question in Palestine," *International Journal of Middle East Studies* 20, no. 2 (1988): 197–220, at 200–202.

12. Charles Anderson, "Will the Real Palestinian Peasantry Please Sit Down? Towards a New History of British Rule in Palestine, 1917–1936," LSE Middle East Centre Paper, 2015; Dov Gavish, *A Survey of Palestine under the British Mandate, 1920–1948* (New York: Routledge, 2005), 163; Stein, *The Land Question in Palestine, 1917–1939*.

13. Adler, "The Tenants of Wadi Hawarith"; Munir Fakher Eldin, "Communities of Owners: Land Law, Governance, and Politics in Palestine, 1858–1948," PhD diss., New York University, 2008.

14. Sherene Seikaly, *Men of Capital: Scarcity and Economy in Mandate Palestine* (Stanford: Stanford University Press, 2015).

15. Eldin, "Communities of Owners"; Ylana Miller, *Government and Society in Rural Palestine, 1920–1948* (Austin: University of Texas Press, 1985), 19; Sreemati Mitter, "Bankrupt: Financial Life in Late Mandate Palestine," *International Journal of Middle East Studies* 52, no. 2 (2020): 289–310.

16. Eldin, "Communities of Owners"; Munir Fakher Eldin, "The Middle Class and the Land Struggle in Palestine: Revisiting the Colonial Encounter in the Beisan Valley, 1908–1948," *Comparative Studies of South Asia, Africa and the Middle East* 43, no. 3 (December 1, 2023): 249–61.

17. By 1948, the Zionist movement had purchased 6 percent of Mandate Palestine, and 20 percent of the arable land. See Rashid Khalidi, "A Question of Land," *Journal of Palestine Studies* 17, no. 1 (1987): 146–49. On the legal dispossession of the

rest, see Geremy Forman and Alexandre Kedar, "From Arab Land to 'Israel Lands': The Legal Dispossession of the Palestinians Displaced by Israel in the Wake of 1948," *Environment and Planning D: Society and Space* 22, no. 6 (2004): 809–30.

18. Forman and Kedar, "From Arab Land to 'Israel Lands,' " 823–25.

19. Since 1967, for strategic legal and political reasons, the Israeli state has refrained from formally declaring sovereign rule over the West Bank and Gaza Strip. Amahl Bishara, "Sovereignty and Popular Sovereignty for Palestinians and Beyond," *Cultural Anthropology* 32, no. 3 (2017): 349–58.

20. These legal changes have been well documented. See Yehezkel Lein and Eyal Weizman, "Land Grab: Israel's Settlement Policy in the West Bank" (Jerusalem: B'Tselem, 2002); Nir Shalev, "Under the Guise of Legality: Israel's Declarations of State Land in the West Bank" (Jerusalem: B'Tselem, February 2012); Raja Shehadeh, "The Land Law of Palestine: An Analysis of the Definition of State Lands," *Journal of Palestine Studies* 11, no. 2 (1982): 82–99.

21. In 1985, 41 percent of the land was under "direct possession of the Israelis" through "state lands, requisitions, closure, and compulsory purchase," while an addition 11 percent faced significant restrictions. See Usama Halabi, Aron Turner, and Meron Benvenisti, *Land Alienation in the West Bank: A Legal and Spatial Analysis* (Jerusalem: West Bank Data Base Project, 1985), 85–87.

22. Since the 2000s, researchers working for B'Tselem have provided some of the best documentation and analysis of state lands doctrine. The Israeli state does not provide publicly available data as to the mechanisms or total area of state lands, and calculations come from Lein and Weizman, "Land Grab"; Eyal Hareuveni, "By Hook and by Crook: Israeli Settlement Policy in the West Bank" (Jerusalem: B'Tselem, 2010). The final calculation is drawn from B'Tselem and Forensic Architecture, "Divide and Conquer: The Shattering of Palestinian Space," https://conquer-and-divide.btselem.org/map-en.html.

23. Walter Lehn and Uri Davis, *The Jewish National Fund* (London: Kegan Paul International, 1988). In 1971, the JNF's subsidiary Hemnutah (registered in Ramallah in 1971) sought to quietly purchase land from West Bank Palestinians. Press accounts indicate that there may have been a "land craze" in the early 1970s fueled by the JNF and speculators. Whatever market may have existed crashed after a Jordanian law instated enforceable punishments on land sellers and many sales were revealed to be fraudulent. A detailed account appeared in 1976 in *Shu'un Filistiniyya* (Palestinian Affairs) narrating the problem of unregistered land, brokers, and an attempt by urban landlords to sell land to an Israeli buyer. See Saleh Abduljawwad, "Tajarib min al-ʾArd al-Muhtala: Beit Diqqu that al-Qamh al-Asfar" (Experiences from the Occupied Land: The Yellow Wheat of Beit Diqqu), *Shu'un Filistiniyya* 55 (1976): 95–104.

24. Eli Tavor, "Private Enterprise Settlements: Israelis Change Shekels into Villas

in West Bank," *Al-Fajr Weekly*, November 30, 1981. On early Zionist entrepreneurial-ism, see Katz, *The "Business" of Settlement*.

25. Raja Shehadeh, *Occupier's Law: Israel and the West Bank*, 2nd ed. (Washing-ton, DC: Institute for Palestine Studies, 1988); Mohammed Nazal, *Tasrib al-ʾAradi wa-al-ʿAqarat fi al-Diffa al-Gharbiyya* (The Illicit Transfer of Land and Property in the West Bank), (Ramallah: Self-published, 2016).

26. Plia Albeck, who perhaps did more than any other single individual to ad-vance the expansion of Jewish settlement in the West Bank during the 1980s, had the following to say about private purchases in 1985: "From every 100 land sale transac-tions carried out by Arabs in Judea and Samaria to Jews from Israel, 99 of them are based on forgery. Despite this fact, nine out of ten transactions were approved." See Nazal, *Illicit Transfer*. The quote is taken from "Land in Judea and Samaria," a lecture given on May 28, 1985, at Beit Hapraklit (Attorneys' House).

27. The fact that the Jordanian settlement of title had not been completed before the war meant that much of the land private developers hoped to acquire was not titled. Instead, there were Jordanian tax registers that listed the name of whoever had paid the land tax.

28. In the 1980s, land brokers were often affiliated with the Village Leagues, which gave them access to weapons and, more important, the support of the mili-tary authorities. Salim Tamari, "In League with Zion: Israel's Search for a Native Pillar," *Journal of Palestine Studies* 12, no. 4 (1983): 41–56; Neve Gordon, *Israel's Occu-pation* (Berkeley: University of California Press, 2008).

29. After 1967, the Jordanian government was worried about land sales, and in order to prevent forgeries restricted the reproduction of maps and registration doc-uments. See Fischbach, "The Implications of Jordanian Land Policy for the West Bank," 504. During the 1981 Steadfastness Conference, Ala al-Bakri argued for more attention to be given to the problem of land sales by Palestinians living abroad in Cyprus and North and South America. Arab Thought Forum, *Muʾtamir al-Tanmiyya min Ajl al-Sumud* (Development for Sumud Conference), 149–52. That same year, Elyas Khoury, a respected Palestinian lawyer who litigated a number of influential land cases in the 1980s, accused Hamnutah of using agents to sign power of attorney agreements with Palestinians in South America who had inheritance rights to land in the West Bank. The example he provides is from a village outside of Bethlehem, where such agreements were presented as evidence of a sale even though the land in question was undivided among the heirs. The statement was sent to the Israeli Min-istry of Justice. Presumably written in Hebrew, it was translated into English and published in *Al-Fajr Weekly* in 1981. See Elyas Khoury, "Elias Khouri's Letter: Fight for Land in the Courts and on the Ground," *Al-Fajr Weekly*, February 22, 1981.

30. For reports that give a sense of these operations in the early 1980s, see these articles by Al-Fajr Staff in *Al-Fajr Weekly*: "Israel's Covert Land Grabs Revealed," September 6, 1981; "Highlights of Recent Settlement Activity," October 16, 1981; "End of Israeli Rainbow in West Bank," February 29, 1982; "Anatomy of a Forged Land Deal," April 8, 1983. See also Nura Sus, "Losing the Land to Ten New Settlements," *Al-Fajr Weekly*, January 26, 1981; Tavor, "Private Enterprise Settlements: Israelis Change Shekels into Villas in West Bank"; Amos Levav, "The Israeli Gold Rush," *Al-Fajr Weekly*, January 22, 1982. In 1981, one report claimed that Judea and Samaria for Real Estate and Development was able to sell land it had acquired at $750 per dunum for $3,000, a profit of 300 percent over two or three years. In 1982, a *New York Times* article noted that prices had risen even higher, from an initial price of $1,500 up to $15,000. David Shipler, "Israel Changing Face of West Bank," *New York Times*, September 12, 1982. This boom drew in speculators with little interest in Jewish settlement, and veteran settler leaders worried that these speculators were driving up prices and defrauding buyers. On the relationship between Israeli housing policy, suburban development, and West Bank colonization, see David Newman, "Settlement As Suburbanization: The Banality of Colonization," in *Normalizing Occupation: The Politics of Everyday Life in the West Bank Settlements*, ed. Ariel Handel, Marco Allegra, and Erez Maggor (Bloomington: Indiana University Press, 2017), 34–47.

31. In the summer of 1985, the arrest of three Israelis as part of a land ring—among them the former military governor of Tulkarm—resulted in a scandal that captured the headlines for months in the Israeli and Palestinian press.

32. Nazal estimated that there were at least sixty active companies involved in private land acquisition in the 2010s. From 2005 until 2016, Peace Now and Yesh Din litigated almost a hundred cases against these outposts (or settlements that are established without official recognition or planning from the state, but often retroactively legalized), many of which settler groups attempted to shore up with forged documents attesting to some previous sale. As a result of litigation, new outpost creation came to a halt (for a time), and, according to the lawyer Michael Sfard, "construction on privately owned Palestinian land stopped completely." See Sfard, *The Wall and the Gate*, 338–62.

33. Shlomy Zachary, "Renewing Settlement of Title in Area C in the West Bank: A Breach of International Law and Violation of Palestinians' Rights" (Tel Aviv: Yesh Din, April 2021).

34. Nir Hasson and Hagar Shezaf, "JNF Set to Approve Plan That Could Lead to Palestinians' Eviction," *Haaretz*, August 5, 2021; Times of Israel Staff, "KKL-JNF Leadership Approves Purchase of West Bank Land for Isolated Settlements," *Times of Israel*, April 11, 2021.

35. Within Israel, on the other hand, we find Zionist opposition to market liberalization and land privatization, which is seen as a threat to Jewish control over the land. For an example of this position, see Yossi Katz, *The Jewish National Fund and the History of State Ownership of Land in Israel* (Berlin: De Gruyter and Jerusalem: Hebrew University Magnes Press, 2016).

36. For a discussion of the native "right" to sell, see Nichols, *Theft Is Property!* 33.

37. Arab Thought Forum, *Mu'tamir al-Tanmiyya min Ajl al-Sumud* (Development for Sumud Conference), 148.

38. George Bisharat, "Attorneys for the People, Attorneys for the Land: The Emergence of Cause Lawyering in the Israeli-Occupied Territories," *Cause Lawyering: Political Commitments and Professional Responsibilities* (1998): 453–86. For the history of al-Haq, see Lori Allen, *The Rise and Fall of Human Rights: Cynicism and Politics in Occupied Palestine* (Stanford: Stanford University Press, 2013).

39. For example, Beit Ula (Hebron) faced state confiscation orders for thousands of dunums (6,000, according to contemporary press reports; 4,000, from a resident activist and researcher) as well as private fraud. Residents formed a land defense committee, traveled to Turkey to obtain Ottoman titles, and built a 6 km access road to facilitate protests. Lawyers who assisted the committee included Hanna Nakkara, who had decades of experiences with similar land cases within Israel in the 1950s and 1960s. On Nakkara and his role in defending Palestinian land in the Galilee in those decades, see Geremy Forman, "Israeli Settlement of Title in Arab Areas: The Special Land Settlement Operation in Northern Israel (1955–1967)," PhD diss., University of Haifa, 2005.

40. This is assuming, of course, that they were informed of the confiscation in the first place, which often did not (and does not) occur. See Shehadeh, *Occupier's Law*; Shalev, "Under the Guise of Legality: Israel's Declarations of State Land in the West Bank."

41. Rashmawi, *Al-'Ard: Al-Sabil al-Qanuniyya lil-Hifaz 'Aliha* (Land: The Legal Means to Protect It), 10.

42. Finding this sort of evidence was often place-specific. In southern West Bank, for example, Ottoman deeds played a role in land defense strategies. Through establishing histories of land use based on interviews and field visits, surveyors sought to "update" the borders of the deed (*kushan*), rendering it acceptable as private property. See Paul Kohlbry, "Palestinian Counter-Forensics and the Cruel Paradox of Property," *American Ethnologist* 49, no. 3 (2022): 374–86.

43. The main way of doing so was by attempting to track registration claims in the press. To ensure a first registration claim was legitimate and uncontested, Jordanian law stipulated that it be posted locally and printed in newspapers. Israeli com-

panies nominally adhered to this legal requirement, but rather than print announcements in newspapers that anyone read, they placed them in *al-Anba'*, an Israeli government paper with a limited circulation and one that, at least until Palestinians realized the role it played in fraudulent land transfers, enjoyed no readership to speak of. Lawyers had to hunt for copies of *al-Anba'* to find registration announcements and track down where the next case might be. Nidal Taha, "Tasrib al-'Aradi bi-Turuq al-Ihtiyal wa-al-Tawatu al-Isra'ili al-Rasmi" (The Illicit Transfer of Land by Means of Deception and Official Israeli Collaboration), lecture, Institute for Land and Water, November 8, 1991.

44. Created during nineteenth-century Ottoman reforms, the mukhtar was intended as a liaison between the central government and rural communities. After 1967, Israel turned the office into a way to fight nationalist forces, dismissing most of the individuals who refused to obey the dictates of the military government. In the 1980s, the mukhtar was often involved in the transfer of land to Zionist buyers, taking advantage of registries, documents, and connections with the military government to assist in the forgery of documents.

45. There were numerous incidents covered by the press of the period. See Shaul Ephraim Cohen, *The Politics of Planting: Israeli-Palestinian Competition for Control of Land in the Jerusalem Periphery* (Chicago: University of Chicago Press, 1993); Tamari, "In League with Zion." Cohen notes ten attacks on brokers during the time of his fieldwork in the late 1980s.

46. See Shehadeh, *Occupier's Law*, 215–17. According to a report in *al-Fajr* about the Nablus fire arsonists burned the records of the Nablus civil courts and destroyed thousands of files, among them 330 cases involving land disputes, 80 of which were still pending. In his account, Raja Shehadeh states that 250 cases had already been decided in favor of the Palestinian owners. A headline in *al-Fajr* from January 5, 1985, "Hal Qama Samasira al-Ihtilal bi-Ihraq Mahkama Nablus l-Abada Malafat Qadiya al-'Aradi" (Did Occupation Brokers Burn the Nablus Court to Get Rid of Land Case Files?), captured what everyone assumed. Lawyers organized in protest of what they saw as an attempt to prevent further revelations of fraud, and unsurprisingly the Israeli authorities never located the perpetrators. See also Al-Fajr Staff, "Arson at Nablus District Court Destorys Thousands of Legal Documents," *Al-Fajr Weekly*, January 4, 1985.

47. Abdulhalim had been working for *al-Fajr* and had been investigating land sales, and, for his own protection, requested that his name not be mentioned in the byline. See Al-Sha'ab Staff, "Al-Sahafiyyun al-Falastiniyyun Yuwada'un Shahid al-Safahfa Hassan Abdulhalim" (Palestinian Journalists Bid Farewell to the Martyr of Journalists Hassan Abdulhalim), *al-Sha'ab*, December 23, 1985.

48. "With my own eyes," he writes, "I witnessed men, advanced in age [*shuyukh ta'anin fi al-sin*], cry like children" in his office. Taha, "Tasrib al-ʾAradi."

49. Taha, "Tasrib al-ʾAradi."

50. According to Deborah James, "while an increasingly coercive regime was enforcing a racial order in which African customary law, territorial segregation and the denial of property ownership were tools of subjugation, human rights lawyers and the NGOs with which they worked hand-in-glove were using liberal visions of the law, intersecting with ideas on African customary rights, to subvert this. It was through the interactions between such lawyers and their dispossessed African clients, in the years leading to South Africa's transition, that the connections between land ownership and citizenship were partly forged." Deborah James, *Gaining Ground? Rights and Property in South African Land Reform* (New York: Routledge, 2007), 12.

51. As I will show in the next chapter, titling involved significant changes to property and power since, "to formalize rights," points out Derek Hall, "is to change them and the way they are regulated, and simply 'recognizing what exists' is impossible." Derek Hall, *Land* (New York: Polity, 2013), 124.

52. Susan Christine Goedeken, "Made to Measure? Fitting a Development Project to the Occupied Palestinian Territories," MA thesis, American University of Beirut, 2009. In my conversations with foreign consultants and local staff working on LAP-2, a more ambitious project launched in 2012, I found that both expressed similar positions. See Paul Kohlbry, "Titling in the Ruins: Progress, Deferral, and Nonsovereign Property," *Comparative Studies of South Asia, Africa and the Middle East* 43, no. 3 (2023): 262–74.

53. Nicholas Blomley, "The Territory of Property," *Progress in Human Geography* 40, no. 5 (2016): 593–609, at 602.

54. The free-market liberalism built into colonial land administration prefigures today's neoliberal orthodoxy (sometimes word for word), and the principles of British law continue to be in effect, living on through the Jordanian laws that serve as the legal basis to PA land titling.

55. Giovanni Arrighi argues that capitalism and territorialism are two distinct "models of rule or logics of power." For Arrighi, rulers of territory "identify power with the extent and populousness of their domains" and have an instrumental relationship with capital, engaging with it as a means (among others) for territorial expansion. David Harvey builds on this idea to argue that capitalist imperialism is "a contradictory fusion of the politics of state and empire and the molecular processes of capital accumulation in space and time," each with different actors, interests, goals, and constraints. See Giovanni Arrighi, *The Long Twentieth Century: Money,*

Power, and the Origins of Our Times (New York: Verso Books, 1994); David Harvey, *The New Imperialism* (Oxford: Oxford University Press, 2003).

56. According to Musa Shakarneh, a former judge and the first director of the LWSC, the Oslo Accords divisions were political, not legal; with Jordanian law still in force, the argument goes, the Palestinian Authority has the authority to carry out land titling in the entirety of the West Bank.

57. According to legal scholar Jessica Shoemaker, sovereignty is supposed to "encompasses dominion over territory, and part of a sovereign's right and responsibility is to define, and then protect, the institution of private property ownership for all persons and land within that territorial domain." But this relation is inverted in Indigenous territories in the United States, where "who governs where often turns not on the territorial location of the property, but, rather, on the identity of the owners" and an "owner-based (rather than territory-based) system of property sovereignty." Jessica A. Shoemaker, "Complexity's Shadow: American Indian Property, Sovereignty, and the Future," *Michigan Law Review* 115, no. 4 (2016): 487–552, at 502.

58. Israel National News, "Ad Kan: A Fake Palestinian Land Registry for Area C Is Being Written at This Very Moment," *Israel National News*, January 24, 2023, https://www.israelnationalnews.com/news/366380. The settler NGO Regavim makes a similar argument. See Avraham Binyamin, Yonah Admoni, and Yishai Hemo, "The War of Attrition: The Palestinian Authority's Program for Establishing an Arab State in Area C" (Regavim, 2019).

59. Regavim, "600 PA Employees Engaged in Land Registration of Area C," *Regavim* (blog), November 23, 2020, https://www.regavim.org/idfs-civil-administration -hundreds-of-pa-employees-engaged-in-land-registration-of-area-c/.

60. Zachary, "Renewing Settlement of Title in Area C in the West Bank: A Breach of International Law and Violation of Palestinians' Rights."

61. Ministry of Intelligence, "The Palestinian Campaign for Area C—Shaping a Security Reality on the Ground, Description and Implications" (Jerusalem: State of Israel, n.d).

62. Hin Habib, "Qara'a Fi al-Athar al-Maliyya Wa-l-Iqtisadiyya al-Mutawaqʻa Wa-l-Tahadiyyat al-Musabha l-Taswiyya al-'Aradi Wa-Tasjiliha Fi al-Diffa al-Gharbiyya" (A Reading in the Expected Financial and Economic Impact and Challenges Associated with Land Settlement and Registration in the West Bank) (Ramallah: Palestine Economic Policy Research Institute (MAS), 2019); Kohlbry, "Titling in the Ruins."

63. For a longer discussion of UCI and TABO, see Paul Kohlbry, "Selling Rural Palestine: Land Devaluation, Ethical Investment, and the Limits of Human Rights," *Antipode* 55, no. 3 (2023): 897–915.

64. This language comes from TABO's website.

65. For these images, see the hundreds of pictures uploaded to Palestine Remembered: https://www.palestineremembered.com/tags/Palestinian-Land-Deeds.html.

66. Halabi, Turner, and Benvenisti, *Land Alienation in the West Bank*, 1.

67. Through interviews with residents as well as with lawyers from Ramallah familiar with the characters who operated in the land market, I learned that well-known individuals as well as a handful of residents brokered transactions and bought and sold land themselves. Brokerage was one activity among many; they also worked as lawyers, or had small "real estate" offices, and in addition to mediating deals, they made a living buying and selling land.

68. James C. Scott, *The Moral Economy of the Peasant: Rebellion and Subsistence in Southeast Asia* (New Haven: Yale University Press, 1976).

69. Government of Palestine and Sami Hadawi, *Village Statistics 1945: A Classification of Land and Area Ownership in Palestine* (Beirut: PLO Research Center, 1970), 7. After 1948 Hadawi worked with the United Nations to calculate the extent of Palestinian losses, and went on to publish extensively on the issue. The culmination of this work is Sami Hadawi, *Palestinian Rights and Losses in 1948: A Comprehensive Study* (Saqi Books, 1988).

70. In 1980, the UN published its report "Acquisition of Land in Palestine," noting that the "more than 4 million dunams of the land abandoned by the Palestinians [...] is the private property of Palestinian Arabs." Committee on the Exercise of the Inalienable Rights of the Palestinian People (CEIRPP), "Acquisition of Land in Palestine" (New York: United Nations, 1980).

71. Shehadeh, *Occupier's Law*, 21.

72. Meron Benvenisti, Ziad Abu-Zayed, and Danny Rubinstein, *The West Bank Handbook: A Political Lexicon* (Jerusalem: Jerusalem Post, 1986), 113; Peace Now, "Settlement Are Built on Private Palestinian Land," *Peace Now* (blog), March 14, 2007, https://peacenow.org.il/en/settlement-are-built-on-private-palestinian-land.

73. Julia Frankel, "Israel Turbocharges West Bank Settlement Expansion with Largest Land Grab in Decades," *AP News*, July 3, 2024, https://apnews.com/article/israel-palestinians-hamas-war-news-07-03-2024-033deab379a16efdf9989de8d6eaf0f8.

74. George E. Bisharat, "Land, Law, and Legitimacy in Israel and the Occupied Territories," *American University Law Review* 43, no. 2 (1994): 467–561; Usama Halabi, *Musadarat al-ʾAradi fi al-Diffa al-Gharbiyya al-Muhtala* (Land Confiscation in the Occupied West Bank) (Jerusalem: Arab Studies Society, 1986); Halabi, Turner, and Benvenisti, *Land Alienation in the West Bank*; Ala al-Bakri and Hanan Riyyan, *Al-Audaʿ al-Qanuniyya l-Milkiyya l-ʾAradi fi al-Diffa al-Gharbiyya* (The Legal Principles of Land Ownership in the West Bank) (Jerusalem: Arab Studies Society, 1982); Ihsan Atiyya, *Musadarat al-ʾAradi fi al-Manatiq al-Muhtala* (Land Confiscation in

the Occupied Areas: 1967–1980) (Jerusalem: Arab Studies Society, 1980); Shehadeh, *Occupier's Law*. For a discussion of this work, see Kohlbry, "Palestinian Counter-Forensics and the Cruel Paradox of Property."

75. Bhandar, *Colonial Lives of Property*; Gary Fields, *Enclosure: Palestinian Landscapes in a Historical Mirror* (Berkeley: University of California Press, 2017); Eyal Weizman, *Hollow Land: Israel's Architecture of Occupation* (New York: Verso, 2007).

Chapter 3

1. Robert Blackey, "Fanon and Cabral: A Contrast in Theories of Revolution for Africa," *The Journal of Modern African Studies* 12, no. 2 (1974): 191–209; James C. Scott, *The Moral Economy of the Peasant: Rebellion and Subsistence in Southeast Asia* (New Haven: Yale University Press, 1976); Eric R. Wolf, *Peasant Wars of the Twentieth Century* (New York: Harper & Row, 1973).

2. Ramachandra Guha, *The Unquiet Woods: Ecological Change and Peasant Resistance in the Himalaya* (Oxford: Oxford University Press, 1989); James C. Scott, *Weapons of the Weak: Everyday Forms of Peasant Resistance* (New Haven: Yale University Press, 1985). For a helpful summary of the peasant resistance literature, see Donald S. Moore, "Subaltern Struggles and the Politics of Place: Remapping Resistance in Zimbabwe's Eastern Highlands," *Cultural Anthropology* 13, no. 3 (1998): 344–81.

3. Michael F. Brown, "On Resisting Resistance," *American Anthropologist* 98, no. 4 (1996): 729–35, at 729.

4. For a few overviews, see Marc Edelman, Carlos Oya, and Saturnino M Borras, "Global Land Grabs: Historical Processes, Theoretical and Methodological Implications and Current Trajectories," *Third World Quarterly* 34, no. 9 (2013): 1517–31; Charles Geisler and Fouad Makki, "People, Power, and Land: New Enclosures on a Global Scale," *Rural Sociology* 79, no. 1 (2014): 28–33; Ben White et al., "The New Enclosures: Critical Perspectives on Corporate Land Deals," *The Journal of Peasant Studies* 39, no. 3–4 (2012): 619–47.

5. Lila Abu-Lughod, "The Romance of Resistance: Tracing Transformations of Power through Bedouin Women," *American Ethnologist* 17, no. 1 (1990): 41–55.

6. Brown, "On Resisting Resistance."

7. Ruth Hall et al., "Resistance, Acquiescence or Incorporation? An Introduction to Land Grabbing and Political Reactions 'from Below,'" *The Journal of Peasant Studies* 42, no. 3–4 (2015): 467–88. On the critique of peasant idealization, see Natalia Mamonova, "Resistance or Adaptation? Ukrainian Peasants' Responses to Large-Scale Land Acquisitions," *The Journal of Peasant Studies* 42, no. 3–4 (2015): 607–34.

8. Sherry B. Ortner, "Resistance and the Problem of Ethnographic Refusal," *Comparative Studies in Society and History* 37, no. 1 (1995): 173–93, at 179.

9. Ortner, "Resistance and the Problem of Ethnographic Refusal," 180.

10. Ortner, "Resistance and the Problem of Ethnographic Refusal," 187.

11. Ortner, "Resistance and the Problem of Ethnographic Refusal," 187–88.

12. For similar critiques of this sort of framing of the commons, see Michael Levien, *Dispossession without Development: Land Grabs in Neoliberal India* (Oxford: Oxford University Press, 2018); Karen Rignall, *An Elusive Common: Land, Politics, and Agrarian Rurality in a Moroccan Oasis* (Ithaca: Cornell University Press, 2021).

13. Gary Fields, "Landscaping Palestine: Reflections of Enclosure in a Historical Mirror," *International Journal of Middle East Studies* 42, no. 01 (2010): 63–82, at 72.

14. Linda Tabar and Samia Al-Botmeh, "Real Estate Development through Land Grabs: Predatory Accumulation and Precarity in Palestine," *New Political Economy* 26, no. 5 (2021): 783-796.

15. Khaldun Bshara, "Rural Urbanization: The Commodification of Land in Post-Oslo Palestine," in *Reclaiming Space: The 50 Village Project in Rural Palestine*, ed. Khaldun Bshara and Suad Amiry (Ramallah: Riwaq, 2015), 93–103, at 95.

16. Ortner, "Resistance and the Problem of Ethnographic Refusal," 179.

17. Marc Edelman, "Bringing the Moral Economy Back In . . . to the Study of 21st-Century Transnational Peasant Movements," *American Anthropologist* 107, no. 3 (2005): 331–45, at 332.

18. According to the Ottoman legal classification, *mulk* is akin to freehold property, while *miri* is technically the property of the state to which cultivators enjoyed usufruct rights. In practice, both types of land have been treated as privately owned (to varying degrees) since as early as the 1800s. On this history in the highlands, see Beshara Doumani, *Rediscovering Palestine: Merchants and Peasants in Jabal Nablus, 1700–1900* (Berkeley: University of California Press, 1995); Susynne McElrone, "From the Pages of the Defter: A Social History of Rural Property Tenure and the Implementation of Tanzimat Land Reform in Hebron, Palestine (1858–1900)," PhD diss., New York University, 2016. According to Raja Shehadeh, while the "theoretical basis of the Palestinian land law was never altered, several amendments during the Turkish, British, and Jordanian regimes, Jordanian Law No. 49 of 1953, for example, removed any practical difference that existed between the powers of the owner of mulk land and the owner of miri land," and today the only substantive difference that remains involves inheritance. See Raja Shehadeh, *Occupier's Law: Israel and the West Bank*, 2nd ed. (Washington, DC: Institute for Palestine Studies, 1988), 24.

19. One man explained how people used to secure these transactions in the absence of a registry. The buyer and the seller would agree on a sale price, but record a higher price on the written contract. The idea was that, in the case that someone with rights to the land objected in the future, then the buyer would be compensated for any improvements by receiving the higher written price.

20. Eric R. Wolf, "Types of Latin American Peasantry: A Preliminary Discussion," *American Anthropologist* 57, no. 3 (1955): 452–71, at 457.

21. Hin Habib, "Qaraʾa Fi al-Athar al-Maliyya Wa-l-Iqtisadiyya al-Mutawaqʿa Wa-l-Tahadiyyat al-Musabha l-Taswiyya al-ʾAradi Wa-Tasjiliha Fi al-Diffa al-Gharbiyya" (A Reading in the Expected Financial and Economic Impact and Challenges Associated with Land Settlement and Registration in the West Bank) (Ramallah: Palestine Economic Policy Research Institute [MAS], 2019).

22. Paul Kohlbry, "Selling Rural Palestine: Land Devaluation, Ethical Investment, and the Limits of Human Rights," *Antipode* 55, no. 3 (2023): 897–915.

23. Michael Heinrich, *An Introduction to the Three Volumes of Karl Marx's Capital* (New York: NYU Press, 2004), 40.

24. Michael Levien, "Fictitious But Not Utopian: Land Commodification and Dispossession in Rural India," in *Land Fictions: The Commodification of Land in City and Country*, ed. D. Asher Ghertner and Robert W. Lake (Ithaca: Cornell University Press, 2021), 26–43, at 27.

25. Suad Amiry, "Space, Kinship and Gender: The Social Dimension of Peasant Architecture in Palestine," PhD diss., University of Edinburgh, 1987, 52–53.

26. When I interviewed one of the World Bank project managers for LAP-2 in 2013, she told me that one of the lessons drawn from Qarawa was the importance of "informal committees" in assisting the survey teams, a lesson that informed later iterations of land titling. LAP-2 sought to formalize and build out the mechanisms of dispute resolution, generating all sorts of plans to integrate local sources of authority into the project, and hiring additional lawyers and social workers to work in what the Bank called "social facilitation" teams.

27. Abu Ijbal's responsibilities also likely included coordinating for the survey teams. In Farkha, Dura, and other survey teams I spent time with, the guide not only knew boundaries and resolved disputes, but knew whom to call (and whom not to call) and what to say to get people to show up. A good guide was indispensable in moving titling forward; a bad one could wreck the process by getting in fights with people, and not having one often saw work grind to a halt.

28. In the 1920s and 1930s, indebtedness to wealthy landlords was the main form of differentiation in the north Ramallah villages, with peasants losing land to the powerful families of Deir Ghassana and Beit Reema. See Salim Tamari, "The Dislocation and Re-constitution of a Peasantry: The Social Economy of Agrarian Palestine in the Central Highlands and the Jordan Valley, 1960–1980," PhD diss., University of Manchester, 1983, 226. Also see Amiry, "Space, Kinship and Gender." During the years of Jordanian rule in Qarawa, those I interviewed spoke about debt, not to landlords, but to moneylenders and merchants. In these stories, people said that peasants were simple or ignorant—they did not know any better. They also had little

choice but to borrow. One man told me how his father had lost control of his land in 1953, and how they eventually were able to reacquire it in 1970, presumably with savings from working in Israel or abroad.

29. In his conversations with elderly peasant rebels about land sales to Zionists during the Mandate, Ted Swedenburg notes similar sentiments about land and honor. See Ted Swedenburg, *Memories of Revolt: The 1936–1939 Rebellion and the Palestinian National Past* (Fayetteville: University of Arkansas Press, 2003), 74–75.

30. It is likely that these absentee owners were solicited precisely because their potential lack of knowledge about the current state of the land market would cause them to sell at below-market rates. Such a practice is common in Ramallah, where brokers will contact Palestinians living in the United States or Jordan and offer to buy them out of their shares, hoping that the person they are talking to will be unaware of how valuable the land is or may become.

31. Scott, *Weapons of the Weak,* 178–79. Many scholars of Palestine working in the refugee camps of Lebanon, the urban neighborhoods of Amman, and the villages of the West Bank have noted how older men and women often construct an idyllic memory of the village past, which they often interpret as a kind of psychic antidote for the bleakness of the present. See Falestin Naïli, "Memories of Home and Stories of Displacement: The Women of Artas and the 'Peasant Past,' " *Journal of Palestine Studies* 38, no. 4 (2009): 63–74; Swedenburg, *Memories of Revolt,* 25; Rosemary Sayigh, *The Palestinians: From Peasants to Revolutionaries* (London: Zed Books, 1979), 1–2; Rochelle Davis, *Palestinian Village Histories: Geographies of the Displaced* (Stanford: Stanford University Press, 2011), 72–73.

32. Women's Centre for Legal Aid and Counselling (WCLAC), "Palestinian Women and Inheritance" (Ramallah: WCLAC, 2014). In the survey, 50 percent had to wait five years, and 15 percent took as long as ten. Land can be lost de jure when a woman is pressured to sign her rights away (*takharruj*), or de facto when she is denied practical decision-making power.

33. In Dura, a town in the southern highlands, one of the young social workers related stories of men walking out during a public meeting when she raised the issue of women's rights. Surveyors in Salfit told me that in Khirbet Qeis, a combination of a high number of nonresident landowners and the refusal of brothers to grant sisters inheritance rights had slowed operations almost to a halt.

34. "An *important unintended* outcome of the project was the legitimacy it has provided to women's voices on their legal rights," went the World Bank appraisal, and "the project empowered these women with ownership, gaving [*sic*] them greater social influence, and raised public awareness about women's rights. The project also institutionalized the practice of the inclusion of at least one woman as member of

the land settlement committee and village council." See World Bank, "Implementation Completion and Results Report on a Learning and Innovation (Grant) in the Amount of US$3.0Million to West Bank and Gaza for a Land Administration Project" (Washington, DC: World Bank, June 25, 2009), 7 (original emphasis). What remains puzzling to me about this "unintended outcome" is that, long before LAP-1 began in Palestine, the idea that land privatization would support women's rights was well established in development circles, and in the World Bank's own projects. See Bina Agarwal, *A Field of One's Own: Gender and Land Rights in South Asia* (Cambridge, UK: Cambridge University Press, 1994); World Bank, "Engendering Development: Through Gender Equality in Rights, Resources, and Voice" (Washington, DC: World Bank, 2001); Ann Whitehead and Dzodzi Tsikata, "Policy Discourses on Women's Land Rights in Sub-Saharan Africa: The Implications of the Re-turn to the Customary," *Journal of Agrarian Change* 3, no. 1–2 (2003): 67–112; Shahra Razavi, "Engendering the Political Economy of Agrarian Change," *The Journal of Peasant Studies* 36, no. 1 (2009): 197–226.

35. In his history of land settlement in Jordan, Michael Fischbach recounts that these were the very ways that men circumvented registering rights in the name of female heirs. See Michael R. Fischbach, *State, Society, and Land in Jordan* (Boston: Brill, 2000).

36. As anthropologist Annelies Moors has shown, the decision to claim an inheritance right is not a simple question of ownership; instead, the choices that women make to claim (or not to claim) are based on relations of familial support and dependence that shift along with the rural political economy. Annelies Moors, *Women, Property and Islam: Palestinian Experiences, 1920–1990* (Cambridge, UK: Cambridge University Press, 1995), 3. Moors shows how, as wage labor overtook farming in the 1980s, the structural position of the wife shifted from a productive member of the household (that is, a worker on the family farm) to a consumer, shifting relations of dependence from the natal household to the home of the groom. Understanding how this changed gendered relations of dependence, Moors points out, is the only way to understand why women pursued, or chose not to pursue, inheritance claims.

37. James Scott connects the idiom of "eating" to exploitation, and Michael Levien connects it to land speculation. See Scott, *Weapons of the Weak,* 187; and Michael Levien, *Dispossession without Development: Land Grabs in Neoliberal India* (Oxford: Oxford University Press, 2018), 191–93.

38. A few people suggested to me that higher land prices were part of the reason the group of women in Qarawa had decided it was worthwhile to press legal claims. This explanation seems likely, although due to the sensitivity of such conflicts I was never able to verify it with those involved.

39. James Ferguson and Akhil Gupta, "Spatializing States: Toward an Ethnography of Neoliberal Governmentality," *American Ethnologist* 29, no. 4 (2002): 981–1002; James Ferguson, *Global Shadows: Africa in the Neoliberal World Order* (Durham, NC: Duke University Press, 2006); Karen Ho, *Liquidated: An Ethnography of Wall Street* (Durham, NC: Duke University Press, 2009).

40. Vandana Shiva, *Earth Democracy: Justice, Sustainability, and Peace* (London: Zed Books, 2016).

41. Marc Edelman, *Peasants against Globalization: Rural Social Movements in Costa Rica* (Stanford: Stanford University Press, 1999); Stuart Kirsch, "Indigenous Movements and the Risks of Counterglobalization: Tracking the Campaign against Papua New Guinea's Ok Tedi Mine," *American Ethnologist* 34, no. 2 (2007): 303–21; Tania Murray Li, *Land's End: Capitalist Relations on an Indigenous Frontier* (Durham, NC: Duke University Press, 2014); Wendy Wolford, *This Land Is Ours Now: Social Mobilization and the Meanings of Land in Brazil* (Durham, NC: Duke University Press, 2010).

Chapter 4

1. Michel-Rolph Trouillot, *Peasants and Capital: Dominica in the World Economy* (Baltimore: Johns Hopkins University Press, 1988), 5–6.

2. On this point, see Martha Mundy and Richard Saumarez Smith, *Governing Property, Making the Modern State: Law, Administration and Production in Ottoman Syria* (London: IB Tauris, 2007); James C. Scott, *Seeing like a State: How Certain Schemes to Improve the Human Condition Have Failed* (New Haven: Yale University Press, 1998).

3. On revolt, see Eric R. Wolf, *Peasant Wars of the Twentieth Century* (New York: Harper & Row, 1973). On agrarian movements and land reform, see Jo Guldi, *The Long Land War: The Global Struggle for Occupancy Rights* (New Haven: Yale University Press, 2022); Donald Anthony Low, *The Egalitarian Moment: Asia and Africa, 1950–1980* (Cambridge, UK: Cambridge University Press, 1996). Andrew Sartori, in his study of the "property-constituting powers of labor" argues that "the concatenation of imperial discourses of property with agrarian political energies generated the condition of possibility for a strong embrace of Lockean discourses of property in agrarian Bengal in the early twentieth century." Andrew Sartori, *Liberalism in Empire: An Alternative History* (Berkeley: University of California Press, 2014).

4. Wendy Wolford, "Land Reform in the Time of Neoliberalism: A Many-Splendored Thing," *Antipode* 39, no. 3 (2007): 550–70.

5. Bina Agarwal, *A Field of One's Own: Gender and Land Rights in South Asia* (Cambridge, UK: Cambridge University Press, 1994); Kregg Hetherington, *Guerrilla*

Auditors: The Politics of Transparency in Neoliberal Paraguay (Durham, NC: Duke University Press, 2011). The notion of settling unproductive land is also an important part of the Brazilian colonization of the Amazon. After the 1964 coup, the new military government created the legal and infrastructural means for settlers to acquire land in the Amazon under the exact same slogan as early Zionism: "land without people to people without land" (*terra sem homens para homens sem terra*). See Jeremy M. Campbell, *Conjuring Property: Speculation and Environmental Futures in the Brazilian Amazon* (Seattle: University of Washington Press, 2015), 35–36.

6. Sharad Chari, *Fraternal Capital: Peasant-Workers, Self-Made Men, and Globalization in Provincial India* (Stanford: Stanford University Press, 2004), 238.

7. Tania Murray Li, *Land's End: Capitalist Relations on an Indigenous Frontier* (Durham, NC: Duke University Press, 2014), 15.

8. Donald S. Moore, "Subaltern Struggles and the Politics of Place: Remapping Resistance in Zimbabwe's Eastern Highlands," *Cultural Anthropology* 13, no. 3 (1998): 344–81.

9. In Palestine, there are still clear distinctions between urban (*madani*), and rural (*falahi*) Arabic dialects, as well as regional variations that identify a person as hailing from a specific region in the West Bank. Both are distinct from Standard Arabic (*fusha*), which is the Arabic used for newspapers, literature, and broadcast media across the Arabic-speaking world.

10. Older farmers, as well as lawyers and Jordanian cartographers, made this distinction between land cultivated for grains (*falaha*) that needed to be replanted yearly and land planted with trees (*mazrua'* or *mu'amara*). Munir Naser notes that for peasants, *falaha* meant "plowing the land before scattering seeds." See Munir Naser, "Al-Nashat al-Zira'i l-Falah Bir Zeit 'ala Mudar al-Sina" (The Agricultural Activities of the Birzeit Peasant over the Year), *Heritage and Society* 1 (1974): 70–80.

11. Anand Pandian, *Crooked Stalks: Cultivating Virtue in South India* (Durham, NC: Duke University Press, 2009), 5.

12. For Tim Ingold, this is essential to the definition of landscape, or what he calls a "dwelling perspective" in which "the landscape is constituted as an enduring record of—and testimony to—the lives and works of past generations who have dwelt within it, and in so doing, have left there something of themselves." This chapter adopts the starting point suggested by Ingold: "For anthropologists, to adopt a perspective of this kind means bringing to bear the knowledge born of immediate experience, by privileging the understanding that people derive from their lived, everyday involvement in the world." See Tim Ingold, "The Temporality of the Landscape," *World Archaeology* 25, no. 2 (1993): 152–74, at 153.

13. Amy Singer, *Palestinian Peasants and Ottoman Officials: Rural Administra-*

tion around Sixteenth-Century Jerusalem (Cambridge, UK: Cambridge University Press, 1994), 43.

14. Mundy and Smith, *Governing Property, Making the Modern State*, 14 and 37–38.

15. Richard Clifford Tute, *The Ottoman Land Laws, with a Commentary on the Ottoman Land Code of the 7th Ramadan 1274* (Jerusalem: Greek Convent Press, 1927), 97–98. The Land Code defined *mewat* (literally, "dead land") as "vacant (khali) land, such as mountains, rocky places, stony fields, pernallik and grazing ground." By defining "improvement" and recognizing rights derived from "enclosure," the law allowed that "anyone who is in need of such land can with the leave of the Official plough it up gratuitously and cultivate it on the condition that the legal ownership (raqabe) [*sic*] shall belong to the Treasury."

16. For the highlands, see Suad Amiry, "Space, Kinship and Gender: The Social Dimension of Peasant Architecture in Palestine," PhD diss., University of Edinburgh, 1987. More broadly, see Martha Mundy, "Village Land and Individual Title: Musha' and Ottoman Land Registration in the 'Ajlun District," in *Village, Steppe and State: The Social Origins of Modern Jordan,* ed. Eugene Rogan and Tariq Tell (London: Bloomsbury Academic, 1994), 58–79; James C. Scott, *Seeing Like a State: How Certain Schemes to Improve the Human Condition Have Failed* (New Haven: Yale University Press, 1998).

17. Scott Atran, "Hamula Organisation and Masha'a Tenure in Palestine," *Man* (1986): 271–95; Susynne McElrone, "From the Pages of the Defter: A Social History of Rural Property Tenure and the Implementation of Tanzimat Land Reform in Hebron, Palestine (1858–1900)," PhD diss., New York University, 2016. While much of the scholarly debate over *masha'* has focused on the periodic redistribution of land to village shareholders, the term did not always refer to this kind of landholding. While it has often been assumed that *masha'* was less widespread in the highlands due to the prevalence of tree crops, McElrone suggests otherwise. For a review of the *masha'* debates, see Amos Nadan, "Reconsidering Peasant Communes in the Levant, c. 1850s–1940s," *The Economic History Review* 74, no. 1 (2021): 34–59.

18. On *masha'* in the highlands, see Sarah Graham-Brown, "The Political Economy of the Jabal Nablus, 1920–48," in *Studies in the Economic and Social History of Palestine in the Nineteenth and Twentieth Centuries*, ed. Roger Owen (Carbondale: Southern Illinois University Press, 1982), 88–176; McElrone, "From the Pages of the Defter: A Social History of Rural Property Tenure and the Implementation of Tanzimat Land Reform in Hebron, Palestine (1858–1900)."

19. Andrew S. Mathews, *Trees Are Shape Shifters: How Cultivation, Climate Change, and Disaster Create Landscapes* (New Haven: Yale University Press, 2022), 17. From building to grafting, his description of another Mediterranean landscape, the chestnut terraces in Italy, applies quite well to the Palestinian highlands.

20. Shukri Arraf and Sami Khalil Mari, *Al-ʾArd, al-Insan wa-al-Juhd: Dirasa li-Hadaratina al-Madiya ʿala Ardina* (Land, Man, and Effort: A Study of Material Culture on Our Land) (Akka: Maktabat wa-Matbaʿat Abu Rahmun, 1982), 47–48.

21. Akram Fouad Khater, *Inventing Home: Emigration, Gender, and the Middle Class in Lebanon, 1870–1920* (Berkeley: University of California Press, 2001), 26 and 125. Co-planting agreements may include different trees. In Lebanon, for example, co-planting agreements focused on the foundation of the silk trade: mulberry trees. The arrangement would last five to seven years, during which peasants would tend the trees and could use the ground beneath to plant field crops, acquiring a quarter of the land from the landlord when the trees matured.

22. These agreements assumed what James Scott has called "the right of subsistence," the obligation of the powerful to allow the poor to meet their subsistence needs. See James C. Scott, *The Moral Economy of the Peasant: Rebellion and Subsistence in Southeast Asia* (New Haven: Yale University Press, 1976). In the 1960s, for instance, a farmer from Farkha related how a powerful Nablus family took control of a huge portion of village agricultural land after residents, who had put up their olive trees as collateral, defaulted. Creditors seized the land beneath as well and, in contravention of established practice, prevented villagers from intercropping around the trees. Nadan mentions something similar in the Galilee. "In one case, for example, when olive trees were given as security but not the land they were on, the moneylender found that a 'mysterious' arson attack had occurred on the plantation, and that all his (the moneylender's) trees were destroyed. Accordingly, the peasant who owned the land continued to cultivate it with no further obligation to the moneylender." See Amos Nadan, "Merchants and Peasants in the Nazareth Region, 1922–47," *The Journal of Peasant Studies* 34, no. 1 (2007): 51–68.

23. Salim Tamari, "The Dislocation and Re-Constitution of a Peasantry: The Social Economy of Agrarian Palestine in the Central Highlands and the Jordan Valley, 1960–1980," PhD diss., University of Manchester, 1983, 147–48. According to Sarah Graham-Brown, sharecropping was more common in the nineteenth century, but by the late 1920s co-planting arrangements increased the numbers of smallholders immensely. She also notes that in Jabal Nablus planters acquired land, while in other areas planters may have only acquired trees. See Graham-Brown, "The Political Economy of the Jabal Nablus, 1920–48," 120. Ottoman land law recognized the possible separation between rights to the ground and rights to what grew upon it, and contained various provisions for dealing with overlapping claims. Frederic Maurice Goadby and Moses J. Doukhan, *The Land Law of Palestine* (Jerusalem: Shoshany's Printing Co., 1935), 22–23.

24. Noura Alkhalili, "Enclosures from Below: The Mushaaʾ in Contemporary Palestine," *Antipode* 49, no. 5 (2017): 1103–24.

25. By the 1960s, for example, co-planting was declining. The Jordanian government had specific forms one could fill out to register these agreements with the authorities. By the time the settlement of title began in the West Bank, new co-planting agreements were less common. The Nablus village of Burqa, for example, possesses complete copies of the schedule of rights, published as part of the Jordanian settlement of title in 1963. Of the hundreds of plots that make up the village's 18,700 dunums, I counted only 36 ongoing agreements. In the margins, the Jordanian settlement officer recorded the parties to the agreement, the amount of dunums (aside from a few larger agreements of 31 and 54 dunums, most were no more than 10), and the length of contract (10, 13, and 15 years). While several older farmers I interviewed had acquired land through these kinds of agreements decades before, everyone I spoke with agreed that it was a thing of the past, when land was plentiful, and labor was scarce.

26. Abdulla M. Lutfiyya, *Baytin: A Jordanian Village* (London: Mouton, 1966), 126–27; Joel S. Migdal, *Palestinian Society and Politics* (Princeton: Princeton University Press, 1980), 66.

27. The number of nurseries growing olive trees increased from eight in 1967 to forty-seven by 1986. See Jeffrey Drew Reger, "Planting Palestine: The Political Economy of Olive Culture in the 20th-Century Galilee and West Bank," PhD diss., Georgetown University, 2018, 465. In addition, according to Hisham Awartani, in the late 1970s a "major technological breakthrough following the introduction of forced-rooted cuttings by the use of growth stimulating hormones" rapidly increased the number of saplings produced per year in three nurseries. See Awartani, "Agricultural Development in the West Bank," 223.

28. My interlocutor recalled that it was 3 kilos for women for sorting the picked olives (*laquta*) and 4 kilos for men, who picked them from the trees (*jadad*). Another said 2 and 3 kilos.

29. On the expansion of olive tree planting in the West Bank through the 1980s, see Reger, "Planting Palestine." Current statistics show the continued expansion of olive tree planting, especially in areas that were not historically olive regions. See Palestinian Authority Ministry of Agriculture and Palestinian Central Bureau of Statistics, "Agriculture Census: 2021" (Ramallah: Palestinian Central Bureau of Statistics/Ministry of Agriculture, 2023).

30. Katherine Verdery, *The Vanishing Hectare: Property and Value in Postsocialist Transylvania* (Ithaca: Cornell University Press, 2003), 178–81. Verdery argues that effective ownership "was something that enabled them to create order, to control their own labor and its products, and to feel a sense of mastery." Appearances mattered greatly. "In this system of values, having a field of fine and well-weeded crops

that all could see was a way of exhibiting mastery and asserting superior status over those with less or no land, or with poor labor capacity."

31. A surveyor who worked for the Jordanians told me that in the 1950s and 1960s, they had at times calculated the value of the trees and the land, partitioned the area, and then allowed both the owners of the land and the owners of the trees the opportunity to purchase these new, smaller plots.

32. As Raymond Craib has shown in Mexico, rural people resisted *and* invited, engaged, and sometimes exploited those sent to map and title their lands. "Those being 'mapped' did not simply ignore or acquiesce, " he argues; instead, they used state cartographic projects to fix their own ideas of "property, territory, identity, and history" in the landscape. Raymond B. Craib, *Cartographic Mexico: A History of State Fixations and Fugitive Landscapes* (Durham, NC: Duke University Press, 2004), 12.

33. On these procedures and the role of cultivation, see Usama Halabi, Aron Turner, and Meron Benvenisti, *Land Alienation in the West Bank: A Legal and Spatial Analysis* (Jerusalem: West Bank Data Base Project, 1985). On measurement and calculation, see Irus Braverman, " 'The Tree Is the Enemy Soldier': A Sociolegal Making of War Landscapes in the Occupied West Bank," *Law & Society Review* 42, no. 3 (2008): 449–82; Nir Shalev, "Under the Guise of Legality: Israel's Declarations of State Land in the West Bank" (Jerusalem: B'Tselem, February 2012).

34. The Palestinian press carried many stories about these sorts of things in the 1980s. For academic studies, see Shaul Ephraim Cohen, *The Politics of Planting: Israeli-Palestinian Competition for Control of Land in the Jerusalem Periphery* (Chicago: University of Chicago Press, 1993); Fadia Panosetti and Laurence Roudart, "Evolving Regimes of Land Use and Property in the West Bank," *Jerusalem Quarterly* 89 (2022): 10–31. Such activities set the stage for the politics of planting that would play out in the 1990s and beyond. On this later era, see Irus Braverman, *Planted Flags: Trees, Land, and Law in Israel/Palestine* (Cambridge, UK: Cambridge University Press, 2009). And for an overview and critique of the legalism of the cultivation literature, see Omar Loren Tesdell, "Shadow Spaces: Territory, Sovereignty, and the Question of Palestinian Cultivation," PhD diss., University of Minnesota, 2013.

35. Abdulrahman Abu Arafeh, "Siyasat al-Sira' 'ala al-'Ard fi al-Diffa al-Muhtala" (The Politics of Land Struggle in the Occupied West Bank), *Samed al-Iqtisadi* 46 (December 1983): 53–72.

36. Abdulrahman Abu Arafeh, Yusuf al-Azzeh, and Dawood Istanbuli, "Al-Waqa' al-Zira'iyya fi al-Minatiq al-Muhtala wa-Dururat al-Tanmiyya" (The Agricultural Situation in the Occupied Areas and the Requirements of Development), in *Mu'tamir al-Tanmiyya min Ajl al-Sumud* (Development for Sumud Conference) (Jerusalem: Arab Thought Forum, 1983), 55.

37. Alain Epp Weaver and Sonia K. Weaver, *Salt & Sign: Mennonite Central Committee in Palestine, 1949–1999* (Akron, PA: Mennonite Central Committee, 1999). In a proposed development plan from 1982, Awartani calculated that the Community Development Fund and the MCC had contributed half of the 200,000 saplings that were planted per year. Hisham Awartani, "Khuta Muqtaraha li-l-Tatwir al-Zira' fi al-Diffa al-Gharbiyya wa-Qita' Ghazza" (Proposed Plan for Agricultural Development in the West Bank and Gaza Strip), (Rural Research Center/Birzeit University Research Center, 1982).

38. Caroline Abu-Sada, "Cultivating Dependence: Palestinian Agriculture under the Israeli Occupation," in *The Power of Inclusive Exclusion: Anatomy of Israeli Rule in the Occupied Palestinian Territories*, ed. Sari Hanafi, Adi Ophir, and Michal Givoni (New York: Zone Books, 2009), 413–29; Glenn E. Robinson, "The Role of the Professional Middle Class in the Mobilization of Palestinian Society: The Medical and Agricultural Committees," *International Journal of Middle East Studies* 25, no. 2 (1993): 301–26.

39. *Al-Fajr Weekly*, May 3–9, 1981.

40. Said A. Assaf, "A Study on the Recent Growing of a Rapidly Propagating Olive Cultivar Mis-Named 'Improved Nabali' and Its Effect on Impeding the West Bank Olive Industry," in *Acta Horticulturae* 356 (1994): 432–37.

41. This account is based on interviews with Fayyad Fayyad, the head of the Palestinian Olive Oil Council. Mustafa Tamaizh brought this issue to my attention in Hebron.

42. Weaver and Weaver, *Salt & Sign*.

43. One was for Elon Moreh, in which he "persuaded the affected farmers to sign affidavits delegating" the lawyer Elias Khoury as their legal representative. The subsequent Israeli Supreme Court decision remains to this day one of the most consequential rulings for Palestinian land rights. See Weaver and Weaver, *Salt & Sign*.

44. In Hebron, for example, a former employee of the Jordanian Ministry of Agriculture named Salah al-Sharif produced such reports. In another example, in the northern Ramallah villages, PARC helped provide evidence of prior cultivation to residents of the village of Kobar to prevent Israeli land confiscation. On the latter, see Ismail Daiq, "Dur Al-Munazamat al-Jamhariyya fi al-Tanmiyya al-Rifiyya li-l-Ard al-Muhtala" (The Role of Mass Organizations in Rural Development for Occupied Land), *Samed al-Iqtisadi* 61 (June 1986): 41–53.

45. al-Alul, *Istislah wa-Istiglal Aradi al-Diffa al-Gharbiyya* (Land Reclamation and Use in the West Bank), 10.

46. For an overview of the ideas, see Raja Khalidi, "The Economics of Palestinian Liberation," *Jacobin*, 2014, http://jacobinmag.com/2014/10/the-economics-of-pales-

tinian-liberation/. This included the creation of light industry, skills training, and education primarily in the refugee camps in Lebanon, as well as the establishment of agricultural cooperatives in several African countries. On Lebanon, see Rosemary Sayigh, *The Palestinians: From Peasants to Revolutionaries* (London: Zed Books, 1979). On PLO agricultural projects in Africa see Cheryl A. Rubenberg, "The Civilian Infrastructure of the Palestine Liberation Organization: An Analysis of the PLO in Lebanon until June 1982," *Journal of Palestine Studies* 12, no. 3 (1983): 54–78. The UN Conference on Trade and Development (UNCTAD)—according to Vijay Prashad, established in 1964 as an organ to lead an "anti-imperialist strategy for economic development" in the Third World—began to produce research that could clarify the challenges Palestinians faced in building up economic self-sufficiency, both in exile and at home. Vijay Prashad, *The Darker Nations: A People's History of the Third World* (New York: New Press, 2007), 45.

47. Yusif Sayigh, "Dispossession and Pauperisation: The Palestinian Economy under Occupation," and Ibrahim Dakkak, "Development from Within: A Strategy for Survival," both in *The Palestinian Economy: Studies in Development under Prolonged Occupation*, ed. George T. Abed (London: Routledge, 1988).

48. According to Omar Tesdell, this cohort of thinkers largely missed the point about rain-fed agriculture. He argues that the "biological, reproductive, and geomorphological properties of rainfed production" should not be seen as obstacles or limits, but instead as offering "qualities of durability in sustaining an attachment to farmland." The focus on "the political economy of Palestinian agriculture," he continues, renders "embodied practice and accumulated experience of cultivation" invisible. See Tesdell, "Shadow Spaces," 145–54.

49. Abu Arafeh, al-Azzeh, and Istanbuli, "The Agricultural Situation," 56.

50. Awartani, "Agricultural Development in the West Bank," 338.

51. Awartani, "Agricultural Development in the West Bank," 59–60.

52. al-Alul, *Istislah wa-Istiglal Aradi al-Diffa al-Gharbiyya* (Land Reclamation and Use in the West Bank), 35. Through land reclamation, he claimed, an additional 2.6 million dunums of land—which, under Israeli categorizations, were deemed to be unfit for agriculture and thus (potential) state land—could be brought into use. For a discussion of these theories of land reclamation, see Paul Kohlbry, "To Cover the Land in Green: Rain-Fed Agriculture and Anti-Colonial Land Reclamation in Palestine," *The Journal of Peasant Studies* 50, no. 7 (2023): 2666–2684.

53. See, for instance, Abu Arafeh, "The Politics of Land Struggle in the Occupied West Bank" (Siyasat al-Sira' 'ala al-'Ard Fil Diffa al-Muhtela), 40; Awartani, "Agricultural Development in the West Bank," 336; al-Alul, *Istislah wa-Istiglal Aradi al-Diffa al-Gharbiyya* (Land Reclamation and Use in the West Bank), 3. Abu Arafeh argued

that Palestinian development required a different "equation" (*mu'adila*) and set of standards that pushed for extensive land use. For al-'Alul, reclamation efforts were crucial for confronting "Zionist expansion" and should be supported regardless of their "economic feasibility" and required costs. In a study of land reclamation published in 1992, researchers asked people to explain why they carried out land reclamation. The highest percentage stated economic reasons, and the second, at 75 percent, responded that they sought "protection from confiscation." See Munir Awwad, *Istislah al-'Aradi al-Zira'iyya* (The Reclamation of Agricultural Lands) (Nablus: Rural Research Center, 1992).

54. Jamal Talab and Nure al-'Uqbi, *Al-Zaitun taht al-Ihtilal* (The Olive under Occupation) (Jerusalem: Arab Studies Society, n.d.).

55. Assaf, "A Study on the Recent Growing of a Rapidly Propagating Olive Cultivar Mis-Named 'Improved Nabali' and Its Effect on Impeding the West Bank Olive Industry."

56. Land Research Center, "Ravaging 10 Dunums in Farkha Village / Salfit Governorate," October 7, 2019, http://poica.org/2019/10/ravaging-10-dunums-in-farkha-village-salit-governorate/.

57. For the competition framing, see Braverman, *Planted Flags: Trees, Land, and Law in Israel/Palestine*; Cohen, *The Politics of Planting*. For an example of a similar argument that adopts a settler colonial framing, see Ghada Sasa, "Oppressive Pines: Uprooting Israeli Green Colonialism and Implanting Palestinian A'wna," *Politics* 43, no. 2 (2023): 219–35.

58. As Tamari points out, by the 1980s wages and remittances were what allowed people to become "village entrepreneurs," allowing them to put money into village or, ideally, urban property. See Tamari, "The Dislocation and Re-Constitution of a Peasantry: The Social Economy of Agrarian Palestine in the Central Highlands and the Jordan Valley, 1960–1980," 82.

59. Importantly, as Bhandar argues, the legal category of cultivation and the racial logic that "subtends" it has long outlived the economic formation of agrarian capitalism that gave rise to it. See Brenna Bhandar, *Colonial Lives of Property: Law, Land, and Racial Regimes of Ownership* (Durham, NC: Duke University Press, 2018), 113. There are many accounts of the various ways the "improvement" circulated across European empires. See Diana K. Davis, *The Arid Lands: History, Power, Knowledge* (Cambridge, MA: MIT Press, 2016); Richard Drayton, *Nature's Government: Science, Imperial Britain, and the "Improvement" of the World* (New Haven: Yale University Press, 2000); John C. Weaver, *Great Land Rush and the Making of the Modern World, 1650–1900* (Montreal: McGill-Queen's University Press, 2003).

60. The reasons are partially biographical. Locke, more than other important

theorists of classical liberalism, was highly knowledgeable about and directly involved in the practical aspects of colonial settlement throughout his life. See David
Armitage, "John Locke, Carolina, and the Two Treatises of Government," *Political
Theory* 32, no. 5 (October 2004): 602–27; James Tully, *An Approach to Political Philos-
ophy: Locke in Contexts* (Cambridge, UK: Cambridge University Press, 1993), 140–44.
For many, Locke's liberalism amounts to little more than colonial apologetics. See,
for example, Domenico Losurdo, *Liberalism: A Counter-History* (London: Verso
Books, 2014).

61. For Locke, uncultivated land was endemic to America. He asks (rhetorically)
whether a thousand acres of such uncultivated land could produce as much as ten
acres of cultivated land in Devonshire. His answer is, of course, no, as the native has
failed to join "the rest of mankind, in the consent of the use of their common money"
and as such lands "lie waste, and are more than the people, who dwell on it do, or can
make use of, and so still lie in common." See John Locke, *Locke: Two Treatises of Government Student Edition* (Cambridge, UK: Cambridge University Press, 1988), 294
and 299. Such ideas circulated in the colonies before Locke wrote his famous text,
and it was only much later that they could coalesce into a powerful narrative that
justified European conquest and was formalized into law. See Tully, *An Approach to
Political Philosophy*, 157. Nor was it the dominant mode of thought among early settlers, who often had little choice but to purchase land from Indigenous sellers. Only
at the beginning of the 1800s, under very different configurations of military power,
settler sovereignty, and capital, would Lockean ideas would become hegemonic in
settler thought. See Stuart Banner, *How the Indians Lost Their Land: Law and Power
on the Frontier* (Cambridge, MA: Harvard University Press, 2007).

62. For examples, see Davis, *The Arid Lands*; Tania Murray Li, *The Will to Improve: Governmentality, Development, and the Practice of Politics* (Durham, NC: Duke
University Press, 2007).

63. For the Zionist movement, it was less Locke and more German idealism, but
the result was the same. On this point, and for a discussion of improvement and Zionism, see Bhandar, *Colonial Lives of Property*.

64. For early historiography that sought to establish the presence and productivity of Arab agriculture, see Nabil Badran, "Al-Rif al-Filastini Qabal al-Harb al-'Alami
al-Ula" (The Palestinian Countryside before the First World War), *Shu'un Filistiniyya*
7 (1972): 116–29; Khalil Abu Rajili, "al-Zira' al-'Arabi Fi Filastin Qabal Qiam Dawla
Israel" (Arab Agriculture in Palestine before the Founding of the State of Israel),
Shu'un Filistiniyya 11 (1972): 128–43. For a sense of how improvement continues to
reappear in various guises, see Alan George, " 'Making the Desert Bloom': A Myth
Examined," *Journal of Palestine Studies* 8, no. 2 (1979): 88–100; Sara Salazar Hughes,

Stepha Velednitsky, and Amelia Arden Green, "Greenwashing in Palestine/Israel: Settler Colonialism and Environmental Injustice in the Age of Climate Catastrophe," *Environment and Planning E: Nature and Space* 6, no. 1 (2023): 495–513; Lila Sharif, "Vanishing Palestine," *Critical Ethnic Studies* 2, no. 1 (2016): 17–39; Manal Shqair, "Arab-Israeli Eco-Normalization: Greenwashing Settler Colonialism in Palestine and the Jawlan," in *Dismantling Green Colonialism*, ed. Hamza Hamouchene and Katie Sandwell (London: Pluto Press, 2023), 67–87.

65. John Bellamy Foster, "Marx, Value, and Nature," *Monthly Review* 70, no. 3 (2018): 122–36.

66. Foster, "Marx, Value, and Nature," 124.

67. For an example, see Li, *Land's End*, 86.

68. On Locke, capitalism, and the idea of possessive individualism, see C. B. Macpherson, *The Political Theory of Possessive Individualism: Hobbes to Locke* (Oxford: Oxford University Press, 1989). The Lockean model always assumed a male, property-owning subject. See Carole Pateman, *The Sexual Contract* (Stanford: Stanford University Press, 1988).

69. Low, *The Egalitarian Moment*.

Chapter 5

1. Jim Handy, " 'Almost Idiotic Wretchedness': A Long History of Blaming Peasants," *The Journal of Peasant Studies* 36, no. 2 (2009): 325–44.

2. Salim Tamari, "Soul of the Nation: The Fallah in the Eyes of the Urban Intelligentsia," *Review of Middle East Studies* 5, no. 5 (1992): 74–83.

3. Frantz Fanon, *The Wretched of the Earth* (New York: Grove Press, 2004), 67 and 88.

4. Charles Clermont-Ganneau, "The Arabs in Palestine," *Palestine Exploration Quarterly* 7, no. 4 (1875): 199–214, at 208 and 214. For a discussion of biblical archeology and its racial ideology, see Nadia Abu El-Haj, *Facts on the Ground: Archaeological Practice and Territorial Self-Fashioning in Israeli Society* (Chicago: University of Chicago Press, 2008).

5. Salim Tamari charged the Palestinian folklorists of the 1970s with producing a "reified ethnographic corpus" that was blind to "economic changes" and "historical nuance." See Salim Tamari, "Lepers, Lunatics, and Saints: The Nativist Ethnography of Tawfiq Canaan and His Circle," in *Mountain against the Sea: Essays on Palestinian Society and Culture* (Berkeley: University of California Press, 2009), 93–112, at 111. He has similar critical words for the national movement. See Tamari, "Soul of the Nation: The Fallah in the Eyes of the Urban Intelligentsia," 78. Ted Swedenburg showed how the "romanticized peasant" became ubiquitous in Palestinian national

culture precisely "through an erasure of internal difference and a forgetting of social antagonisms." Ted Swedenburg, "The Palestinian Peasant as National Signifier," *Anthropological Quarterly* 63, no. 1 (1990): 18–30. For a similar critique directed at the middle-class fetishization of local food, see Rayya El Zein, "Developing a Palestinian Resistance Economy through Agricultural Labor," *Journal of Palestine Studies* 46, no. 3 (2017): 7–26. Most recently, Kareem Rabie has pointed has out that both private developers and their critics "rely on a version of Palestinian history that has obscured class and economic change." See Kareem Rabie, *Palestine Is Throwing a Party and the Whole World Is Invited: Capital and State Building in the West Bank* (Durham, NC: Duke University Press, 2021), 159.

6. Jeff Halper, *War against the People: Israel, the Palestinians and Global Pacification* (London: Pluto Press, 2016); Antony Loewenstein, *The Palestine Laboratory: How Israel Exports the Technology of Occupation around the World* (New York: Verso, 2023); Darryl Li, "The Gaza Strip As Laboratory: Notes in the Wake of Disengagement," *Journal of Palestine Studies* 35, no. 2 (2006): 38–55.

7. Sam Grey and Raj Patel, "Food Sovereignty As Decolonization: Some Contributions from Indigenous Movements to Food System and Development Politics," *Agriculture and Human Values* 32, no. 3 (2015): 431–44. This has been the case for a long time, with people rebuilding crops and knowledge after genocide. For an example, see David A. Chang, *The Color of the Land: Race, Nation, and the Politics of Landownership in Oklahoma, 1832–1929* (Chapel Hill: University of North Carolina Press, 2010).

8. Owusu Bandele and Gail Myers, "Roots!" and Dãnia Davy et al., "Resistance," both in *Land Justice: Re-imagining Land, Food, and the Commons*, ed. Justine M. Williams and Eric Holt-Giménez (Oakland, CA: Food First Books, 2017), 44–66 and 67–91, respectively; Russell Rickford, " 'We Can't Grow Food on All This Concrete': The Land Question, Agrarianism, and Black Nationalist Thought in the Late 1960s and 1970s," *Journal of American History* 103, no. 4 (2017): 956–80.

9. David E. Gilbert, "Laborers Becoming 'Peasants': Agroecological Politics in a Sumatran Plantation Zone," *The Journal of Peasant Studies* 47, no. 5 (2020): 1030–51.

10. Leila Farsakh, *Palestinian Labour Migration to Israel: Labour, Land and Occupation* (London: Routledge, 2005), 85.

11. It was Sarah Roy who coined the term "de-development," quoted in Farsakh, *Palestinian Labour Migration*, 40.

12. Farsakh, *Palestinian Labour Migration*, 85–86. She writes that the area of cultivated land fell from 2.43 million dunums to 1.79 million between 1965 and 1992, and that agriculture's share of West Bank GDP fell from 35 percent in 1970 to 16 percent in 1991.

13. Farsakh, *Palestinian Labour Migration*, 4.

14. Salim Tamari, "Building Other People's Homes: The Palestinian Peasant's Household and Work in Israel," *Journal of Palestine Studies* 11, no. 1 (1981): 31–66, at 56.

15. Walid Rabie, "Mawsem al-Tin fi Biladi" (The Fig Season in My Country), *Heritage and Society* 4 (1975): 3–16.

16. Annelies Moors, *Women, Property and Islam: Palestinian Experiences, 1920–1990* (Cambridge, UK: Cambridge University Press, 1995).

17. This, in turn, gave rise to worries about the corrupting influence of Israeli cities—drugs, women, and other illicit activities—on the youth. For mentions of these influences, see Beshara Doumani, "Family and Politics in Salfit," in *Intifada: The Palestinian Uprising against Israeli Occupation*, ed. Joel Beinin and Zachary Lockman (Boston: South End Press, 1989), 143–54, at 147; Rema Hammami, "From Immodesty to Collaboration: Hamas, the Women's Movement, and National Identity in the Intifada," in *Political Islam: Essays from Middle East Report,* ed. Joel Beinin and Joe Stork (Berkeley: University of California Press, 1997), 194–210; Tobias Kelly, *Law, Violence and Sovereignty among West Bank Palestinians* (Cambridge, UK: Cambridge University Press, 2006); Tamari, "Building Other People's Homes."

18. Marisa Escribano and Nazmi El-Joubeh, "Migration and Change in a West Bank Village: The Case of Deir Dibwan," *Journal of Palestine Studies* 11, no. 1 (1981): 150–60.

19. Al-Fajr Staff, "Olive Harvest: Generations Meeting under the Olive Tree," *Al-Fajr Weekly*, November 1, 1985.

20. On place and "land rhetoric" see Barbara McKean Parmenter, *Giving Voice to Stones: Place and Identity in Palestinian Literature* (Austin: University of Texas Press, 1994).

21. While I did not systematically investigate this phenomenon, it frequently came up in my interviews. In his dissertation, Salim Tamari notes that rural people sought to invest in urban real estate. See Salim Tamari, "The Dislocation and Re-constitution of a Peasantry: The Social Economy of Agrarian Palestine in the Central Highlands and the Jordan Valley, 1960–1980," PhD diss., University of Manchester, 1983.

22. Joel S. Migdal, *Palestinian Society and Politics* (Princeton: Princeton University Press, 1980).

23. Sahar Khalifeh, *Wild Thorns* (London: Al Saqi Books, 1985). Tamari records an interview with a former tenant farmer who voices a similar critique. See Tamari, "The Dislocation and Re-constitution of a Peasantry: The Social Economy of Agrarian Palestine in the Central Highlands and the Jordan Valley, 1960–1980."

24. Andy Clarno, *Neoliberal Apartheid: Palestine/Israel and South Africa after 1994* (Chicago: University of Chicago Press, 2017); Farsakh, *Palestinian Labour Migration to Israel.*

25. Yael Berda, *Living Emergency: Israel's Permit Regime in the Occupied West Bank* (Stanford: Stanford University Press, 2017); Kelly, *Law, Violence and Sovereignty among West Bank Palestinians*; Sobhi Samour, "The Palestinian Economy between Settler Colonial Invasion and Neoliberal Management," PhD diss., School of Oriental and African Studies (SOAS), 2016.

26. Ethan Morton-Jerome, "The Struggle for Palestinian Workers' Rights in Israeli Settlements: The Case of Maan v. Zarfati Garage," *Jerusalem Quarterly* 86 (2021): 79–96; Andrew Ross, *Stone Men: Palestinians Who Built the Houses of Zion* (New York: Verso, 2019).

27. Dawn Chatty, *Displacement and Dispossession in the Modern Middle East* (Cambridge, UK: Cambridge University Press, 2010).

28. Rob Nixon, *Slow Violence and the Environmentalism of the Poor* (Cambridge, MA: Harvard University Press, 2011), 19.

29. Diana Allan, *Refugees of the Revolution: Experiences of Palestinian Exile* (Stanford: Stanford University Press, 2013); Rosemary Sayigh, *The Palestinians: From Peasants to Revolutionaries* (London: Zed Books, 1979).

30. Sumaya Farhat-Naser, *Zaytun Filastin wa-Mushkilatuha* (Olives of Palestine and Their Problems) (Birzeit: Birzeit University, 1980).

31. Abu Kishk would later detail how the Israeli state had dispossessed Palestinians inside Israel, and likely had that precedent in mind. See Bakir Abu Kishk, "Arab Land and Israeli Policy," *Journal of Palestine Studies* 11, no. 1 (1981): 124–35.

32. The conference was a series of workshops from 1981 to 1982 held at universities and centers in the West Bank in which researchers presented a series of papers covering all aspects of the economy in the occupied territories. Arab Thought Forum, ed., *Mu'tamir al-Tanmiyya min Ajl al-Sumud* (Development for Sumud Conference) (Jerusalem: Arab Thought Forum, 1983), 148. The papers, as well as abbreviated discussion minutes from the meetings, were published in Arabic in 1983.

33. Abdulrahman Abu Arafeh, Yusuf al-Azzeh, and Dawood Istanbuli, "Al-Waqaʿ al-Ziraʿiyya fil-Minatiq al-Muhtala wa-Dururat al-Tanmiyya" (The Agricultural Situation in the Occupied Areas and the Requirements of Development)," in *Mu'tamir al-Tanmiyya min Ajl al-Sumud* (Development for Sumud Conference) (Jerusalem: Arab Thought Forum, 1983), 39.

34. A complete history of the voluntary work movement has yet to be written. In addition to interviews with voluntary work activists, this section draws on the following: Tamir Sorek, *The Optimist: A Social Biography of Tawfiq Zayyad* (Stanford: Stanford University Press, 2020); Lisa Taraki, "The Development of Political Consciousness among Palestinians in the Occupied Territories, 1967–1987," in *Intifada: Palestine at the Crossroads*, ed. Jamal Nassar and Roger Heacock (New York: Praeger,

1990), 53–72; Linda Tabar, "People's Power: Lessons from the First Intifada," in *Critical Readings of Development under Colonialism: Towards a Political Economy for Liberation in the Occupied Palestinian Territories*, ed. Linda Tabar and Omar Jabary Salamanca (Ramallah: Rosa Luxemburg Foundation, 2015), 135–72.

35. Voluntary work and "work parties" are common in peasant communities elsewhere. See Daniel Jaffee, *Brewing Justice: Fair Trade Coffee, Sustainability and Survival* (Berkeley: University of California Press, 2014); Wendy Wolford, *This Land Is Ours Now: Social Mobilization and the Meanings of Land in Brazil* (Durham, NC: Duke University Press, 2010); Marygold Walsh-Dilley, "Negotiating Hybridity in Highland Bolivia: Indigenous Moral Economy and the Expanding Market for Quinoa," *The Journal of Peasant Studies* 40, no. 4 (2013): 659–82.

36. Atran, for example, argues that this kind of cooperation and coordination was inseparable from *masha'* and the need to plant and harvest certain crops on schedule. See Scott Atran, "Hamula Organisation and Masha'a Tenure in Palestine," *Man* (1986): 271–95. Barghouti described it to me like this: "Voluntary work had the same idea as aid (*'awna*), which was part of the Palestinian cultural inheritance (*mawruth al-thaqafi*) [. . .] when the peasant (*fallah*) would finish his harvest, and would have free time, he would go and help others."

37. Atran, "Hamula Organisation and Masha'a Tenure in Palestine," 281; Amiry, "Space, Kinship and Gender," 63.

38. Amiry, "Space, Kinship and Gender," 144–51.

39. Birgit Schaebler, "Practicing Musha: Common Lands and the Common Good in Southern Syria under the Ottomans and the French," in *New Perspectives on Property and Land in the Middle East*, ed. Roger Owen and Martin Bunton (Cambridge, MA: Harvard University Press, 2000), 241–312.

40. Taraki, "The Development of Political Consciousness among Palestinians in the Occupied Territories, 1967–1987."

41. Leena Dallasheh, "Persevering through Colonial Transition: Nazareth's Palestinian Residents after 1948," *Journal of Palestine Studies* 45, no. 2 (2016): 8–23.

42. Sorek, *The Optimist*, 98.

43. On the political and legal developments leading up to Land Day, see Geremy Forman, "Israeli Settlement of Title in Arab Areas: The Special Land Settlement Operation in Northern Israel (1955–1967)," PhD diss., University of Haifa, 2005.

44. Cited in Sorek, *The Optimist*, 99.

45. Taraki, "The Development of Political Consciousness among Palestinians in the Occupied Territories, 1967–1987."

46. Al-Fajr Staff, "Two Hundred Arrested during Voluntary Work," *Al-Fajr Weekly*, May 24, 1981.

47. Al-Fajr Staff, "Volunteers Work on Kobar's Land," *Al-Fajr Weekly*, September 21, 1984.

48. On this point, and the importance of voluntary work within a broader revolutionary collective politics, see Tabar, "People's Power: Lessons from the First Intifada."

49. PARC Bulletin, n.d., cited in Samir Abed-Rabbo and Doris Safie, eds., *The Palestinian Uprising: FACTS Information Committee, Jerusalem* (Belmont: Association of Arab-American University Graduates, 1990), 291.

50. PARC Bulletin, n.d., cited in Abed-Rabbo and Safie, *The Palestinian Uprising*, 295.

51. Ismail Daiq, "Dur Al-Munazzamat al-Jamhariyya fi al-Tanmiyya al-Rifiyya li-l-Ard al-Muhtalla" (The Role of Mass Organizations in Rural Development for Occupied Land), *Samed al-Iqtisadi* 61 (June 1986): 41–53.

52. Arab Thought Forum, *Mu'tamir al-Tanmiyya min Ajl al-Sumud* (Development for Sumud Conference), 137; and Awartani, "Khuta Muqtaraha li-l-Tatwir al-Zira' fi al-Diffa al-Gharbiyya wa-Qita' Ghazza" (Proposed Plan for Agricultural Development in the West Bank and Gaza Strip), 24.

53. Glenn E. Robinson, "The Role of the Professional Middle Class in the Mobilization of Palestinian Society: The Medical and Agricultural Committees," *International Journal of Middle East Studies* 25, no. 2 (1993): 301–26, at 312.

54. Ghassan Jarrar, "Mulahazat Hawl al-Mashakil al-Rifiyya fi al-Minatiq al-Muhtala" (Notes on Rural Problems in the Occupied Territories), *Samed al-Iqtisadi* 61 (June 1986): 17–33.

55. Jarrar, "Notes on Rural Problems," 28.

56. Robinson, "The Role of the Professional Middle Class in the Mobilization of Palestinian Society," 314.

57. Adel Samara and Shehada Awda, *Al-Himayya al-Sha'biyya* (Popular Protection) (Damascus: Dar Kan'an li-l-Darasat wa-l-Nashr, 1988), 114.

58. Samara and Awda *Popular Protection*. Samara is one of the few thinkers whom I have found discussing the collectivization of property. In an early article, he would argue that peasant culture contains a contradictory position on private ownership. On the one hand, he wrote, peasant culture is infused with cooperative labor, a spirit of volunteerism, and a value of common and public land. On the other hand, there is an element that sanctifies private ownership. For Samara, this kind of individualism could be potentially overcome by the shared attachment to village land. See Adel Samara, "Hawl 'Alaqa al-Iqtisad bi-l-Turath al-Sha'bi" (About the Relationship of the Economy to Popular Culture), *Heritage and Society* 1, no. 1 (1974): 80–84.

59. Taraki, "The Development of Political Consciousness among Palestinians in

the Occupied Territories, 1967–1987"; Tabar, "People's Power: Lessons from the First Intifada."

60. PARC Bulletin, May 1988, cited in Abed-Rabbo and Safie, *The Palestinian Uprising*, 300.

61. Anthropologists Nisreen Mazzawi and Amalia Sa'ar, in their history of the *hawakir* in Nazareth, write that "until 1948 the *hakura* was an essential and integral part of the home in Nazareth. It provided food, was a source of income in times of need, and constituted a major locus of social life, particularly for women." Nisreen Mazzawi and Amalia Sa'ar, "The Ḥawākīr of Nazareth: The History and Contemporary Face of a Cultural Ecological Institution," *International Journal of Middle East Studies* 50, no. 3 (2018): 537–56. The *hakura* (pl. *hawakir*) refers to a plot of land adjacent to the home for cultivating fruit trees and vegetables. In the highlands, the *hawakir* once formed a ring around the village, separating the built-up area from the surrounding agricultural lands. See Amiry, "Space, Kinship and Gender." PARC reported distributing "600,000 vegetable seedings (mainly tomato, eggplant, and pepper) and 250,000 packets of seeds." See PARC Interim Report, June 1988, cited in Abed-Rabbo and Safie, *The Palestinian Uprising*, 303.

62. PARC Interim Report, June 1988, cited in Abed-Rabbo and Safie, *The Palestinian Uprising*, 302.

63. Robinson, "The Role of the Professional Middle Class in the Mobilization of Palestinian Society."

64. Rema Hammami, "NGOs: The Professionalisation of Politics," *Race and Class* 37 (1995): 51–63.

65. In the 1990s, Israel began to develop an "industrial" olive sector based on a new cultivar that responded well to irrigation. See Natalia Gutkowski, *Struggling for Time: Environmental Governance and Agrarian Resistance in Israel/Palestine* (Stanford: Stanford University Press, 2024). Jordan, once the main market for Palestinian oil, also created its own olive sector, and only imported Palestinian oil during poor harvests. Cheaper oil produced by Spanish and North African growers also cut into the internal market. See UNCTAD, "The Besieged Palestinian Agricultural Sector" (New York: United Nations, 2015); Jeffrey Drew Reger, "Planting Palestine: The Political Economy of Olive Culture in the 20th Century Galilee and West Bank," PhD diss., Georgetown University, 2018.

66. Jehad Yousif Alayasa, "Building on the Strengths of Indigenous Knowledge to Promote Sustainable Development in Crisis Conditions from the Community Level: The Case of Palestine," PhD diss., Portland State University, 2012, 112.

67. This crisis was also the impetus for the creation of Canaan Fair Trade in Jenin, which has been a leader in the development of organic and fair-trade olive oil

in Palestine. See Gabi Kirk, "Commodifying Indigeneity? Settler Colonialism and Racial Capitalism in Fair Trade Farming in Palestine," *Historical Materialism* 31, no. 2 (2023): 236–68, at 253.

68. On the work that goes into creating these markets, see Anne Meneley, "Blood, Sweat and Tears in a Bottle of Palestinian Extra-Virgin Olive Oil," *Food, Culture & Society* 14, no. 2 (2011): 275–92; Kirk, "Commodifying Indigeneity?"

69. Farhat-Naser, in her important survey of olive production in the 1980s, reports low levels of chemical fertilizer use in the 1980s, and recommends increasing its use to increase productivity. See Sumaya Farhat-Naser, *Zaytun Filastin wa-Mushkilatuha* (Olives of Palestine and Their Problems) (Birzeit: Birzeit University Press, 1980). What farmers in the central highlands told me was quite similar to what farmers in Jenin explained to Gabi Kirk: "Farmers who sell their olive oil to Canaan must maintain organic certification, which every farmer I spoke to said was not a problem because of how their existing farming practices, which they learned before Canaan was founded, fit well with organic production." Kirk, "Commodifying Indigeneity?" 254.

70. As anthropologist Anne Meneley has explained, the need to cater to international standards—in particular, "extra virgin"—has created a new group of Palestinian experts who face the task of making Palestinian oil appeal to the tastes and, more important, regulatory standards of Western consumers. See Anne Meneley, "Discourses of Distinction in Contemporary Palestinian Extra-Virgin Olive Oil Production," *Food and Foodways* 22, no. 1–2 (2014): 48–64.

71. It was funded in part by Oxfam, through its "Grove to Market" initiative, with support from the Applied Research Institute—Jerusalem (ARIJ), a large Palestinian NGO.

72. A century ago, a missionary would describe terraced agriculture in the highlands this way: "In the districts where vine and fruit-trees are grown, the terraces add much to the beauty of the hillsides. A row of fig-trees, mulberries, etc., will often be seen planted near the outer edge, where the soil is deepest, and in the spaces between them and the wall of the terrace above vegetables will be grown, or the land will be ploughed, and corn, lentils, or other crops, sown there. Vines are commonly planted close to the outer wall, the branches being trained so that they hang down over it. In the early summer, when the vines are in their fresh green foliage, the picture, as one looks at such a terraced hillside from below, with cascade after cascade of brilliant verdure relieved by the darker hue of the olive and fig, the warm red-brown colour of the soil, and the gray of the stone walls peeping out here and there, is very beautiful." See Charles Thomas Wilson, *Peasant Life in the Holy Land* (London: E. P. Dutton, 1906), 200.

73. Fatima AbdulKarim, "The Palestinian Ecovillage Putting Grassroots Democ-

racy into Action," *+972 Magazine*, January 10, 2023, https://www.972mag.com/farkha-ecovillage-democracy-communism/; Alice Gray, "Green Resistance: Building Palestine's First Eco-Village," *The New Arab*, December 17, 2015, https://www.newarab.com/analysis/green-resistance-building-palestines-first-eco-village.

74. Marc Edelman, "What Is a Peasant? What Are Peasantries? A Briefing Paper on Issues of Definition," paper presented at First Session of the Intergovernmental Working Group on a United Nations Declaration on the Rights of Peasants and Other People Working in Rural Areas, Geneva, July, 2013, 15–19.

75. Annette Aurelie Desmarais, *La Via Campesina: Globalization and the Power of Peasants* (London: Pluto Press, 2007), 38–39.

76. Fanon, *The Wretched of the Earth,* 65.

77. Mourid Barghouti, *I Saw Ramallah* (New York: American University in Cairo Press, 2000).

Conclusion

1. Madeleine Fairbairn, *Fields of Gold: Financing the Global Land Rush* (Ithaca: Cornell University Press, 2020); Michael Levien, *Dispossession without Development: Land Grabs in Neoliberal India* (Oxford: Oxford University Press, 2018). Scholars are also returning to older struggles for land for insights. See Kristin Ross, *The Commune Form: The Transformation of Everyday Life* (New York: Verso, 2024).

2. Ricardo Jacobs, "An Urban Proletariat with Peasant Characteristics: Land Occupations and Livestock Raising in South Africa," *The Journal of Peasant Studies* 45, no. 5–6 (2018): 884–903; Matthew C. Canfield, *Translating Food Sovereignty: Cultivating Justice in an Age of Transnational Governance* (Stanford: Stanford University Press, 2022).

3. Courtney Fullilove, " 'Famine Foods' and the Values of Biodiversity Preservation in Israel-Palestine," *Isis* 113, no. 3 (2022): 625–36; Courtney Fullilove and Abdallah Alimari, "Baladi Seeds in the oPt: Populations as Objects of Preservation and Units of Analysis," in *Towards Responsible Plant Data Linkage: Data Challenges for Agricultural Research and Development*, ed. Hugh Williamson and Sabina Leonelli (Cham, Switzerland: Springer, 2023), 65–84; Anne Meneley, "Hope in the Ruins: Seeds, Plants, and Possibilities of Regeneration," *Environment and Planning E: Nature and Space* 4, no. 1 (2021): 158–72.

4. Birzeit University, "Young Activists Examine Models to Implement a Resistance Economy," June 10, 2022, https://www.birzeit.edu/en/news/young-activists-examine-models-implement-resistance-economy; Nadine Fattaleh and Adam Albarghouthi, "Agroecology, from Palestine to the Diaspora," *Science for the People Magazine* (blog), August 1, 2022, https://magazine.scienceforthepeople.org/vol25-1-the-soil-and-worker/agroecology-from-palestine-to-the-diaspora/; Abeer Musleh,

"Reviving the 'Hakora': Local Farming and Collaborative Efforts," *Sharing Society: The Impact of Collaborative Collective Actions in the Transformation of Contemporary Societies* (2019): 68–78.

5. Nabil Abu Shammala, "Status of Farmers in Border Areas in the Gaza Strip from a Food Sovereignty Perspective" (Ramallah: Dalia, n.d.); Tariq Dana, "Localising the Economy as a Resistance Response: A Contribution to the 'Resistance Economy' Debate in the Occupied Palestinian Territories," *Journal of Peacebuilding & Development* 15, no. 2 (2020): 192–204; Tariq Dana, "A Resistance Economy: What Is It and Can It Provide an Alternative?" *Rosa Luxemburg Stiftung PAL Papers Series* (2014); Faiq Mari, "Mashaʿ of the Periphery: Collective Labor and Property in Palestinian Liberation Struggle," PhD diss., ETH Zurich, 2024; Fathi Nimer, "Food Sovereignty in a Palestinian Economy of Resistance," *Al-Shabaka*, 2024, https://al-shabaka.org/briefs/food-sovereignty-in-a-palestinian-economy-of-resistance/; Alaa Tartir et al., "Defeating Dependency, Creating a Resistance Economy," *Al-Shabaka,* February 13, 2012, https://al-shabaka.org/briefs/defeating-dependency-creating-resistance-economy/; Timothy Seidel, "Settler Colonialism and Land-Based Struggle in Palestine: Toward a Decolonial Political Economy," in *Political Economy of Palestine: Critical, Interdisciplinary, and Decolonial Perspectives*, ed. Alaa Tartir, Tariq Dana, and Timothy Seidel (London: Palgrave Macmillan, 2021), 81–107.

6. Ali Abunimah, *The Battle for Justice in Palestine* (Chicago: Haymarket Books, 2014), 120–24.

7. Vivien Sansour and Alaa Tartir, "Palestinian Farmers: A Last Stronghold of Resistance," *Al-Shabaka* (blog), 2014, https://al-shabaka.org/briefs/palestinian-farmers-a-last-stronghold-of-resistance/.

8. Abunimah, *The Battle for Justice in Palestine*, 123.

9. Ruba Anabtawi, "Hijrat al-ʿUdwi: Hin Tazriʿ al-ʾArd al-Filastiniyya al-Ghithaʾ al-Nazif l-Yatamatiʿ bi-al-Amiriki wa-al-Yabani" (Organic Migration: When Palestinian Land Grows Clean Food for Americans and Japanese to Enjoy), *Environment and Development Horizons*, March 1, 2019, https://www.maan-ctr.org/magazine/article/2161/; Gabi Kirk, "Commodifying Indigeneity? Settler Colonialism and Racial Capitalism in Fair Trade Farming in Palestine," *Historical Materialism* 31, no. 2 (2023): 236–68.

10. Rayya El Zein, "Developing a Palestinian Resistance Economy through Agricultural Labor," *Journal of Palestine Studies* 46, no. 3 (2017): 7–26.

11. Salim Tamari, "The Dislocation and Re-Constitution of a Peasantry: The Social Economy of Agrarian Palestine in the Central Highlands and the Jordan Valley, 1960–1980," PhD diss., University of Manchester, 1983, 274–78.

12. MIFTAH, "The Jordan Valley" (Ramallah: MIFTAH, 2017), https://www.miftah.org/Display.cfm?DocId=26418&CategoryId=4.

13. Julie Trottier, Nelly Leblond, and Yaakov Garb, "The Political Role of Date Palm Trees in the Jordan Valley: The Transformation of Palestinian Land and Water Tenure in Agriculture Made Invisible by Epistemic Violence," *Environment and Planning E: Nature and Space* 3, no. 1 (2020): 114–40. On earlier phases of capitalist agriculture in the Valley, see Alex Pollock, "Realist Methodology and the Articulation of Modes of Production: An Analysis of Palestinian Peasant Household Production in the North Jordan Valley of the Occupied West Bank/the Central Highlands of Palestine," PhD diss., University of Strathclyde, 1987.

14. Gabi Kirk and Paul Kohlbry, "Situating the Transnational in Agrarian Palestine," in *Resisting Domination in Palestine: Mechanisms and Techniques of Control, Coloniality and Settler Colonialism*, ed. Alaa Tartir, Timothy Seidel, and Tariq Dana (New York: Bloomsbury, 2024).

15. Hadeel Hunaiti, "Arab Jahalin: From the Nakba to the Wall" (Ramallah: Stop the Wall, 2008), 34–38.

16. Hisham Awartani, *The Agricultural Sector of the West Bank and the Gaza Strip* (Geneva: UNCTAD, 1993), 38.

17. Natalia Gutkowski, "Bodies That Count: Administering Multispecies in Palestine/Israel's Borderlands," *Environment and Planning E: Nature and Space* (2020): 4, no. 1 (2021): 135-157; Hunaiti, "Arab Jahalin: From the Nakba to the Wall."

18. Neve Gordon, *Israel's Occupation* (Berkeley: University of California Press, 2008), 6.

19. Paul Kohlbry, "Selling Rural Palestine: Land Devaluation, Ethical Investment, and the Limits of Human Rights," *Antipode* 55, no. 3 (2023): 897–915.

20. Ahmed Alsammak, "Palestinians Aim to Prove Right of Return with Ancestral Land Titles," *Middle East Eye*, September 23, 2021, https://www.middleeasteye.net/news/israel-palestine-land-titles-kushan-baladi-right-return; *Kushan Baladi: Mubadara l-Tawthiq Haq al-Filistini b-Ardi* (Kushan Baladi: An Initiative to Document the Palestinian Right to Land) (2021), https://www.youtube.com/watch?v=KX-MAt2Zzw_A.

21. Rema Hammami, "Between Heaven and Earth: Transformations in Religiosity and Labor among Southern Palestinian Peasant and Refugee Women, 1920–1993," PhD diss., Temple University, 1994; Joan Mandell, "Gaza: Israel's Soweto," *MERIP*, October 20, 1985, https://merip.org/1985/10/gaza-israels-soweto/.

22. Hammami, "Between Heaven and Earth"; Sara M. Roy, *The Gaza Strip: The Political Economy of de-Development* (Washington, DC: Institute for Palestine Studies, 1995).

23. Ron J. Smith and Martin Isleem, "Farming the Front Line: Gaza's Activist Farmers in the No Go Zones," *City* 21, no. 3–4 (July 4, 2017): 448–65.

24. Shourideh Molavi, *Environmental Warfare in Gaza: Colonial Violence and New Landscapes of Resistance* (London: Pluto Press, 2024).

25. For a work on the previous wars, dated shortly after it was published, see Jean-Pierre Filiu, "The Twelve Wars on Gaza," *Journal of Palestine Studies* 44, no. 1 (2014): 52–60. While there has been much written about the genocide in Gaza, South Africa's case against Israel in the International Court of Justice by South Africa remains one of the most powerful accounts. It too was dated quickly.

26. Jason Burke and Malak A. Tantesh, "Gaza Food Production 'Decimated' with 70% of Farmland Hit, UN Finds," *The Guardian*, November 21, 2024; He Yin et al., "Evaluating War-Induced Damage to Agricultural Land in the Gaza Strip since October 2023 Using PlanetScope and SkySat Imagery," *Science of Remote Sensing* 11 (June 1, 2025): 100199. The Food and Agriculture Organization (FAO) of the United Nations has also carried out regular analyses of war's effects on agricultural land. The latest at the time of writing was FAO and UNITAR, "Agricultural Damage Assessment in the Gaza Strip from October 7th 2023 to September 1st 2024," 2024, https://openknowledge.fao.org/handle/20.500.14283/cd2592en.

27. Christian Henderson, "Israel's Weapon of Hunger in Gaza," *Agrarian Conversations* (blog), 2021, https://www.peasantjournal.org/news/israel's-weapon-of-hunger-in-gaza/.

28. Mandell, "Gaza," 11. In the 1980s, when Israel was expanding settlements in the area, settlers used excavators to bury cultivated areas, while the government attempted to convince farmers to bury it themselves, and then rent the land back from the state. Al-Fajr Staff, "Mowasi Land Threatend," *Al-Fajr Weekly*, April 29, 1981.

29. Fred Pearce, "As War Halts, the Environmental Devastation in Gaza Runs Deep," *Yale E360* (blog), February 26, 2025, https://e360.yale.edu/features/gaza-war-environment.

30. Pearce, "As War Halts, the Environmental Devastation in Gaza Runs Deep."

31. Luke Carneal, "A Picture of Farming in Gaza Today: In Remembrance of Youssef Saqr Abu Rabie," *Jadaliyya* (blog), November 11, 2024, https://www.jadaliyya.com/Details/46334.

32. " 'This Is My Only Hope' Says Palestinian Who Farms to Combat Hunger," *Al-Jazeera*, August 2, 2024.

33. Hadeel Awni Atallah, "Youssef Abu Rabie: Al-Ghazi Lan Yatarajai Lakin Nafad al-Buthur Yunthir Bil-Tawaquf" (Youssef Abu Rabie: Gazans Will Not Retreat, But Seed Saving Risks Coming to a Halt), *Environment and Development Horizons*, September 1, 2024, https://www.maan-ctr.org/magazine/article/4342/.

34. Carneal, "A Picture of Farming in Gaza Today."

35. Julia Frankel, "Israel Turbocharges West Bank Settlement Expansion with

Largest Land Grab in Decades," *AP News*, July 3, 2024, https://apnews.com/article/israel-palestinians-hamas-war-news-07-03-2024-033deab379a16efdf9989de8d6eafof8; Amira Hass, "How Palestinians Near Bethlehem Are Expelled From Their Land," *Haaretz*, May 25, 2024; Kerem Navot, "An Israeli Roadblock: How Israel Took Control over the Bethlehem Area?" n.d., https://www.keremnavot.org/israeli-roadblock.

36. Violeta Colman et al., "We Will Return: An Analysis of the Escalating Forced Displacement of Palestinian Communities in the West Bank since the Genocide in Gaza" (Ramallah: Stop the Wall, 2024); Hamdan Ballal Al-Huraini, "Settler-Soldier Militias Threaten Susiya with Death and Displacement," *+972 Magazine*, October 31, 2023, https://www.972mag.com/susiya-settler-soldier-militia-displacement/. For earlier analyses of displacement, see Land Research Center (LRC), "al-Bur al-Istitaniyat al-Raʿiat Nuqtat al-Intilaq l-Nahb al-Mazid min al-ʾAradi al- Filastiniyya" (Pastoral Settlement Outposts as a Starting Point for Increased Theft of Palestinian Land), (Halhul: Land Research Center, July 2023); Stop the Wall, "The Palestinian Periphery: Home Demolitions and Settler Colonialism in the Jordan Valley and South Hebron Hills" (Ramallah: Stop the Wall, 2017).

37. Peter Beaumont and Quique Kierszenbaum, " 'Last Nail in the Coffin': Israeli Settlers Push on with Fresh West Bank Land Grab," *The Guardian*, February 13, 2025; Hagar Shezaf, "Israeli Settlers Pressured, the Cabinet Approved. Now Annexation Is Creeping into West Bank's Area B," *Haaretz*, December 30, 2024.

38. Christian Lund, *Nine-Tenths of the Law: Enduring Dispossession In Indonesia* (New Haven: Yale University Press, 2020), 4.

References

Archives and Libraries

Birzeit University Library, Birzeit, West Bank, Palestine

Department of Statistics Archival Library, Amman, Jordan

Hashemite Hall, University of Jordan Library, Amman

Israel State Archive, Jerusalem

Inash al-Usra Archive, Ramallah, West Bank, Palestine

al-Najah National University Library, Nablus, West Bank, Palestine

National Library of Israel, Jerusalem

Periodicals

(consulted in samples between 1979 and 1987)

al-Anba'

al-Fajr

Al-Fajr Weekly

al-Quds

al-Sha'ab

Books and Articles

Abduljawwad, Saleh. "Tajarib min al-'Ard al-Muhtala: Beit Diqqu that al-Qamh al-Asfar" (Experiences from the Occupied Land: The Yellow Wheat of Beit Diqqu). *Shu'un Filistiniyya* 55 (1976): 95–104.

AbdulKarim, Fatima. "The Palestinian Ecovillage Putting Grassroots Democracy

into Action." *+972 Magazine*, January 10, 2023. https://www.972mag.com/farkha
-ecovillage-democracy-communism/.

Abed-Rabbo, Samir, and Doris Safie, eds. *The Palestinian Uprising: FACTS Information Committee, Jerusalem*. Belmont: Association of Arab-American University
Graduates, 1990.

Abu Arafeh, Abudulrahman. "Siyasat al-Sira' 'ala al-'Ard fi al-Diffa al-Muhtala" (The
Politics of Land Struggle in the Occupied West Bank). *Samed al-Iqtisadi* 46 (December 1983): 53–72.

Abu Arafeh, Abdulrahman, Yusuf al-Azzeh, and Dawood Istanbuli. "Al-Waqa' al-
Zira'iyya fi al-Minatiq al-Muhtala wa-Dururat al-Tanmiyya." (The Agricultural
Situation in the Occupied Areas and the Requirements of Development). In
Mu'tamir al-Tanmiyya min Ajl al-Sumud (Development for Sumud Conference).
Jerusalem: Arab Thought Forum, 1983.

Abu El-Haj, Nadia. *Facts on the Ground: Archaeological Practice and Territorial Self-
Fashioning in Israeli Society*. Chicago: University of Chicago Press, 2008.

Abu Kishk, Bakir. "Arab Land and Israeli Policy." *Journal of Palestine Studies* 11, no. 1
(1981): 124–35.

Abu-Lughod, Lila. "The Romance of Resistance: Tracing Transformations of Power
through Bedouin Women." *American Ethnologist* 17, no. 1 (1990): 41–55.

———. "Zones of Theory in the Anthropology of the Arab World." *Annual Review of
Anthropology* 18 (1989): 267–306.

Abunimah, Ali. *The Battle for Justice in Palestine*. Chicago: Haymarket Books, 2014.

Abu Rajili, Khalil. "Al-Zira' al-'Arabi fi Filastin Qabal Qiam Dawlat Israel" (Arab Agriculture in Palestine Before the Founding of the State of Israel). *Shu'un Filistiniyya* 11 (1972): 128–43.

Abu-Sada, Caroline. "Cultivating Dependence: Palestinian Agriculture under the Israeli Occupation." In *The Power of Inclusive Exclusion: Anatomy of Israeli Rule in
the Occupied Palestinian Territories*, edited by Sari Hanafi, Adi Ophir, and Michal
Givoni, 413–29. New York: Zone Books, 2009.

Abu Shammala, Nabil. "Status of Farmers in Border Areas in the Gaza Strip from a
Food Sovereignty Perspective." Ramallah: Dalia, n.d.

Adler, Raya. "The Tenants of Wadi Hawarith: Another View of the Land Question in
Palestine." *International Journal of Middle East Studies* 20, no. 2 (1988): 197–220.

Agarwal, Bina. *A Field of One's Own: Gender and Land Rights in South Asia*. Cambridge, UK: Cambridge University Press, 1994.

Ajl, Max. "Does the Arab Region Have an Agrarian Question?" *The Journal of Peasant
Studies* 48, no. 5 (2021): 955–83.

Akram-Lodhi, A. Haroon. "The Ties That Bind? Agroecology and the Agrarian Question in the Twenty-First Century." *The Journal of Peasant Studies* 48, no. 4 (2021): 687–714.

Al-Alul, Khalil. *Istislah wa-Istiglal 'Aradi al-Diffa al-Gharbiyya* (Land Reclamation and Use in the West Bank). Jerusalem: Arab Thought Forum, 1987.

Alayasa, Jehad Yousif. "Building on the Strengths of Indigenous Knowledge to Promote Sustainable Development in Crisis Conditions from the Community Level: The Case of Palestine." PhD diss., Portland State University, 2012.

Alden Wily, Liz. "Looking Back to See Forward: The Legal Niceties of Land Theft in Land Rushes." *The Journal of Peasant Studies* 39, no. 3–4 (2012): 751–75.

al-Fajr Staff. "Anatomy of a Forged Land Deal." *Al-Fajr Weekly*, April 8, 1983.

———. "Arson at Nablus District Court Destroys Thousands of Legal Documents." *Al-Fajr Weekly*, January 4, 1985.

———. "Hal Qama Samasira al-Ihtilal bi-Ihraq Mahkama Nablus l-Abada Malafat Qadiya al-'Aradi?" (Did Occupation Brokers Burn the Nablus Court to Get Rid of Land Case Files?). *Al-Fajr*, January 5, 1985.

———. "End of Israeli Rainbow in West Bank." *Al-Fajr Weekly*, February 29, 1982.

———. "Highlights of Recent Settlement Activity." *Al-Fajr Weekly*, October 16, 1981.

———. "Israel's Covert Land Grabs Revealed." *Al-Fajr Weekly*, September 6, 1981.

———. "Mowasi Land Threatened." *Al-Fajr Weekly*, April 29, 1981.

———. "Olive Harvest: Generations Meeting under the Olive Tree." *Al-Fajr Weekly*, November 1, 1985.

———. "Two Hundred Arrested during Voluntary Work." *Al-Fajr Weekly*, May 24, 1981.

———. "Volunteers Work on Kobar's Land." *Al-Fajr Weekly*, September 21, 1984.

Alff, Kristen. "Changing Capitalist Structures and Settler-Colonial Land Purchases in Northern Palestine, 1897–1922." *International Journal of Middle East Studies* 55, no. 4 (2023): 675–92.

Al-Huraini, Hamdan Ballal. "Settler-Soldier Militias Threaten Susiya with Death and Displacement." *+972 Magazine*, October 31, 2023. https://www.972mag.com/ susiya-settler-soldier-militia-displacement/.

Alkhalili, Noura. "Enclosures from Below: The Mushaa' in Contemporary Palestine." *Antipode* 49, no. 5 (2017): 1103–24.

———. "Protection from Below: On Waqf between Theft and Morality." *Jerusalem Quarterly* 70 (2017): 62.

Allan, Diana. "Introduction: Past Continuous." In *Voices of the Nakba*, edited by Diana Allan, 1–19. London: Pluto Press, 2021.

———. *Refugees of the Revolution: Experiences of Palestinian Exile*. Stanford: Stanford University Press, 2013.

Allen, Lori. *The Rise and Fall of Human Rights: Cynicism and Politics in Occupied Palestine*. Stanford: Stanford University Press, 2013.

Allweil, Yael. "Neoliberal Settlement as Violent State Project." *ACME: An International Journal for Critical Geographies* 19, no. 1 (2020): 70–105.

Alqamar, Luna. "Farming as Resistance: Reviving Indigenous Agricultural Practices in Palestine." *Vice*, July 12, 2018. https://www.vice.com/en/article/3kyzej/farming-as-resistance-reviving-indigenous-agricultural-practices-in-palestine.

Alsammak, Ahmed. "Palestinians Aim to Prove Right of Return with Ancestral Land Titles." *Middle East Eye*, September 23, 2021. https://www.middleeasteye.net/news/israel-palestine-land-titles-kushan-baladi-right-return.

al-Sha'ab Staff. "Al-Sahafiyyun al-Falastiniyyun Yuwada'un Shahid al-Sahafa Hassan Abdulhalim" (Palestinian Journalists Bid Farewell to the Martyr of Journalists Hassan Abdulhalim). *Al-Sha'ab*, December 23, 1985.

Altieri, Miguel A. "Applying Agroecology to Enhance the Productivity of Peasant Farming Systems in Latin America." *Environment, Development and Sustainability* 1, no. 3–4 (1999): 197–217.

Amira, Saad. "The Slow Violence of Israeli Settler-Colonialism and the Political Ecology of Ethnic Cleansing in the West Bank." *Settler Colonial Studies* 11, no. 4 (2021): 512–32.

Amiry, Suad. "Space, Kinship and Gender: The Social Dimension of Peasant Architecture in Palestine." PhD diss., University of Edinburgh, 1987.

Anabtawi, Ruba. "Hijrat al-'Udwi: Hin Tazri' al-'Ard al-Filastiniyya al-Ghitha' al-Nazif l-Yatamati' bi-al-Amiriki wa-al-Yabani" (Organic Migration: When Palestinian Land Grows Clean Food for Americans and Japanese to Enjoy). *Environment and Development Horizons*, March 1, 2019. https://www.maan-ctr.org/magazine/article/2161/.

Anderson, Charles. "From Petition to Confrontation: The Palestinian National Movement and the Rise of Mass Politics, 1929–1939." PhD diss., New York University, 2013.

———. "When Palestinians Became Human Shields: Counterinsurgency, Racialization, and the Great Revolt (1936–1939)." *Comparative Studies in Society and History* 63, no. 3 (2021): 625–54.

———. "Will the Real Palestinian Peasantry Please Sit Down? Towards a New History of British Rule in Palestine, 1917–1936," LSE Middle East Centre Paper, 2015.

Arab Thought Forum, ed. *Mu'tamir al-Tanmiyya min Ajl al-Sumud* (Development for Sumud Conference). Jerusalem: Arab Thought Forum, 1983.

Araghi, Farshad A. "Global Depeasantization, 1945–1990." *The Sociological Quarterly* 36, no. 2 (1995): 337–68.

Armitage, David. "John Locke, Carolina, and the Two Treatises of Government." *Political Theory* 32, no. 5 (2004): 602–27.

Arraf, Shukri, and Sami Khalil Mari. *Al-ʾArd, al-Insan wa-al-Juhd: Dirasa li-Hadaratina al-Madiya ʿala Ardina* (Land, Man, and Effort: A Study of Our Material Culture on Our Land). Akka: Maktabat wa-Matbaʿat Abu Rahmun, 1982.

Arrighi, Giovanni. "Labour Supplies in Historical Perspective: A Study of the Proletarianization of the African Peasantry in Rhodesia." *The Journal of Development Studies* 6, no. 3 (1970): 197–234.

———. *The Long Twentieth Century: Money, Power, and the Origins of Our Times*. New York: Verso Books, 1994.

Asad, Talal. "Anthropological Texts and Ideological Problems: An Analysis of Cohen on Arab Villages in Israel." *Economy and Society* 4, no. 3 (1975): 251–82.

Assaf, Said A. "A Study on the Recent Growing of a Rapidly Propagating Olive Cultivar Mis-Named 'Improved Nabali' and Its Effect on Impeding the West Bank Olive Industry." *Acta Horticulturae* 356 (1994): 432–37.

Atallah, Hadeel Awni. "Youssef Abu Rabie: Al-Ghazi Lan Yatarajai Lakin Nafad al-Buthur Yunthir Bil-Tawaquf" (Youssef Abu Rabie: Gazans Will Not Retreat, But Seed Saving Risks Coming to a Halt). *Environment and Development Horizons*, September 1, 2024. https://www.maan-ctr.org/magazine/article/4342/.

Atiyya, Ihsan. *Musadarat al-ʾAradi fi al-Manatiq al-Muhtala* (Land Confiscation in the Occupied Areas: 1967–1980). Jerusalem: Arab Studies Society, 1980.

Atran, Scott. "Hamula Organisation and Mashaʾa Tenure in Palestine." *Man* (1986): 271–95.

Atshan, Saʾed. "The Anthropological Rise of Palestine." *Journal of Palestine Studies* 50, no. 4 (2021): 3–31.

Awartani, Hisham. "Agricultural Development in the West Bank: An Economic and Political Study of the Development of Rain-Fed Farming in the West Bank." PhD diss., University of Bradford, 1982.

———. *The Agricultural Sector of the West Bank and the Gaza Strip*. Geneva: UNCTAD, 1993.

———. "Khuta Muqtaraha li-l-Tatwir al-Ziraʿ fi al-Diffa al-Gharbiyya wa-Qitaʿ Ghazza" (Proposed Plan for Agricultural Development in the West Bank and Gaza Strip). Rural Research Center/Birzeit University Research Center, 1982.

Awwad, Munir. *Istislah al-ʾAradi al-Ziraʿiyya* (The Reclamation of Agricultural Lands). Nablus: Rural Research Center, 1992.

Baconi, Tareq. *Hamas Contained: The Rise and Pacification of Palestinian Resistance*. Stanford: Stanford University Press, 2018.

Badran, Nabil. "Al-Rif al-Filastini Qabal al-Harb al-ʿAlami al-ʾUla" (The Palestinian Countryside Before the First World War). *Shuʾun Filistiniyya* 7 (1972): 116–29.

Al-Bakri, Ala, and Hanan Riyyan. *al-Audaʿ al-Qanuniyya l-Milkiyya al-ʾAradi fi al-Diffa al-Gharbiyya* (The Legal Principles of Land Ownership in the West Bank). Jerusalem: Arab Studies Society, 1982.

Balakrishnan, Sai. "Recombinant Urbanization: Agrarian–Urban Landed Property and Uneven Development in India." *International Journal of Urban and Regional Research* 43, no. 4 (2019): 617–32.

Bandele, Owusu, and Gail Myers. "Roots!" In *Land Justice: Re-imagining Land, Food, and the Commons*, edited by Justine M. Williams and Eric Holt-Giménez, 44–66. Oakland, CA: Food First Books, 2017.

Banner, Stuart. *How the Indians Lost Their Land: Law and Power on the Frontier*. Cambridge, MA: Harvard University Press, 2007.

———. *Possessing the Pacific: Land, Settlers, and Indigenous People from Australia to Alaska*. Cambridge, MA: Harvard University Press, 2009.

Barghouti, Mourid. *I Saw Ramallah*. New York: American University in Cairo Press, 2000.

Beaumont, Peter, and Quique Kierszenbaum. " 'Last Nail in the Coffin': Israeli Settlers Push on with Fresh West Bank Land Grab." *The Guardian*, February 13, 2025.

Benvenisti, Meron. *Sacred Landscape: The Buried History of the Holy Land since 1948*. Berkeley: University of California Press, 2000.

Benvenisti, Meron, Ziad Abu-Zayed, and Danny Rubinstein. *The West Bank Handbook: A Political Lexicon*. Jerusalem: The Jerusalem Post, 1986.

Berda, Yael. *Living Emergency: Israel's Permit Regime in the Occupied West Bank*. Stanford: Stanford University Press, 2017.

Bernstein, Henry. "Agrarian Questions from Transition to Globalization." In *Peasants and Globalization*, edited by A. Haroon Akram-Lodhi and Cristóbal Kay, 251–73. New York: Routledge, 2012.

———. *Class Dynamics of Agrarian Change*. Sterling, CT: Kumarian Press, 2010.

Bernstein, Henry, and Terence J. Byres. "From Peasant Studies to Agrarian Change." *Journal of Agrarian Change* 1, no. 1 (2001): 1–56.

Bhandar, Brenna. *Colonial Lives of Property: Law, Land, and Racial Regimes of Ownership*. Durham, NC: Duke University Press, 2018.

Binyamin, Avraham, Yonah Admoni, and Yishai Hemo. "The War of Attrition: The Palestinian Authority's Program for Establishing an Arab State in Area C." Regavim, 2019.

Birzeit University. "Young Activists Examine Models to Implement a Resistance Economy," June 10, 2022. https://www.birzeit.edu/en/news/young-activists-examine-models-implement-resistance-economy.

Bishara, Amahl. "Sovereignty and Popular Sovereignty for Palestinians and Beyond." *Cultural Anthropology* 32, no. 3 (2017): 349–58.

Bisharat, George. "Attorneys for the People, Attorneys for the Land: The Emergence of Cause Lawyering in the Israeli-Occupied Territories." *Cause Lawyering: Political Commitments and Professional Responsibilities* (1998): 453–86.

———. "Land, Law, and Legitimacy in Israel and the Occupied Territories." *American University Law Review* 43, no. 2 (1994): 467–561.

Blackey, Robert. "Fanon and Cabral: A Contrast in Theories of Revolution for Africa." *The Journal of Modern African Studies* 12, no. 2 (1974): 191–209.

Blaikie, Piers, and Harold Brookfield. *Land Degradation and Society*. London: Methuen, 1987.

Blomley, Nicholas. "The Territory of Property." *Progress in Human Geography* 40, no. 5 (2016): 593–609.

Borras, Saturnino M., Jr., Ruth Hall, Ian Scoones, Ben White, and Wendy Wolford. "Towards a Better Understanding of Global Land Grabbing: An Editorial Introduction." *The Journal of Peasant Studies* 38, no. 2 (2011): 209–16.

Bou Akar, Hiba. *For the War Yet to Come: Planning Beirut's Frontiers*. Stanford: Stanford University Press, 2018.

Braverman, Irus. *Planted Flags: Trees, Land, and Law in Israel/Palestine*. Cambridge, UK: Cambridge University Press, 2009.

———. "'The Tree Is the Enemy Soldier': A Sociolegal Making of War Landscapes in the Occupied West Bank." *Law & Society Review* 42, no. 3 (2008): 449–82.

Brown, Michael. "On Resisting Resistance." *American Anthropologist* 98, no. 4 (1996): 729–35.

Bryceson, Deborah. "Peasant Theories and Smallholder Policies: Past and Present." In *Disappearing Peasantries? Rural Labour in Africa, Asia and Latin America*, edited by Deborah Bryceson, Cristóbal Kay, and Jos Mooij, 1–36. London: Intermediate Technology Publications, 2000.

Bshara, Khaldun. "Rural Urbanization: The Commodification of Land in Post-Oslo Palestine." In *Reclaiming Space: The 50 Village Project in Rural Palestine*, edited by Khaldun Bshara and Suad Amiry, 93–103. Ramallah: Riwaq, 2015.

Bunton, Martin. *Colonial Land Policies in Palestine 1917–1936*. Oxford: Oxford University Press, 2007.

Burke, Jason, and Malak A. Tantesh. "Gaza Food Production 'Decimated' with 70% of Farmland Hit, UN Finds." *The Guardian*, November 21, 2024.

Büssow, Johann. *Hamidian Palestine: Politics and Society in the District of Jerusalem 1872–1908*. Boston: Brill, 2011.

Calis, Irene. "Routine and Rupture: The Everyday Workings of Abyssal (Dis)order in the Palestinian Food Basket." *American Ethnologist* 44, no. 1 (2017): 65–76.

Campbell, Jeremy M. *Conjuring Property: Speculation and Environmental Futures in the Brazilian Amazon*. Seattle: University of Washington Press, 2015.

Canfield, Matthew C. *Translating Food Sovereignty: Cultivating Justice in an Age of Transnational Governance.* Stanford: Stanford University Press, 2022.

Carneal, Luke. "A Picture of Farming in Gaza Today: In Remembrance of Youssef Saqr Abu Rabie." *Jadaliyya* (blog), November 11, 2024. https://www.jadaliyya.com/Details/46334.

Carpenter, Michael J. *Palestinian Popular Struggle: Unarmed and Participatory.* London: Routledge, 2018.

Chang, David A. *The Color of the Land: Race, Nation, and the Politics of Landownership in Oklahoma, 1832–1929.* Chapel Hill: University of North Carolina Press, 2010.

Chari, Sharad. *Fraternal Capital: Peasant-Workers, Self-Made Men, and Globalization in Provincial India.* Stanford: Stanford University Press, 2004.

Chatty, Dawn. *Displacement and Dispossession in the Modern Middle East.* Cambridge: Cambridge University Press, 2010.

Chen, Chris. "The Limit Point of Capitalist Equality." *Endnotes* 3 (2013): 202–23.

Clarno, Andy. *Neoliberal Apartheid: Palestine/Israel and South Africa after 1994.* Chicago: University of Chicago Press, 2017.

Clermont-Ganneau, Charles. "The Arabs in Palestine." *Palestine Exploration Quarterly* 7, no. 4 (1875): 199–214.

Clover, Joshua. *Riot. Strike. Riot: The New Era of Uprisings.* New York: Verso Books, 2016.

Cohen, Shaul Ephraim. *The Politics of Planting: Israeli-Palestinian Competition for Control of Land in the Jerusalem Periphery.* Chicago: University of Chicago Press, 1993.

Collins, John. *Global Palestine.* London: Hurst, 2011.

———. *Occupied by Memory: The Intifada Generation and the Palestinian State of Emergency.* New York: NYU Press, 2004.

Colman, Violeta, Maren Mantovani, Mohammad Mousa, and Nati Peña Boero. "We Will Return: An Analysis of the Escalating Forced Displacement of Palestinian Communities in the West Bank since the Genocide in Gaza." Ramallah: Stop the Wall, 2024.

Committee on the Exercise of the Inalienable Rights of the Palestinian People (CEIRPP). "Acquisition of Land in Palestine." New York: United Nations, 1980.

Craib, Raymond B. *Cartographic Mexico: A History of State Fixations and Fugitive Landscapes.* Durham, NC: Duke University Press, 2004.

Cronon, William. *Changes in the Land: Indians, Colonists, and the Ecology of New England.* New York: Hill & Wang, 2011.

Daiq, Ismail. "Dur al-Munazamat al-Jamhariyya fi al-Tanmiyya al-Rifiyya li-l-'Ard al-Muhtala" (The Role of Mass Organizations in Rural Development for Occupied Land). *Samed al-Iqtisadi* 61 (June 1986): 41–53.

———. *The Local Knowledge System for Plant Protection and Soil Conservation in Rain-Fed Agriculture in the West Bank, Palestine*. Berlin: Margraf, 2005.

Dakkak, Ibrahim. "Development from Within: A Strategy for Survival." In *The Palestinian Economy: Studies in Development under Prolonged Occupation*, edited by George T. Abed, 287–310. London: Routledge, 1988.

Dallasheh, Leena. "Persevering through Colonial Transition: Nazareth's Palestinian Residents after 1948." *Journal of Palestine Studies* 45, no. 2 (2016): 8–23.

Dana, Tariq. "Localising the Economy as a Resistance Response: A Contribution to the 'Resistance Economy' Debate in the Occupied Palestinian Territories." *Journal of Peacebuilding & Development* 15, no. 2 (2020): 192–204.

———. "A Resistance Economy: What Is It and Can It Provide an Alternative?" *Rosa Luxemburg Stiftung PAL Papers Series*, 2014.

Davis, Diana K. *The Arid Lands: History, Power, Knowledge*. Cambridge, MA: MIT Press, 2016.

Davis, Mike. *Planet of Slums*. New York: Verso, 2006.

Davis, Rochelle. *Palestinian Village Histories: Geographies of the Displaced*. Stanford: Stanford University Press, 2011.

Davis, Uri. "Rawabi Remains Settler-Colonial Sub-Contractor." *BDS Movement* (blog), March 31, 2011. https://bdsmovement.net/news/rawabi-remains-settler-colonial-sub-contractor.

Davy, Dãnia, Savonala Horne, Tracy Lloyd McCurty, and Edward Pennick. "Resistance." In *Land Justice: Re-Imagining Land, Food, and the Commons*, edited by Justine M. Williams and Eric Holt-Giménez, 67–91. Oakland, CA: Food First Books, 2017.

De Angelis, Massimo. "Marx and Primitive Accumulation: The Continuous Character of Capital's Enclosures." *The Commoner* 2, no. 01 (2001): 1–22.

———. *Omnia Sunt Communia: On the Commons and the Transformation to Postcapitalism*. London: Zed Books, 2017.

Desmarais, Annette Aurelie. *La Via Campesina: Globalization and the Power of Peasants*. London: Pluto Press, 2007.

Doumani, Beshara. "Endowing Family: Waqf, Property Devolution, and Gender in Greater Syria, 1800 to 1860." *Comparative Studies in Society and History* 40, no. 1 (1998): 3–41.

———. "Family and Politics in Salfit." In *Intifada: The Palestinian Uprising against Israeli Occupation*, edited by Joel Beinin and Zachary Lockman, 143–54. Boston: South End Press, 1989.

———. "Palestine versus the Palestinians? The Iron Laws and Ironies of a People Denied." *Journal of Palestine Studies* 36, no. 4 (2007): 49–64.

———. *Rediscovering Palestine: Merchants and Peasants in Jabal Nablus, 1700–1900*. Berkeley: University of California Press, 1995.

Doumani, Beshara, and Paul Kohlbry. "Introduction: Claiming Property, Claiming Palestine." *Comparative Studies of South Asia, Africa and the Middle East* 43, no. 3 (2023): 245–48.

Drayton, Richard. *Nature's Government: Science, Imperial Britain, and the "Improvement" of the World.* New Haven: Yale University Press, 2000.

Dunbar-Ortiz, Roxanne. *An Indigenous Peoples' History of the United States.* Boston: Beacon Press, 2014.

Edelman, Marc. "Bringing the Moral Economy Back In ... to the Study of 21st-Century Transnational Peasant Movements." *American Anthropologist* 107, no. 3 (2005): 331–45.

———. *Peasant Politics of the Twenty-First Century: Transnational Social Movements and Agrarian Change.* Ithaca: Cornell University Press, 2024.

———. *Peasants against Globalization: Rural Social Movements in Costa Rica.* Stanford: Stanford University Press, 1999.

———. "What Is a Peasant? What Are Peasantries? A Briefing Paper on Issues of Definition." Paper presented at First Session of the Intergovernmental Working Group on a United Nations Declaration on the Rights of Peasants and Other People Working in Rural Areas, Geneva, July 2013, 15–19.

Edelman, Marc, Carlos Oya, and Saturnino M Borras. "Global Land Grabs: Historical Processes, Theoretical and Methodological Implications and Current Trajectories." *Third World Quarterly* 34, no. 9 (October 2013): 1517–31.

Eldin, Munir Fakher. "Communities of Owners: Land Law, Governance, and Politics in Palestine, 1858–1948." PhD diss., New York University, 2008.

———. "The Middle Class and the Land Struggle in Palestine: Revisiting the Colonial Encounter in the Beisan Valley, 1908–1948." *Comparative Studies of South Asia, Africa and the Middle East* 43, no. 3 (December 1, 2023): 249–61.

El Zein, Rayya. "Developing a Palestinian Resistance Economy through Agricultural Labor." *Journal of Palestine Studies* 46, no. 3 (2017): 7–26.

Erakat, Noura. *Justice for Some: Law and the Question of Palestine.* Stanford: Stanford University Press, 2019.

Escribano, Marisa, and Nazmi El-Joubeh. "Migration and Change in a West Bank Village: The Case of Deir Dibwan." *Journal of Palestine Studies* 11, no. 1 (1981): 150–60.

Eyal, Gil. *The Disenchantment of the Orient: Expertise in Arab Affairs and the Israeli State.* Stanford: Stanford University Press, 2006.

Fairbairn, Madeleine. *Fields of Gold: Financing the Global Land Rush.* Ithaca: Cornell University Press, 2020.

Fanon, Frantz. *The Wretched of the Earth.* New York: Grove Press, 2004.

FAO and UNITAR. "Agricultural Damage Assessment in the Gaza Strip from October 7th 2023 to September 1st 2024," 2024. https://openknowledge.fao.org/handle/20.500.14283/cd2592en.

Farha, Leilani. "Area C Is Everything: Planning for the Future of Palestine." Oslo: Norwegian Refugee Council, 2023.

Farhat-Naser, Sumaya. *Zaytun Filastin wa-Mushkilatuha* (Olives of Palestine and Their Problems). Birzeit: Birzeit University, 1980.

Farsakh, Leila. *Palestinian Labour Migration to Israel: Labour, Land and Occupation.* London: Routledge, 2005.

Fattaleh, Nadine, and Adam Albarghouthi. "Agroecology, from Palestine to the Diaspora." *Science for the People Magazine* (blog), August 1, 2022. https://magazine.scienceforthepeople.org/vol25-1-the-soil-and-worker/agroecology-from-palestine-to-the-diaspora/.

Federici, Silvia. "Palestine Is the World (2002)." *PM Press* (blog), March 14, 2024. https://blog.pmpress.org/2024/03/14/palestine-is-the-world-2002/.

———. *Re-Enchanting the World: Feminism and the Politics of the Commons.* Oakland, CA: PM Press, 2018.

Ferguson, James. *Global Shadows: Africa in the Neoliberal World Order.* Durham, NC: Duke University Press, 2006.

Ferguson, James, and Akhil Gupta. "Spatializing States: Toward an Ethnography of Neoliberal Governmentality." *American Ethnologist* 29, no. 4 (2002): 981–1002.

Fields, Gary. *Enclosure: Palestinian Landscapes in a Historical Mirror.* Berkeley: University of California Press, 2017.

———. "Landscaping Palestine: Reflections of Enclosure in a Historical Mirror." *International Journal of Middle East Studies* 42, no. 01 (2010): 63–82.

Filiu, Jean-Pierre. "The Twelve Wars on Gaza." *Journal of Palestine Studies* 44, no. 1 (2014): 52–60.

Fischbach, Michael R. "The Implications of Jordanian Land Policy for the West Bank." *Middle East Journal* 48, no. 3 (1994): 492–509.

———. *State, Society, and Land in Jordan.* Boston: Brill, 2000.

Forman, Geremy. "Israeli Settlement of Title in Arab Areas: The Special Land Settlement Operation in Northern Israel (1955–1967)." PhD diss., University of Haifa, 2005.

———. "Settlement of the Title in the Galilee: Dowson's Colonial Guiding Principles." *Israel Studies* 7, no. 3 (2002): 61–83.

Forman, Geremy, and Alexandre Kedar. "From Arab Land to 'Israel Lands': The Legal Dispossession of the Palestinians Displaced by Israel in the Wake of 1948." *Environment and Planning D: Society and Space* 22, no. 6 (2004): 809–30.

Foster, John Bellamy. *Marx's Ecology: Materialism and Nature*. New York: Monthly Review Press, 2000.

———. "Marx, Value, and Nature." *Monthly Review* 70, no. 3 (2018): 122–36.

Franco, Jennifer, and Saturnino M. Borras Jr. "A 'Land Sovereignty' Alternative? Towards a Peoples' Counter-Enclosure." Amsterdam: Transnational Institute, July 2012. https://repub.eur.nl/pub/38546/.

Frankel, Julia. "Israel Turbocharges West Bank Settlement Expansion with Largest Land Grab in Decades." *AP News*, July 3, 2024. https://apnews.com/article/israel-palestinians-hamas-war-news-07-03-2024-033deab379a16efdf9989de8d6eaf0f8.

Friedmann, Harriet. "Origins of Peasant Studies." In *Handbook of Critical Agrarian Studies*, edited by A. Haroon Akram-Lodhi, Kristina Dietz, Bettina Engels, and Ben M. McKay, 15–24. Northampton, MA: Edward Elgar Publishing, 2021.

Fullilove, Courtney. "'Famine Foods' and the Values of Biodiversity Preservation in Israel-Palestine." *Isis* 113, no. 3 (2022): 625–36.

Fullilove, Courtney, and Abdallah Alimari. "Baladi Seeds in the oPt: Populations as Objects of Preservation and Units of Analysis." In *Towards Responsible Plant Data Linkage: Data Challenges for Agricultural Research and Development*, edited by Hugh Williamson and Sabina Leonelli, 65–84. Cham, Switzerland: Springer, 2023.

Furani, Khaled, and Dan Rabinowitz. "The Ethnographic Arriving of Palestine." *Annual Review of Anthropology* 40 (2011): 475–91.

Gavish, Dov. *A Survey of Palestine under the British Mandate, 1920–1948*. New York: Routledge, 2005.

Geisler, Charles, and Fouad Makki. "People, Power, and Land: New Enclosures on a Global Scale." *Rural Sociology* 79, no. 1 (2014): 28–33.

George, Alan. "'Making the Desert Bloom': A Myth Examined." *Journal of Palestine Studies* 8, no. 2 (January 1, 1979): 88–100.

Ghertner, D. Asher, and Robert W. Lake. "Introduction: Land Fictions and the Politics of Commodification in City and Country." In *Land Fictions: The Commodification of Land in City and Country*, edited by D. Asher Ghertner and Robert W. Lake, 1–25. Ithaca: Cornell University Press, 2021.

Gilbert, David E. "Laborers Becoming 'Peasants': Agroecological Politics in a Sumatran Plantation Zone." *The Journal of Peasant Studies* 47, no. 5 (2020): 1030–51.

Gilmore, Ruth Wilson. *Golden Gulag: Prisons, Surplus, Crisis, and Opposition in Globalizing California*. Berkeley: University of California Press, 2007.

Glavanis, Kathy, and Pandeli Glavanis, eds. *The Rural Middle East: Peasant Lives and Modes of Production*. London: Zed Books/Birzeit University, 1989.

Gliessman, Stephen R. *Agroecology: The Ecology of Sustainable Food Systems*. 3rd ed. Boca Raton: CRC Press, 2014.

Goadby, Frederic Maurice, and Moses J. Doukhan. *The Land Law of Palestine*. Jerusalem: Shoshany's Printing Co., 1935.

Goedeken, Susan Christine. "Made to Measure? Fitting a Development Project to the Occupied Palestinian Territories." MA thesis, American University of Beirut, 2009.

Gordon, Neve. *Israel's Occupation*. Berkeley: University of California Press, 2008.

Government of Palestine and Sami Hadawi. *Village Statistics 1945: A Classification of Land and Area Ownership in Palestine*. Beirut: Palestine Liberation Organization Research Center, 1970.

Govindrajan, Radhika. *Animal Intimacies: Interspecies Relatedness in India's Central Himalayas*. Chicago: University of Chicago Press, 2019.

Graham-Brown, Sarah. "The Political Economy of the Jabal Nablus, 1920–48." In *Studies in the Economic and Social History of Palestine in the Nineteenth and Twentieth Centuries*, edited by Roger Owen, 88–176. Carbondale: Southern Illinois University Press, 1982.

Grandia, Liza. *Enclosed: Conservation, Cattle, and Commerce among the Q'eqchi' Maya Lowlanders*. Seattle: University of Washington Press, 2012.

Grandinetti, Tina. "The Palestinian Middle Class in Rawabi: Depoliticizing the Occupation." *Alternatives* 40, no. 1 (2015): 63–78.

Gray, Alice. "Green Resistance: Building Palestine's First Eco-Village." *The New Arab*, December 17, 2015. https://www.newarab.com/analysis/green-resistance-building-palestines-first-eco-village.

Greer, Allan. *Property and Dispossession: Natives, Empires and Land in Early Modern North America*. Cambridge, UK: Cambridge University Press, 2018.

Grey, Sam, and Raj Patel. "Food Sovereignty as Decolonization: Some Contributions from Indigenous Movements to Food System and Development Politics." *Agriculture and Human Values* 32, no. 3 (2015): 431–44.

Guha, Ramachandra. *The Unquiet Woods: Ecological Change and Peasant Resistance in the Himalaya*. Oxford: Oxford University Press, 1989.

Guldi, Jo. *The Long Land War: The Global Struggle for Occupancy Rights*. New Haven: Yale University Press, 2022.

Gutkowski, Natalia. "Bodies That Count: Administering Multispecies in Palestine/Israel's Borderlands." *Environment and Planning E: Nature and Space* 4, no. 1 (2021): 135–57.

———. *Struggling for Time: Environmental Governance and Agrarian Resistance in Israel/Palestine*. Stanford: Stanford University Press, 2024.

Habib, Hin. "Qara'a fi al-Athar al-Maliyya wa-l-Iqtisadiyya al-Mutawaq'a wa-l-Tahadiyyat al-Musabha l-Taswiyya al-'Aradi wa-Tasjiliha fi al-Diffa al-Gharbiyya" (A Reading in the Expected Financial and Economic Impact and Challenges Associated with Land Settlement and Registration in the West Bank). Ramallah: Palestine Economic Policy Research Institute (MAS), 2019.

Hadawi, Sami. *Palestinian Rights and Losses in 1948: A Comprehensive Study*. London: Saqi Books, 1988.

Haddad, Toufic. *Palestine Ltd.: Neoliberalism and Nationalism in the Occupied Territory*. London: IB Tauris, 2016.

Hajjar, Lisa. "Human Rights in Israel/Palestine: The History and Politics of a Movement." *Journal of Palestine Studies* 30, no. 4 (2001): 21–38.

Halabi, Usama. *Musadarat al-'Aradi fi al-Diffa al-Gharbiyya al-Muhtala* (Land Confiscation in the Occupied West Bank). Jerusalem: Arab Studies Society, 1986.

Halabi, Usama, Aron Turner, and Meron Benvenisti. *Land Alienation in the West Bank: A Legal and Spatial Analysis*. Jerusalem: West Bank Data Base Project, 1985.

Hale, Charles R. "Neoliberal Multiculturalism." *PoLAR: Political and Legal Anthropology Review* 28, no. 1 (2005): 10–19.

Hall, Derek. *Land*. New York: Polity, 2013.

———. "Primitive Accumulation, Accumulation by Dispossession and the Global Land Grab." *Third World Quarterly* 34, no. 9 (2013): 1582–1604.

Hall, Ruth, Marc Edelman, Saturnino M. Borras Jr., Ian Scoones, Ben White, and Wendy Wolford. "Resistance, Acquiescence or Incorporation? An Introduction to Land Grabbing and Political Reactions 'from Below.'" *The Journal of Peasant Studies* 42, no. 3–4 (2015): 467–88.

Halper, Jeff. "The 94 Percent Solution." *Middle East Report* 216 (Autumn 2000): 14–19.

———. *War against the People: Israel, the Palestinians and Global Pacification*. London: Pluto Press, 2016.

———. "Warehousing a 'Surplus People.'" *Palestine Chronicle*, September 11, 2008. https://www.palestinechronicle.com/warehousing-a-surplus-people/.

Hammami, Rema. "Between Heaven and Earth: Transformations in Religiosity and Labor among Southern Palestinian Peasant and Refugee Women, 1920–1993." PhD diss., Temple University, 1994.

———. "NGOs: The Professionalisation of Politics." *Race and Class* 37 (1995): 51–63.

———. "Women, the Hijab and the Intifada." *Middle East Report*, no. 164/5 (1990): 24–28.

Handel, Ariel, Marco Allegra, and Erez Maggor. *Normalizing Occupation: The Politics of Everyday Life in the West Bank Settlements*. Bloomington: Indiana University Press, 2017.

Handy, Jim. " 'Almost Idiotic Wretchedness': A Long History of Blaming Peasants." *The Journal of Peasant Studies* 36, no. 2 (2009): 325–44.

Hanieh, Adam. "The Internationalisation of Gulf Capital and Palestinian Class Formation." *Capital & Class* 35, no. 1 (2011): 81–106.

———. *Lineages of Revolt: Issues of Contemporary Capitalism in the Middle East.* Chicago: Haymarket Books, 2013.

Harb, Samir. "Imaginary and Autonomy: Urbanisation, Construction, and Cement Production in Palestine." PhD diss., University of Manchester, 2020.

Hareuveni, Eyal. "By Hook and by Crook: Israeli Settlement Policy in the West Bank." Jerusalem: B'Tselem, 2010.

———. "Foul Play: Neglect of Wastewater Treatment in the West Bank." Jerusalem: B'Tselem, 2009.

Harker, Christopher. *Spacing Debt: Obligations, Violence, and Endurance in Ramallah, Palestine.* Durham, NC: Duke University Press, 2020.

Harvey, David. *The New Imperialism.* Oxford: Oxford University Press, 2003.

Hass, Amira. "How Palestinians Near Bethlehem Are Expelled from Their Land." *Haaretz*, May 25, 2024.

Hasson, Nir, and Hagar Shezaf. "JNF Set to Approve Plan That Could Lead to Palestinians' Eviction." *Haaretz*, August 5, 2021.

Hattem, Ben. "The Wild Boar and Feces Epidemic in Palestine." *Vice* (blog), January 3, 2014. https://www.vice.com/en/article/exmnya/the-wild-boar-and-feces-epidemic-in-palestine.

Heinrich, Michael. *An Introduction to the Three Volumes of Karl Marx's Capital.* New York: NYU Press, 2004.

Henderson, Christian. "Israel's Weapon of Hunger in Gaza." *Agrarian Conversations* (blog), 2021. https://www.peasantjournal.org/news/israel's-weapon-of-hunger-in-gaza/.

Hetherington, Kregg. *Guerrilla Auditors: The Politics of Transparency in Neoliberal Paraguay.* Durham, NC: Duke University Press, 2011.

Hilal, Jamil. *Al-Diffa al-Gharbiyya: Al-Tarkib al-Ijtima'i wa-al-Iqtisadi (1948–1974)* (West Bank: Economic and Social Structure). Beirut: Palestine Liberation Organization Research Center, 1974.

———. "West Bank and Gaza Strip Social Formation under Jordanian and Egyptian Rule (1948–1967)." *Review of Middle East Studies* 5 (1992): 33–73.

Ho, Karen. *Liquidated: An Ethnography of Wall Street.* Durham, NC: Duke University Press, 2009.

Hughes, Sara Salazar, Stepha Velednitsky, and Amelia Arden Green. "Greenwashing in Palestine/Israel: Settler Colonialism and Environmental Injustice in the Age of Climate Catastrophe." *Environment and Planning E: Nature and Space* 6, no. 1 (2023): 495–513.

Human Rights Watch. "A Threshold Crossed: Israeli Authorities and the Crimes of Apartheid and Persecution." Human Rights Watch, 2021.

Hunaiti, Hadeel. "Arab Jahalin: From the Nakba to the Wall." Ramallah: Stop the Wall, 2008.

Ingold, Tim. "The Temporality of the Landscape." *World Archaeology* 25, no. 2 (1993): 152–74.

Israel National News. "Ad Kan: A Fake Palestinian Land Registry for Area C Is Being Written at This Very Moment." *Israel National News*, January 24, 2023. https://www.israelnationalnews.com/news/366380.

Istanbuli, Dawood. "Al-Insan al-Zira'i" (The Agricultural Individual). In *Mu'tamir al-Tanmiyya min Ajl al-Sumud* (Development for Sumud Conference). Arab Thought Forum, 1982.

Jaber, D. A. "Settler Colonialism and Ecocide: Case Study of Al-Khader, Palestine." *Settler Colonial Studies* 9, no. 1 (2019): 135–54.

Jacobs, Ricardo. "An Urban Proletariat with Peasant Characteristics: Land Occupations and Livestock Raising in South Africa." *The Journal of Peasant Studies* 45, no. 5–6 (2018): 884–903.

Jaffee, Daniel. *Brewing Justice: Fair Trade Coffee, Sustainability and Survival.* Berkeley: University of California Press, 2014.

James, Deborah. *Gaining Ground? Rights and Property in South African Land Reform.* New York: Routledge, 2007.

Jansen, Kees, Mark Vicol, and Lisette Nikol. "Autonomy and Repeasantization: Conceptual, Analytical, and Methodological Problems." *Journal of Agrarian Change* 22, no. 3 (2022): 489–505.

Jarrar, Ghassan. "Mulahazat Hawl al-Mashakil al-Rifiyya fi al-Minatiq al-Muhtala" (Notes on Rural Problems in the Occupied Territories). *Samed Al-Iqtisadi* 61 (June 1986): 17–33.

Jiryis, Sabri. "The Legal Structure for the Expropriation and Absorption of Arab Lands in Israel." *Journal of Palestine Studies* 2, no. 4 (1973): 82–104.

Johnson, Penny. *Companions in Conflict: Animals in Occupied Palestine.* New York: Melville House Publishing, 2019.

Katz, Yossi. *The "Business" of Settlement: Private Entrepreneurship in the Jewish Settlement of Palestine, 1900–1914.* Jerusalem: Hebrew University Magnes Press, 1994.

———. *The Jewish National Fund and the History of State Ownership of Land in Israel.* Berlin: De Gruyter and Jerusalem: Hebrew University Magnes Press, 2016.

Kelly, Tobias. *Law, Violence and Sovereignty among West Bank Palestinians.* Cambridge, UK: Cambridge University Press, 2006.

Kerem Navot. "An Israeli Roadblock: How Israel Took Control over the Bethlehem Area?" n.d. https://www.keremnavot.org/israeli-roadblock.

Khalidi, Raja. "The Economics of Palestinian Liberation." *Jacobin*, 2014. http://jacobinmag.com/2014/10/the-economics-of-palestinian-liberation/.

Khalidi, Raja, and Sobhi Samour. "Neoliberalism as Liberation: The Statehood Program and the Remaking of the Palestinian National Movement." *Journal of Palestine Studies* 40, no. 2 (2011): 6–25.

Khalidi, Rashid. *The Hundred Years' War on Palestine: A History of Settler Colonialism and Resistance, 1917–2017*. New York: Metropolitan Books, 2020.

———. *Palestinian Identity: The Construction of Modern National Consciousness*. New York: Columbia University Press, 1997.

———. "A Question of Land." *Journal of Palestine Studies* 17, no. 1 (1987): 146–49.

Khalifeh, Sahar. *Wild Thorns*. London: Al Saqi Books, 1985.

Khater, Akram Fouad. *Inventing Home: Emigration, Gender, and the Middle Class in Lebanon, 1870–1920*. Berkeley: University of California Press, 2001.

Khoury, Elyas. "Elias Khouri's Letter: Fight for Land in the Courts and on the Ground." *Al-Fajr Weekly*, February 22, 1981.

Kimmerling, Baruch. "Sovereignty, Ownership, and 'Presence' in the Jewish-Arab Territorial Conflict: The Case of Bir'im and Ikrit." *Comparative Political Studies* 10, no. 2 (1977): 155–76.

Kirk, Gabi. "Commodifying Indigeneity? Settler Colonialism and Racial Capitalism in Fair Trade Farming in Palestine." *Historical Materialism* 31, no. 2 (2023): 236–68.

———. "Confronting the Twin Crises of Climate Change and Occupation in Palestine." *Arab Studies Journal* 30, no. 2 (2022): 90–95.

Kirk, Gabi, and Paul Kohlbry. "Situating the Transnational in Agrarian Palestine." In *Resisting Domination in Palestine: Mechanisms and Techniques of Control, Coloniality and Settler Colonialism*, edited by Alaa Tartir, Timothy Seidel, and Tariq Dana. New York: Bloomsbury, 2024.

Kirsch, Stuart. "Indigenous Movements and the Risks of Counterglobalization: Tracking the Campaign against Papua New Guinea's Ok Tedi Mine." *American Ethnologist* 34, no. 2 (2007): 303–21.

Kohlbry, Paul. "Palestinian Counter-Forensics and the Cruel Paradox of Property." *American Ethnologist* 49, no. 3 (2022): 374–86.

———. "Selling Rural Palestine: Land Devaluation, Ethical Investment, and the Limits of Human Rights." *Antipode* 55, no. 3 (2023): 897–915.

———. "Titling in the Ruins: Progress, Deferral, and Nonsovereign Property." *Comparative Studies of South Asia, Africa and the Middle East* 43, no. 3 (December 1, 2023): 262–74.

———. "To Cover the Land in Green: Rain-Fed Agriculture and Anti-Colonial Land

Reclamation in Palestine." *The Journal of Peasant Studies* 50, no. 7 (2023): 2666–2684.

Kurzom, George. *Towards Alternative Self-Reliant Agricultural Development.* Birzeit: Development Studies Program / Birzeit University, 2001.

Kushan Baladi: Mubadara l-Tawthiq Haq al-Filistini bi-ʾArdi (Kushan Baladi: An Initiative to Document the Palestinian Right to Land), 2021. https://www.youtube.com/watch?v=KXMAt2Zzw_A.

Land Research Center (LRC). "Olive Seedlings and Metal Corners Stolen by Settlers in Bruqin Village Land—Salfit Governorate—POICA," June 6, 2020. http://poica.org/2020/06/olive-seedlings-and-metal-corners-stolen-by-settlers-in-bruqin-village-land-salfit-governorate/.

———. "al-Bur al-Istitaniyat al-Raʿiat Nuqtat al-Intilaq l-Nahb al-Mazid min al-ʾAradi al- Filastiniyya" (Pastoral Settlement Outposts as a Starting Point for Increased Theft of Palestinian Land). Halhul: Land Research Center, July 2023.

———. "Ravaging 10 Dunums in Farkha Village / Salfit Governorate," October 7, 2019. http://poica.org/2019/10/ravaging-10-dunums-in-farkha-village-salit-governorate/.

La Via Campesina. "La Via Campesina Delegation Visited Palestine in December 2024: Notes from Their Daily Diaries [Part 1]." *La Via Campesina—EN* (blog), January 16, 2025. https://viacampesina.org/en/2025/01/la-via-campesina-delegation-visited-palestine-in-december-2024-notes-from-their-daily-diaries-part-1/.

Leeds, Anthony. "Mythos and Pathos: Some Unpleasantries on Peasantries." In *Peasant Livelihood: Studies in Economic Anthropology and Cultural Ecology,* edited by Rhoda Halperin and James Dow. New York: St. Martin's Press, 1977.

Lehn, Walter, and Uri Davis. *The Jewish National Fund.* London: Kegan Paul International, 1988.

Lein, Yehezkel, and Eyal Weizman. "Land Grab: Israel's Settlement Policy in the West Bank." Jerusalem: B'Tselem, 2002.

Lester-Murad, Nora. "Do Pigs Fly—Or Is This a Matter of Human Rights?" *The View From My Window in Palestine* (blog), December 14, 2012. https://noralestermurad.com/do-pigs-fly-or-is-this-a-matter-of-human-rights/.

Levav, Amos. "The Israeli Gold Rush." *Al-Fajr Weekly,* January 22, 1982.

Levien, Michael. *Dispossession without Development: Land Grabs in Neoliberal India.* Oxford: Oxford University Press, 2018.

———. "Fictitious But Not Utopian: Land Commodification and Dispossession in Rural India." In *Land Fictions: The Commodification of Land in City and Country,* edited by D. Asher Ghertner and Robert W. Lake, 26–43. Ithaca: Cornell University Press, 2021.

Levien, Michael, Michael Watts, and Hairong Yan. "Agrarian Marxism." *The Journal of Peasant Studies* 45, no. 5–6 (2018): 853–83.

Li, Darryl. "The Gaza Strip as Laboratory: Notes in the Wake of Disengagement." *Journal of Palestine Studies* 35, no. 2 (2006): 38–55.

Li, Tania Murray. *Land's End: Capitalist Relations on an Indigenous Frontier.* Durham, NC: Duke University Press, 2014.

———. "To Make Live or Let Die? Rural Dispossession and the Protection of Surplus Populations." *Antipode* 41, no. s1 (2010): 66–93.

———. *The Will to Improve: Governmentality, Development, and the Practice of Politics.* Durham, NC: Duke University Press, 2007.

Linebaugh, Peter. "Palestine and the Commons: Or, Marx and the Musha'a." *CounterPunch,* March 1, 2024. https://www.counterpunch.org/2024/03/01/palestine-the-commons-or-marx-the-mushaa/.

Lloyd, David, and Patrick Wolfe. "Settler Colonial Logics and the Neoliberal Regime." *Settler Colonial Studies* 6, no. 2 (2016): 109–18.

Locke, John. *Locke: Two Treatises of Government (Student Edition).* Cambridge, UK: Cambridge University Press, 1988.

Loewenstein, Antony. *The Palestine Laboratory: How Israel Exports the Technology of Occupation around the World.* New York: Verso, 2023.

Losurdo, Domenico. *Liberalism: A Counter-History.* London: Verso Books, 2014.

Low, Donald Anthony. *The Egalitarian Moment: Asia and Africa, 1950–1980.* Cambridge, UK: Cambridge University Press, 1996.

Lund, Christian. *Nine-Tenths of the Law: Enduring Dispossession in Indonesia.* New Haven: Yale University Press, 2020.

Lustick, Ian. "Israel and the West Bank after Elon Moreh: The Mechanics of De Facto Annexation." *Middle East Journal* 35, no. 4 (1981): 557–77.

Lutfiyya, Abdulla M. *Baytin: A Jordanian Village.* London: Mouton & Co., 1966.

Macpherson, C. B. *The Political Theory of Possessive Individualism: Hobbes to Locke.* Oxford: Oxford University Press, 1989.

Magubane, Bernard, and Nzongola Ntalaja, eds. "Imperialism and the Making of the South African Working Class." In *Proletarianization and Class Struggle in Africa,* 19–56. San Francisco: Synthesis Publications, 1983.

Makhoul, Najwa Hanna. "The Proletarianization of Palestinians in Israel: A Study of Development and Class Formation." PhD diss., MIT, 1978.

Makki, Fouad. "Development by Dispossession: *Terra Nullius* and the Social-Ecology of New Enclosures in Ethiopia." *Rural Sociology* 79, no. 1 (2014): 79–103.

Mamonova, Natalia. "Resistance or Adaptation? Ukrainian Peasants' Responses to Large-Scale Land Acquisitions." *The Journal of Peasant Studies* 42, no. 3–4 (2015): 607–34.

Mamonova, Natalia, and Lee-Ann Sutherland. "Rural Gentrification in Russia: Rene-gotiating Identity, Alternative Food Production and Social Tensions in the Coun-tryside." *Journal of Rural Studies* 42 (2015): 154–65.

Mandell, Joan. "Gaza: Israel's Soweto." *MERIP*, October 20, 1985. https://merip.org/1985/10/gaza-israels-soweto/.

Manna, Jumana. "Where Nature Ends and Settlements Begin." *E-Flux Journal* 113 (No-vember 2020). https://www.e-flux.com/journal/113/360006/where-nature-ends-and-settlements-begin/.

Mari, Faiq. "Masha' of the Periphery: Collective Labor and Property in Palestinian Liberation Struggle." PhD diss., ETH Zurich, 2024.

Marx, Karl, and Ernest Mandel. *Capital: Volume 1: A Critique of Political Economy.* Translated by Ben Fowkes. New York: Penguin Classics, 1992.

Marzin, Jacques, Ahmad Uwaidat, and Jean-Michel Sourisseau. "Study on Small-Scale Agriculture in the Palestinian Territories." Rome: The Food and Agricul-ture Organization of the United Nations (FAO), 2019.

Mathews, Andrew S. *Trees Are Shape Shifters: How Cultivation, Climate Change, and Disaster Create Landscapes.* New Haven: Yale University Press, 2022.

Mazzawi, Nisreen, and Amalia Sa'ar. "The Ḥawākīr of Nazareth: The History and Contemporary Face of a Cultural Ecological Institution." *International Journal of Middle East Studies* 50, no. 3 (2018): 537–56.

Mbembe, Achille. "Necropolitics." Translated by Libby Meintjes. *Public Culture* 15, no. 1 (2003): 11–40.

McElrone, Susynne. "From the Pages of the Defter: A Social History of Rural Property Tenure and the Implementation of Tanzimat Land Reform in Hebron, Palestine (1858–1900)." PhD diss., New York University, 2016.

Meneley, Anne. "Blood, Sweat and Tears in a Bottle of Palestinian Extra-Virgin Olive Oil." *Food, Culture & Society* 14, no. 2 (2011): 275–92.

———. "Discourses of Distinction in Contemporary Palestinian Extra-Virgin Olive Oil Production." *Food and Foodways* 22, no. 1–2 (2014): 48–64.

———. "Hope in the Ruins: Seeds, Plants, and Possibilities of Regeneration." *Envi-ronment and Planning E: Nature and Space* 4, no. 1 (2021): 158–72.

MIFTAH. "The Jordan Valley." Ramallah: MIFTAH, 2017. https://www.miftah.org/Display.cfm?DocId=26418&CategoryId=4.

Migdal, Joel S. *Palestinian Society and Politics.* Princeton: Princeton University Press, 1980.

Miller, Ylana. *Government and Society in Rural Palestine, 1920–1948.* Austin: Univer-sity of Texas Press, 1985.

Ministry of Intelligence. "The Palestinian Campaign for Area C—Shaping a Security

Reality on the Ground, Description and Implications." Jerusalem: State of Israel, n.d.

Mitter, Sreemati. "Bankrupt: Financial Life in Late Mandate Palestine." *International Journal of Middle East Studies* 52, no. 2 (2020): 289–310.

Molavi, Shourideh. *Environmental Warfare in Gaza: Colonial Violence and New Landscapes of Resistance.* London: Pluto Press, 2024.

Moore, Donald S. "Subaltern Struggles and the Politics of Place: Remapping Resistance in Zimbabwe's Eastern Highlands." *Cultural Anthropology* 13, no. 3 (1998): 344–81.

Moors, Annelies. *Women, Property and Islam: Palestinian Experiences, 1920–1990.* Cambridge, UK: Cambridge University Press, 1995.

Morton-Jerome, Ethan. "The Struggle for Palestinian Workers' Rights in Israeli Settlements: The Case of Maan v. Zarfati Garage." *Jerusalem Quarterly* 86 (2021): 79–96.

Mousa, Riyad. "The Dispossession of the Peasantry: Colonial Policies, Settler Capitalism, and Rural Change in Palestine, 1918–1948." PhD diss., University of Utah, 2006.

Mundy, Martha. "Village Land and Individual Title: Musha' Ottoman Land Registration in the 'Ajlun District." In *Village, Steppe and State: The Social Origins of Modern Jordan*, edited by Eugene Rogan and Tariq Tell, 58–79. London: Bloomsbury Academic, 1994.

Mundy, Martha, and Richard Saumarez Smith. *Governing Property, Making the Modern State: Law, Administration and Production in Ottoman Syria.* London: IB Tauris, 2007.

Musleh, Abeer. "Reviving the 'Hakora': Local Farming and Collaborative Efforts." *Sharing Society: The Impact of Collaborative Collective Actions in the Transformation of Contemporary Societies* (2019): 68–78.

Nadan, Amos. "Merchants and Peasants in the Nazareth Region, 1922–47." *The Journal of Peasant Studies* 34, no. 1 (2007): 51–68.

———. "Reconsidering Peasant Communes in the Levant, c. 1850s–1940s." *The Economic History Review* 74, no. 1 (2021): 34–59.

———. "The Route from Informal Peasant Landownership to Formal Tenancy and Eviction in Palestine, 1800s–1947." *Continuity and Change* 36, no. 2 (2021): 233–56.

Nadasdy, Paul. " 'Property' and Aboriginal Land Claims in the Canadian Subarctic: Some Theoretical Considerations." *American Anthropologist* 104, no. 1 (2002): 247–61.

Naïli, Falestin. "Memories of Home and Stories of Displacement: The Women of

Artas and the 'Peasant Past.'" *Journal of Palestine Studies* 38, no. 4 (2009): 63–74.

Nakkara, Hanna. *Mudhakkarat Muhami Filastini: Hanna Dib Naqqarah, Muhami al->Ard wa-al-Sha'ab* (Memoirs of a Palestinian Lawyer: Hanna Deeb Nakkara, Lawyer of the Land and the People. Edited by Atallah Said Copty. 2nd ed. Beirut: Institute for Palestine Studies, 2011.

Naser, Munir. "Al-Nashat al-Zira'i l-Falah Bir Zeit 'ala Mudar al-Sina" (The Agricultural Activities of the Birzeit Peasant over the Year). *Heritage and Society* 1 (1974): 70–80.

Nassar, Maha, Richard Levy, Noel Keough, and Nashaat N. Nassar. "Agricultural Land Use Change and Its Drivers in the Palestinian Landscape under Political Instability, the Case of Tulkarm City." *Journal of Borderlands Studies* 34, no. 3 (2019): 377–94.

Nazal, Mohammed. *Tasrib al->Aradi wa-al-'Aqarat fi al-Diffa al-Gharbiyya* (The Illicit Transfer of Land and Property in the West Bank). Ramallah: Self-published, 2016.

Neeson, Jeanette M. *Commoners: Common Right, Enclosure and Social Change in England, 1700–1820*. Cambridge, UK: Cambridge University Press, 1996.

Netting, Robert McC. *Smallholders, Householders: Farm Families and the Ecology of Intensive, Sustainable Agriculture*. Stanford: Stanford University Press, 1993.

Newman, David. "Settlement as Suburbanization: The Banality of Colonization." In *Normalizing Occupation: The Politics of Everyday Life in the West Bank Settlements*, edited by Marco Allegra, Ariel Handel, and Erez Maggor, 34–47. Bloomington: Indiana University Press, 2017.

Nichols, Robert. *Theft Is Property! Dispossession and Critical Theory*. Durham, NC: Duke University Press, 2020.

Nimer, Fathi. "Food Sovereignty in a Palestinian Economy of Resistance." Al-Shabaka, 2024. https://al-shabaka.org/briefs/food-sovereignty-in-a-palestinian-economy-of-resistance/.

Nixon, Rob. *Slow Violence and the Environmentalism of the Poor*. Cambridge, MA: Harvard University Press, 2011.

Ortner, Sherry B. "Resistance and the Problem of Ethnographic Refusal." *Comparative Studies in Society and History* 37, no. 1 (1995): 173–93.

Palestinian Authority Ministry of Agriculture and Palestinian Central Bureau of Statistics. "Agriculture Census: 2021." Ramallah: Palestinian Central Bureau of Statistics / Ministry of Agriculture, 2023.

Palestinian Grassroots Anti-Apartheid Wall Campaign (Stop the Wall) and Addameer. "Repression Allowed, Resistance Denied: Israel's Suppression of the Popular Movement against the Apartheid Annexation Wall." Ramallah: Stop the Wall, 2009.

Pandian, Anand. *Crooked Stalks: Cultivating Virtue in South India*. Durham, NC: Duke University Press, 2009.

Panosetti, Fadia, and Laurence Roudart. "Evolving Regimes of Land Use and Property in the West Bank." *Jerusalem Quarterly* 89 (2022): 10–31.

———. "Land Struggle and Palestinian Farmers' Livelihoods in the West Bank: Between De-agrarianization and Anti-colonial Resistance." *The Journal of Peasant Studies* (November 10, 2023): 1–23.

Park, K-Sue. "Money, Mortgages, and the Conquest of America." *Law & Social Inquiry* 41, no. 4 (2016): 1006–35.

Parmenter, Barbara McKean. *Giving Voice to Stones: Place and Identity in Palestinian Literature*. Austin: University of Texas Press, 1994.

Pasternak, Shiri. *Grounded Authority: The Algonquins of Barriere Lake against the State*. Minneapolis: University of Minnesota Press, 2017.

Pateman, Carole. *The Sexual Contract*. Stanford: Stanford University Press, 1988.

Peace Now. "Settlement Are Built on Private Palestinian Land." *Peace Now* (blog), March 14, 2007. https://peacenow.org.il/en/settlement-are-built-on-private-palestinian-land.

Pearce, Fred. "As War Halts, the Environmental Devastation in Gaza Runs Deep." *Yale E360* (blog), February 6, 2025. https://e360.yale.edu/features/gaza-war-environment.

———. *The Land Grabbers: The New Fight over Who Owns the Earth*. Boston: Beacon Press, 2012.

Perelman, Michael. *The Invention of Capitalism: Classical Political Economy and the Secret History of Primitive Accumulation*. Durham, NC: Duke University Press, 2000.

Peters, Pauline E. "Land Appropriation, Surplus People and a Battle over Visions of Agrarian Futures in Africa." *The Journal of Peasant Studies* 40, no. 3 (2013): 537–62.

Pollock, Alex. "Realist Methodology and the Articulation of Modes of Production: An Analysis of Palestinian Peasant Household Production in the North Jordan Valley of the Occupied West Bank/the Central Highlands of Palestine." PhD diss., University of Strathclyde, 1987.

Prashad, Vijay. *The Darker Nations: A People's History of the Third World*. New York: New Press, 2007.

Qumsiyeh, Mazin B. *Popular Resistance in Palestine: A History of Hope and Empowerment*. London: Pluto Press, 2011.

Qumsiyeh, Mazin B., and M. Abusarhan. "An Environmental Nakba: The Palestinian Environment under Israeli Colonization." *Science for the People* 1, no. 21 (2020): 1969–89.

Rabie, Kareem. *Palestine Is Throwing a Party and the Whole World Is Invited: Capital and State Building in the West Bank.* Durham, NC: Duke University Press, 2021.

———. "Ramallah's Bubbles." *Jadaliyya* (blog), January 18, 2013. http://www.jadaliyya.com/Details/27839/Ramallah%E2%80%99s-Bubbles.

———. "Remaking Ramallah." *New Left Review* 111 (2018): 43–60.

———. "What Do We Talk About When We Talk About Political Economy?" *Jadaliyya* (blog), September 29, 2015. https://www.jadaliyya.com/Details/32527/What-Do-We-Talk-About-When-We-Talk-About-Political-Economy.

Rabie, Walid. "Mawsim al-Tin Fi Biladi" (The Fig Season in My Country). *Heritage and Society* 4 (1975): 3–16.

Rashmawi, Muna. *Al-'Ard: Al-Sabil al-Qanuniyya lil-Hifaz 'Aliha* (Land: The Legal Means to Protect It). Ramallah: al-Haq, 1982.

Razavi, Shahra. "Engendering the Political Economy of Agrarian Change." *The Journal of Peasant Studies* 36, no. 1 (2009): 197–226.

Regavim. "600 PA Employees Engaged in Land Registration of Area C." *Regavim* (blog), November 23, 2020. https://www.regavim.org/idfs-civil-administration-hundreds-of-pa-employees-engaged-in-land-registration-of-area-c/.

Reger, Jeffrey D. "Olive Cultivation in the Galilee, 1948–1955: Hegemony and Resistance." *Journal of Palestine Studies* 46, no. 4 (2017): 28–45.

———. "Planting Palestine: The Political Economy of Olive Culture in the 20th Century Galilee and West Bank." PhD diss., Georgetown University, 2018.

Rickford, Russell. " 'We Can't Grow Food on All This Concrete': The Land Question, Agrarianism, and Black Nationalist Thought in the Late 1960s and 1970s." *Journal of American History* 103, no. 4 (2017): 956–80.

Rignall, Karen. *An Elusive Common: Land, Politics, and Agrarian Rurality in a Moroccan Oasis.* Ithaca: Cornell University Press, 2021.

Robinson, Glenn E. "The Role of the Professional Middle Class in the Mobilization of Palestinian Society: The Medical and Agricultural Committees." *International Journal of Middle East Studies* 25, no. 2 (1993): 301–26.

Robinson, Shira N. *Citizen Strangers: Palestinians and the Birth of Israel's Liberal Settler State.* Stanford: Stanford University Press, 2013.

Rosenfeld, Henry. "From Peasantry to Wage Labor and Residual Peasantry: The Transformation of an Arab Village." In *Process and Pattern in Culture*, edited by Robert Manners, 211–34. Chicago: Aldine Publishing Co., 1964.

Ross, Andrew. *Stone Men: Palestinians Who Built the Houses of Zion.* New York: Verso, 2019.

Ross, Kristin. *The Commune Form: The Transformation of Everyday Life*. New York: Verso, 2024.

Roy, Sara M. *The Gaza Strip: The Political Economy of De-development*. Washington, DC: Institute for Palestine Studies, 1995.

Rubenberg, Cheryl A. "The Civilian Infrastructure of the Palestine Liberation Organization: An Analysis of the PLO in Lebanon until June 1982." *Journal of Palestine Studies* 12, no. 3 (1983): 54–78.

Safransky, Sara. "Land Justice as a Historical Diagnostic: Thinking with Detroit." In *Social Justice and the City*, edited by Nik Heynen, 199–212. London: Routledge, 2020.

Said, Edward W. *The Question of Palestine*. New York: Vintage, 1992.

Sajadian, China. "Critical Agrarian Studies." In *International Encyclopedia of Human Geography*, edited by Audrey Lynn Kobayashi, 17–23. 2nd ed. Amsterdam: Elsevier, 2020.

Salamanca, Omar Jabary, Mezna Qato, Kareem Rabie, and Sobhi Samour. "Past Is Present: Settler Colonialism in Palestine." *Settler Colonial Studies* 2, no. 1 (2012): 1–8.

Samamreh, Rawan. "Wild Boars in Palestine Are Being Weaponized by Israeli Colonialism." *Mondoweiss* (blog), November 13, 2022. https://mondoweiss.net/2022/11/wild-boars-in-palestine-are-being-weaponized-by-israeli-colonialism/.

Samara, Adel. *Beyond De-linking: Development by Popular Protection vs. Development by State*. Ramallah: al-Mashriq al-A'amil for Cultural and Development Studies, 2005.

———. "Hawl 'Alaqa al-Iqtisad bi-l-Turath al-Sha'bi" (About the Relationship of the Economy to Popular Culture). *Heritage and Society* 1, no. 1 (1974): 80–84.

———. "The Political Economy of the West Bank 1967–1987: From Peripheralization to Development." In *Palestine: Profile of an Occupation*, 7–31. London: Zed Books, 1989.

Samara, Adel, and Shehada Awda. *Al-Himayya al-Sha'biyya* (Popular Protection). Damascus: Dar Kan'an li-l-Darasat wa-l-Nashr, 1988.

Samour, Sobhi. "The Palestinian Economy between Settler Colonial Invasion and Neoliberal Management." PhD diss., School of Oriental and African Studies (SOAS), 2016.

Sansour, Vivien, and Alaa Tartir. "Palestinian Farmers: A Last Stronghold of Resistance." *Al-Shabaka* (blog), 2014. https://al-shabaka.org/briefs/palestinian-farmers-a-last-stronghold-of-resistance/.

Sartori, Andrew. *Liberalism in Empire: An Alternative History*. Berkeley: University of California Press, 2014.

Sasa, Ghada. "Oppressive Pines: Uprooting Israeli Green Colonialism and Implanting Palestinian A'wna." *Politics* 43, no. 2 (May 2023): 219–35.

Sayigh, Rosemary. *The Palestinians: From Peasants to Revolutionaries.* London: Zed Books, 1979.

Sayigh, Yusif. "Dispossession and Pauperisation: The Palestinian Economy under Occupation." In *The Palestinian Economy: Studies in Development under Prolonged Occupation*, edited by George T. Abed. London: Routledge, 1988.

Sayrafı, Imad. "Political Ecology and the Social Solidarity Economies within the Power Matrix in Rural Palestine." Birzeit: Center for Development Studies, Birzeit University, 2022.

Schaebler, Birgit. "Practicing Musha: Common Lands and the Common Good in Southern Syria under the Ottomans and the French." In *New Perspectives on Property and Land in the Middle East*, edited by Roger Owen and Martin Bunton, 241–312. Cambridge, MA: Harvard University Press, 2000.

Scott, James C. *The Moral Economy of the Peasant: Rebellion and Subsistence in Southeast Asia.* New Haven: Yale University Press, 1976.

———. *Seeing Like a State: How Certain Schemes to Improve the Human Condition Have Failed.* New Haven: Yale University Press, 1998.

———. *Weapons of the Weak: Everyday Forms of Peasant Resistance.* New Haven: Yale University Press, 1985.

Seidel, Timothy. "Settler Colonialism and Land-Based Struggle in Palestine: Toward a Decolonial Political Economy." In *Political Economy of Palestine: Critical, Interdisciplinary, and Decolonial Perspectives*, edited by Alaa Tartir, Tariq Dana, and Timothy Seidel, 81–107. London: Palgrave Macmillan, 2021.

Seikaly, Sherene. *Men of Capital: Scarcity and Economy in Mandate Palestine.* Stanford: Stanford University Press, 2015.

Sfard, Michael. "A Guide to Housing, Land and Property Law in Area C of the West Bank." Norwegian Refugee Council, 2012.

———. *The Wall and the Gate: Israel, Palestine, and the Legal Battle for Human Rights.* New York: Metropolitan Books, 2018.

Shafır, Gershon. *Land, Labor and the Origins of the Israeli-Palestinian Conflict, 1882–1914.* Berkeley: University of California Press, 1996.

Shalev, Nir. "Under the Guise of Legality: Israel's Declarations of State Land in the West Bank." Jerusalem: B'Tselem, February 2012.

Shalev, Nir, and Alon Cohen-Lifshitz. "The Prohibited Zone, Israeli Planning Policy in the Palestinian Villages in Area C." Jerusalem: Bimkom—Planners for Planning Rights, 2008.

Shanin, Teodor. *Peasants and Peasant Societies.* Harmondsworth, UK: Penguin Books, 1971.

Sharif, Lila. "Vanishing Palestine." *Critical Ethnic Studies* 2, no. 1 (2016): 17–39.

Shehadeh, Aziz. "From the Court Records: 1. The Concept of State Land in the Occupied Territories." *The Palestine Yearbook of International Law Online* 2, no. 1 (January 1, 1985): 163–87.

Shehadeh, Raja. "The Land Law of Palestine: An Analysis of the Definition of State Lands." *Journal of Palestine Studies* 11, no. 2 (1982): 82–99.

———. *Occupier's Law: Israel and the West Bank*. 2nd ed. Washington, DC: Institute for Palestine Studies, 1988.

Shezaf, Hagar. "Israeli Settlers Pressured, the Cabinet Approved. Now Annexation Is Creeping into West Bank's Area B." *Haaretz*, December 30, 2024.

Shipler, David. "Israel Changing Face of West Bank." *New York Times*, September 12, 1982.

Shiva, Vandana. *Earth Democracy: Justice, Sustainability, and Peace*. North Atlantic Books, 2015.

Shoemaker, Jessica A. "Complexity's Shadow: American Indian Property, Sovereignty, and the Future." *Michigan Law Review* 115, no. 4 (2016): 487–552.

Shqair, Manal. "Arab-Israeli Eco-Normalization: Greenwashing Settler Colonialism in Palestine and the Jawlan." In *Dismantling Green Colonialism*, edited by Hamza Hamouchene and Katie Sandwell, 67–87. London: Pluto Press, 2023.

Singer, Amy. *Palestinian Peasants and Ottoman Officials: Rural Administration around Sixteenth-Century Jerusalem*. Cambridge, UK: Cambridge University Press, 1994.

Slyomovics, Susan. *The Object of Memory: Arab and Jew Narrate the Palestinian Village*. Philadelphia: University of Pennsylvania Press, 1998.

Smith, Ron J., and Martin Isleem. "Farming the Front Line: Gaza's Activist Farmers in the No Go Zones." *City* 21, no. 3–4 (July 4, 2017): 448–65.

Snikersproge, Ieva. "Who Are Neorurals? Or, How Capitalist Time Discipline Dilutes Political Projects and Makes It Difficult to Propose an Alternative." *Economic Anthropology* 10, no. 1 (2023): 65–76.

Sorek, Tamir. *The Optimist: A Social Biography of Tawfiq Zayyad*. Stanford: Stanford University Press, 2020.

Stamatopoulou-Robbins, Sophia. *Waste Siege: The Life of Infrastructure in Palestine*. Stanford: Stanford University Press, 2020.

Stein, Kenneth. *The Land Question in Palestine, 1917–1939*. Chapel Hill: University of North Carolina Press, 1984.

Stoler, Ann Laura. "Plantation Politics and Protest on Sumatra's East Coast." *The Journal of Peasant Studies* 13, no. 2 (1986): 124–43.

———. " 'The Rot Remains': From Ruins to Ruination." In *Imperial Debris: On Ruins and Ruination*, edited by Ann Laura Stoler, 1–35. Durham, NC: Duke University Press, 2013.

Stop the Wall. "The Palestinian Periphery: Home Demolitions and Settler Colonialism in the Jordan Valley and South Hebron Hills." Ramallah: Stop the Wall, 2017.

Sus, Nura. "Losing the Land to Ten New Settlements." *Al-Fajr Weekly*, January 26, 1981.

Swedenburg, Ted. *Memories of Revolt: The 1936–1939 Rebellion and the Palestinian National Past*. University of Arkansas Press: Fayetteville, 2003.

———. "The Palestinian Peasant As National Signifier." *Anthropological Quarterly* 63, no. 1 (1990): 18–30.

Tabar, Linda. "People's Power: Lessons from the First Intifada." In *Critical Readings of Development under Colonialism: Towards a Political Economy for Liberation in the Occupied Palestinian Territories*, edited by Linda Tabar and Omar Jabary Salamanca, 135–72. Ramallah: Rosa Luxemburg Foundation, 2015.

Tabar, Linda, and Samia Al-Botmeh. "Real Estate Development through Land Grabs: Predatory Accumulation and Precarity in Palestine." *New Political Economy* 26, no. 5 (2021): 783–96.

Taha, Nidal. "Tasrib al-'Aradi bi-Turuq al-Ihtiyal wa-al-Tawatu al-Isra'ili al-Rasmi" (The Illicit Transfer of Land by Means of Deception and Official Israeli Collaboration). Lecture presented at Institute for Land and Water, November 8, 1991.

Talab, Jamal, and Nure al-'Uqbi. *Al-Zaitun taht al-Ihtilal* (The Olive under Occupation). Jerusalem: Arab Studies Society, n.d.

Tamari, Salim. "Building Other People's Homes: The Palestinian Peasant's Household and Work in Israel." *Journal of Palestine Studies* 11, no. 1 (1981): 31–66.

———. "The Dislocation and Re-constitution of a Peasantry: The Social Economy of Agrarian Palestine in the Central Highlands and the Jordan Valley, 1960–1980." PhD diss., University of Manchester, 1983.

———. "In League with Zion: Israel's Search for a Native Pillar." *Journal of Palestine Studies* 12, no. 4 (1983): 41–56.

———. "Lepers, Lunatics, and Saints: The Nativist Ethnography of Tawfiq Canaan and His Circle." In *Mountain against the Sea: Essays on Palestinian Society and Culture*, 93–112. Berkeley: University of California Press, 2009.

———. "Soul of the Nation: The Fallah in the Eyes of the Urban Intelligentsia." *Review of Middle East Studies* 5, no. 5 (1992): 74–83.

Taqqu, Rachelle. "Peasants into Workmen: Internal Labor Migration and the Arab Village Community under the Mandate." In *Palestinian Society and Politics*, edited by Joel S. Migdal, 261–85. Princeton: Princeton University Press, 1980.

Taraki, Lisa. "The Development of Political Consciousness among Palestinians in the Occupied Territories, 1967–1987." In *Intifada: Palestine at the Crossroads*, edited by Jamal Nassar and Roger Heacock, 53–72. New York: Praeger, 1990.

————. "Urban Modernity on the Periphery: A New Middle Class Reinvents the Palestinian City." *Social Text* 26, no. 95 (2008): 61–81.

Tartir, Alaa, Sam Bahour, and Samer Abdelnour. "Defeating Dependency, Creating a Resistance Economy." Al-Shabaka, February 13, 2012. https://al-shabaka.org/briefs /defeating-dependency-creating-resistance-economy/.

Tavor, Eli. "Private Enterprise Settlements: Israelis Change Shekels into Villas in West Bank." *Al-Fajr Weekly*, November 30, 1981.

Tawil-Souri, Helga. "Digital Occupation: Gaza's High-Tech Enclosure." *Journal of Palestine Studies* 41, no. 2 (2012): 27–43.

Tesdell, Omar. "Shadow Spaces: Territory, Sovereignty, and the Question of Palestinian Cultivation." PhD diss., University of Minnesota, 2013.

Tesdell, Omar, Yusra Othman, and Saher Alkhoury. "Rainfed Agroecosystem Resilience in the Palestinian West Bank, 1918–2017." *Agroecology and Sustainable Food Systems* 43, no. 1 (2019): 21–39.

" 'This Is My Only Hope' Says Palestinian Who Farms to Combat Hunger." al Jazeera, August 2, 2024.

Thomson, William, Cynthia Gharios, and Rami Zurayk. "From Silk to Concrete: Exploring the Socio-spatial Aspects of the Agrarian Question (s) in Mount Lebanon." *The Journal of Peasant Studies* (2022): 1–23.

Times of Israel Staff. "KKL-JNF Leadership Approves Purchase of West Bank Land for Isolated Settlements." *Times of Israel*, April 11, 2021.

Treleaven, Sarah, and Jamie Levin. "The Impossible Promise of Building a New Palestinian City." *The Walrus*, April 8, 2024. https://thewalrus.ca/rawabi/.

Trottier, Julie, Nelly Leblond, and Yaakov Garb. "The Political Role of Date Palm Trees in the Jordan Valley: The Transformation of Palestinian Land and Water Tenure in Agriculture Made Invisible by Epistemic Violence." *Environment and Planning E: Nature and Space* 3, no. 1 (2020): 114–40.

Trouillot, Michel-Rolph. *Peasants and Capital: Dominica in the World Economy*. Baltimore: Johns Hopkins University Press, 1988.

Tully, James. *An Approach to Political Philosophy: Locke in Contexts*. Cambridge, UK: Cambridge University Press, 1993.

Tute, Richard Clifford. *The Ottoman Land Laws, with a Commentary on the Ottoman Land Code of the 7th Ramadan 1274*. Jerusalem: Greek Convent Press, 1927.

UNCTAD. "The Besieged Palestinian Agricultural Sector." New York: United Nations, 2015.

Van der Ploeg, Jan Douwe. *The New Peasantries: Struggles for Autonomy and Sustainability in an Era of Empire and Globalization*. London: Routledge, 2009.

Verdery, Katherine. *The Vanishing Hectare: Property and Value in Postsocialist Transylvania*. Ithaca: Cornell University Press, 2003.

Wainwright, Joel, and Joe Bryan. "Cartography, Territory, Property: Postcolonial Reflections on Indigenous Counter-Mapping in Nicaragua and Belize." *Cultural Geographies* 16, no. 2 (2009): 153–78.

Walsh-Dilley, Marygold. "Negotiating Hybridity in Highland Bolivia: Indigenous Moral Economy and the Expanding Market for Quinoa." *The Journal of Peasant Studies* 40, no. 4 (2013): 659–82.

Weaver, Alain Epp, and Sonia K. Weaver. *Salt & Sign: Mennonite Central Committee in Palestine, 1949–1999*. Akron, PA: Mennonite Central Committee, 1999.

Weaver, John C. *Great Land Rush and the Making of the Modern World, 1650–1900*. Montreal: McGill-Queen's University Press, 2003.

Weizman, Eyal. *Hollow Land: Israel's Architecture of Occupation*. New York: Verso, 2007.

White, Ben, Saturnino M. Borras Jr., Ruth Hall, Ian Scoones, and Wendy Wolford. "The New Enclosures: Critical Perspectives on Corporate Land Deals." *The Journal of Peasant Studies* 39, no. 3–4 (2012): 619–47.

Whitehead, Ann, and Dzodzi Tsikata. "Policy Discourses on Women's Land Rights in Sub–Saharan Africa: The Implications of the Re-turn to the Customary." *Journal of Agrarian Change* 3, no. 1–2 (2003): 67–112.

Williams, Justine M., and Eric Holt-Giménez, eds. *Land Justice: Re-imagining Land, Food, and the Commons*. Oakland, CA: Food First Books, 2017.

Wilson, Charles Thomas. *Peasant Life in the Holy Land*. London: E. P. Dutton, 1906.

Wolf, Eric R. *Peasant Wars of the Twentieth Century*. New York: Harper & Row, 1973.

———. "Types of Latin American Peasantry: A Preliminary Discussion." *American Anthropologist* 57, no. 3 (1955): 452–71.

Wolfe, Patrick. "Settler Colonialism and the Elimination of the Native." *Journal of Genocide Research* 8, no. 4 (2006): 387–409.

Wolford, Wendy. "Land Reform in the Time of Neoliberalism: A Many-Splendored Thing." *Antipode* 39, no. 3 (2007): 550–70.

———. *This Land Is Ours Now: Social Mobilization and the Meanings of Land in Brazil*. Durham, NC: Duke University Press, 2010.

Wolford, Wendy, Ben White, Ian Scoones, Ruth Hall, Marc Edelman, and Saturnino M. Borras. "Global Land Deals: What Has Been Done, What Has Changed, and What's Next?" *The Journal of Peasant Studies* (2024): 1–38.

Women's Centre for Legal Aid and Counselling (WCLAC). "Palestinian Women and Inheritance." Ramallah: WCLAC, 2014.

World Bank. "Engendering Development: Through Gender Equality in Rights, Resources, and Voice." Washington, DC: World Bank, 2001.

———. "Implementation Completion and Results Report on a Learning and Innovation (Grant) in the Amount of US$3.0 Million to West Bank and Gaza for a Land Administration Project." Washington, DC: World Bank, June 25, 2009.

Yin, He, Lina Eklund, Dimah Habash, Mazin B. Qumsiyeh, and Jamon Van Den Hoek. "Evaluating War-Induced Damage to Agricultural Land in the Gaza Strip since October 2023 Using PlanetScope and SkySat Imagery." *Science of Remote Sensing* 11 (June 1, 2025): 100199.

Zachary, Shlomy. "Renewing Settlement of Title in Area C in the West Bank: A Breach of International Law and Violation of Palestinians' Rights." Tel Aviv: Yesh Din, April 2021.

Zureik, Elia T. "Transformation of Class Structure among the Arabs in Israel: From Peasantry to Proletariat." *Journal of Palestine Studies* 6, no. 1 (1976): 39–66.

Index

Stanford Studies in Middle Eastern and
Islamic Societies and Cultures

Lara Deeb and Sherene Seikaly, editors

For a complete listing of titles in this series, visit the
Stanford University Press website, www.sup.org.